NATIONAL GEOGRAPHIC KiDS

United States Atlas

Fifth Edition

NATIONAL GEOGRAPHIC

WASHINGTON, D.C.

Table of Contents

Northeast: Maine lighthouse, pp. 34–35

Southeast: Manatee in Florida waters, p. 62

Title page: Atlantic sand crab; Lower Falls of the Yellowstone, Wyoming; football player; skyline, Tampa, Florida; sage grouse; skyline, Seattle, Washington State; American girl; Organ Pipe Cactus National Monument, Arizona

It's *your* country. Learn it. Love it. Explore it.

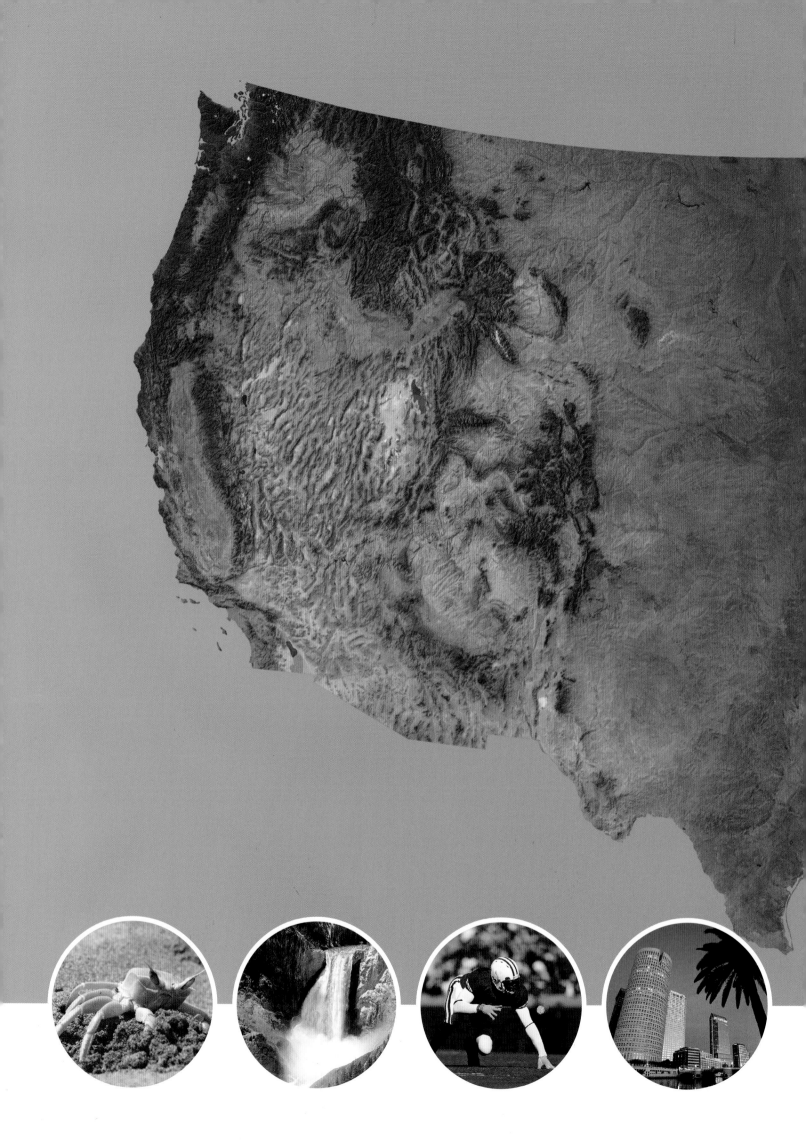

Territories: Festival dancers, American Samoa, pp. 156–157

Southwest: Albuquerque balloon festival, p. 120

Midwest: Illinois hay field with tractor, pp. 88–89

West: Wyoming ranch, p. 152

How to Use This Atlas

This atlas is much more than just another book of maps about the United States. Of course you will find plenty of maps—country, regional, and state—that will help you learn about the people and places that make up our country. But there's much more. This atlas includes essays filled with history and current facts about each state, and photos that provide an up close view of natural and cultural features. In addition, you will discover state flags and nicknames, state flowers and birds, facts and statistics, and even graphs and charts. Follow the captions below and to the right to discover all the special features that are waiting for you in this atlas.

STATE FACT BOX

The fact box is full of key information you need at a glance about a state: its nickname and flag, statehood, statistics about land and population*, racial and ethnic makeup** and other population characteristics, plus some fascinating Geo Whiz facts and the state bird and flower.

Population figures are for 2015 unless otherwise noted; city populations are for city proper unless metropolitan area is specified.
*** Racial percentages total less than 100 percent because very small racial groups are not included. Hispanics are an ethnic group and can be included in any racial group.*

COLOR BARS

Each section of the atlas has its own color to make it easy to move from one to another. Look for the color in the Table of Contents and across the top of the pages in the atlas. The name of the section and the title for each topic or map is in the color bar.

> THE NORTHEAST
> THE SOUTHEAST
> THE MIDWEST
> THE SOUTHWEST
> THE WEST
> THE TERRITORIES

WHERE ARE THE PICTURES?

If you want to know where a picture in any of the regional sections in the atlas was taken, check the map in the regional photo essay. Find the label that describes the photograph you are curious about, and follow the line to its location.

CHARTS AND GRAPHS

The photo essay for each state includes a chart or graph that highlights economic, physical, cultural, or some other type of information related to the state.

BAR SCALE

Each map has a bar scale in miles and kilometers to help you find out how far on Earth's surface it is from one place to another on the map.

YOU ARE HERE

Locator maps show you where each region and state within the region is in relation to the rest of the United States. Regions are shown in the regional color; featured states are in yellow.

MAP SYMBOLS

Maps use symbols to represent many physical, political, and economic features. Below is a complete list of the map symbols used in this atlas. In addition, each state map has its own key featuring symbols for major economic activities. Other abbreviations are listed on page 160.

- **•Aspen** ....town of under 25,000 residents
- **•Frankfort** ....town of 25,000 to 99,999
- **•San Jose** ....city of 100,000 to 999,999
- **•New York** .....city of 1,000,000 and over
- ⊛ National capital
- ⊛ State capital
- ■ Point of interest
- + Mountain peak with elevation above sea level
- • Low point with elevation below sea level
- —— River
- — — Intermittent river
- ┴┴┴ Canal
- ——— Interstate or selected other highway
- - - - Trail
- •••• State or national boundary
- •••••• Continental divide
- Lake and dam
- Intermittent lake
- Dry lake
- Swamp
- Glacier
- National Wild & Scenic River, **N.W.&S.R.**

- Sand
- Lava
- Area below sea level
- Indian Reservation, **I.R.**
- State Park, **S.P.**
  State Historical Park, **S.H.P.**
  State Historic Site, **S.H.S.**
- National Battlefield, **N.B.**
  National Battlefield Park, **N.B.P.**
  National Battlefield Site, **N.B.S.**
  National Historic Site, **N.H.S.**
  National Historical Area, **N.H.A.**
  National Historical Park, **N.H.P.**
  National Lakeshore
  National Military Park, **N.M.P.**
  National Memorial, **NAT. MEM.**
  National Monument, **NAT. MON.**
  National Park, **N.P.**
  National Parkway
  National Preserve
  National Recreation Area, **N.R.A.**
  National River
  National Riverway
  National Scenic Area
  National Seashore
  National Volcanic Monument
- National Forest, **N.F.**
- National Grassland, **N.G.**
- National Wildlife Refuge, **N.W.R.**

Economy Symbols

Fishing		Stone/gravel/cement	
Lobster fishing		Mining	
Shellfish		Coal	
Poultry/eggs		Oil/gas	
Sheep		Hydro-electricity	
Hogs		Machinery	
Dairy cows/products		Metal manufacturing	
Beef cattle		Metal products	
Fruits		Shipbuilding	
Vegetables		Railroad equipment	
Vegetable oil		Motor vehicles/parts	
Peanuts		Rubber/plastics	
Nursery stock		Chemistry	
Wheat		Food processing	
Corn		Clothing/textiles	
Rice		Leather products	
Soybeans		Glass/clay products	
Sugarcane		Jewelry	
Cotton		Electrical equipment	
Tobacco		Computers/electronics	
Coffee		Scientific instruments	
Vineyards		Aircraft/parts	
Maple syrup		Aerospace	
Timber/forest products		Motion picture/music industry	
Furniture		Tourism	
Printing/publishing		Finance/insurance	

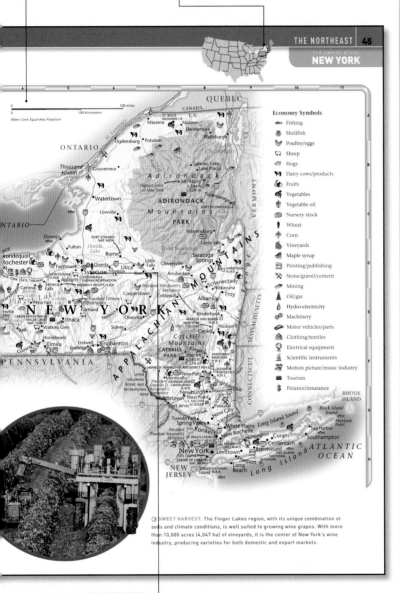

THE NORTHEAST **45**

THE EMPIRE STATE
NEW YORK

QUEBEC
CANADA
ONTARIO
Adirondack
ADIRONDACK Mountains PARK
NEW YORK
APPALACHIAN MOUNTAINS
Catskill Mountains
PENNSYLVANIA
NEW JERSEY
Long Island Sound
Long Island
ATLANTIC OCEAN
RHODE ISLAND

Economy Symbols
- Fishing
- Shellfish
- Poultry/eggs
- Sheep
- Hogs
- Dairy cows/products
- Fruits
- Vegetables
- Vegetable oil
- Nursery stock
- Wheat
- Corn
- Vineyards
- Maple syrup
- Printing/publishing
- Stone/gravel/cement
- Mining
- Oil/gas
- Hydro-electricity
- Machinery
- Motor vehicles/parts
- Clothing/textiles
- Electrical equipment
- Scientific instruments
- Motion picture/music industry
- Tourism
- Finance/insurance

SWEET HARVEST. The Finger Lakes region, with its unique combination of soils and climate conditions, is well suited to growing wine grapes. With more than 10,000 acres (4,047 ha) of vineyards, it is the center of New York's wine industry, producing varieties for both domestic and export markets.

INDEX AND GRID

A grid system makes it easy to find places listed in the index. For example, the listing for Syracuse, New York, is followed by **45** D5. The bold type is the page number; D5 tells you the city is near the point where imaginary lines drawn from D and 5 on the grid bars meet.

The Physical United States

Stretching from the Atlantic Ocean in the east to the Pacific in the west, the United States is the third largest country in area in the world. Its physical diversity ranges from mountains to fertile plains and from tropical forests to dry deserts. Shading on the map indicates changes in elevation, and colors suggest different vegetation patterns.

ALASKA AND HAWAI'I.

In addition to the states located on the main landmass, the United States has two states—Alaska and Hawai'i—that are not directly connected to the other 48 states. If Alaska and Hawai'i were shown in their correct relative sizes and locations, the map would not fit on the page. The locator globe shows the correct relative size and location of each.

Coast Ranges   Sierra Nevada   Great Basin   Rocky Mountains

San Francisco

0 400 miles
0 400 kilometers

Albers Conic Equal-Area Projection

Lake of
the Woods

Red River of the North

Mesabi Ra.

Eagle Mt.
+ 2,301 ft
701 m

Isle Royale

Lake Superior

Keweenaw
Peninsula

Source of the
Mississippi
(Lake Itasca)

Upper Peninsula

Strs. of
Mackinac

Lake Huron

Minnesota

James

Wisconsin

Mississippi

Lake
Winnebago

Lower Peninsula

Lake Michigan

Lake
St. Clair

Lake Erie

Cedar

Platte

C E N T R A L

Des Moines

Illinois

Great Miami

Ohio

Geographical Center
of the 48 Contiguous
• United States

L O W L A N D

Wabash

Smoky Hills

Missouri

Lake of
the Ozarks

Cimarron

Harry S.
Truman
Res.

Ozark Plateau

Ohio

Kentucky
Lake

Lake
Barkley

Tennessee

Cumberland

Magazine Mt.
2,753 ft +
839 m
Ouachita Mts.

Arkansas

Mississippi

Red

Ouachita

Brazos

Trinity

Sabine

Red

C O A S T A L

Alabama Belt

Chattahoochee

Black

Mt. Mitchell
+ 6,684 ft, 2,037 m

Savannah

Altamaha

Colorado

P L A I N

Mississippi
River Delta

Okefenokee
Swamp

Suwannee

Cape
Canaveral

Lake
Okeechobee

The
Everglades

Florida Keys

Lake of
the Woods

Lake
Champlain

Adirondack
Mts.

Green Mts.

Connecticut

Mt. Washington
6,288 ft
1,917 m

Gulf of
Maine

Cape
Cod

Lake Ontario

Niagara
Falls

Allegheny

Catskill
Mts.

Hudson

Long Island

Allegheny Plateau

Susquehanna

Delaware

Potomac

Delaware Bay

⊛ Washington, D.C.

M O U N T A I N S

Chesapeake Bay

James

A P P A L A C H I A N

Cumberland Plateau

Roanoke

Cape
Fear

Great Pee Dee

Cape
Hatteras

Cape
Fear

NATURAL
VEGETATION

NEEDLELEAF FOREST

BROADLEAF FOREST

MIXED FOREST

GRASSLAND

TROPICAL VEGETATION

ARID/SEMIARID

TUNDRA

⊖ CROSS SECTION.

Trace a line from Washington, D.C., to San Francisco.
Locate the features shown in the cross section below.

Washington, D.C.

Great Plains   Ozark Plateau   Appalachian   Atlantic
                                                                 Mountains   Coastal Plain

NATURAL ENVIRONMENT

Natural Environment

A big part of the natural environment of the United States is the climate. With humid areas near the coasts, dry interior regions far from any major water body, and land areas that extend from northern Alaska to southern Florida and Hawai'i, the country experiences great variation in climate. Location is the key. Distance from the Equator, nearness to water, wind patterns, temperature of nearby water bodies, and elevation are things that influence temperature and precipitation. Climate affects the types of vegetation that grow in a particular place and plays a part in soil formation.

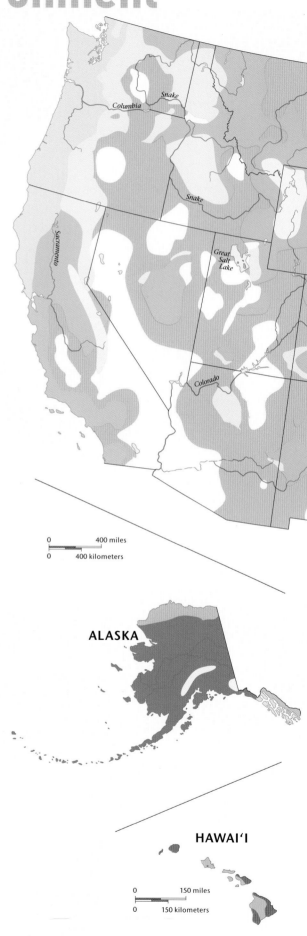

CHANGING CLIMATE

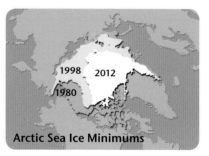

Arctic Sea Ice Minimums

Scientists believe that a warming trend that has occurred in recent decades may be more than a natural cycle and that human activity is a contributing factor. An increase in average temperatures could result in more severe storms, changes in precipitation patterns, and the spread of deserts. Rising temperatures may also play a part in the melting of glaciers, which could lead to a rise in ocean levels and the shrinking of the Arctic ice cover. NASA satellite images indicate that Arctic ice is shrinking as much as 9 percent each decade. Many believe that this puts polar bears at risk, because they normally hunt and raise their young on ice floes.

0   400 miles
0   400 kilometers

Albers Conic Equal-Area Projection

Climate Zones

Tropical
- Tropical wet
- Tropical wet and dry

Dry
- Semiarid
- Arid

Mild
- Marine west coast
- Mediterranean
- Humid subtropical

Continental
- Hot summer
- Warm summer
- Subarctic

Polar
- Tundra and ice

High Elevations
- Highlands

◎ CLIMATE MOSAIC.
The United States includes every major climate type, shown in different colors on the map above.

WARMING UP

Evidence indicates that Earth is experiencing a warming pattern unlike any in recorded history. In 2015 every state reported above average temperatures, and four states saw record-setting averages. Overall the average temperature in the lower 48 states was 2.4°F (1.3°C) warmer than the 20th-century average.

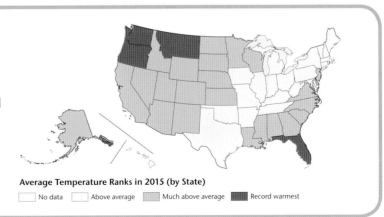

Average Temperature Ranks in 2015 (by State)

No data   Above average   Much above average   Record warmest

Natural Hazards

The natural environment of the United States provides much diversity, but it also poses many dangers, especially when people locate homes and businesses in places at risk of natural disasters. Tornadoes bring destructive winds, and hurricanes bring strong winds, rain, and more; shifting of Earth's crust along fault lines rattles buildings; flood waters and wildfires threaten lives and property. More than one-third of the U.S. population lives in hazardprone areas. Compare this natural hazards map to the population map on pages 16–17.

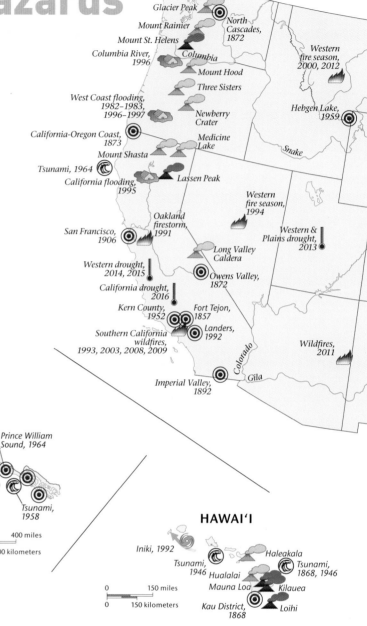

Mount Baker
Glacier Peak
Mount Rainier
North Cascades, 1872
Mount St. Helens
Columbia River, 1996
Columbia
Western fire season, 2000, 2012
Mount Hood
Three Sisters
West Coast flooding, 1982–1983, 1996–1997
Newberry Crater
Hebgen Lake, 1959
California-Oregon Coast, 1873
Medicine Lake
Snake
Mount Shasta
Tsunami, 1964
Lassen Peak
California flooding, 1995
Western fire season, 1994
Oakland firestorm, 1991
San Francisco, 1906
Western & Plains drought, 2013
Long Valley Caldera
Western drought, 2014, 2015
Owens Valley, 1872
California drought, 2016
Kern County, 1952
Fort Tejon, 1857
Southern California wildfires, 1993, 2003, 2008, 2009
Landers, 1992
Wildfires, 2011
Colorado
Imperial Valley, 1892
Gila

ALASKA

Alaska has about 80 major volcanic centers.

More earthquakes occur in Alaska than in the other 49 states combined.

Alaskan wildfires, 2015
Prince William Sound, 1964
Novarupta, 1912
Tsunami, 1964
Tsunami, 1958
Tsunami, 1946, 1957

0   400 miles
0   400 kilometers

HAWAI'I

Iniki, 1992
Haleakala
Tsunami, 1946
Tsunami, 1868, 1946
Hualalai
Mauna Loa
Kilauea
Kau District, 1868
Loihi

0   150 miles
0   150 kilometers

BLIZZARD. Severe storm with bitter cold temperatures and wind-whipped snow and ice particles that reduce visibility to less than 650 feet (198 m), paralyzing transportation systems

FLOOD. Inundation of buildings or roadways caused by overflow of a river or stream swollen by heavy rainfall or rapid snowmelt; may involve displacement of people

DROUGHT. Long and continuous period of abnormally low precipitation, resulting in water shortages that negatively affect people, animals, and plant life; may result in crop loss

HURRICANE. Tropical storm in the Atlantic, Caribbean, Gulf of Mexico, or eastern Pacific with a minimum sustained wind speed of 74 miles an hour (119 km/h)

ICE STORM. Damaging accumulations of ice associated with freezing rain; may pull down trees or utility lines, causing extensive damage and creating dangerous travel conditions

NATURAL HAZARDS

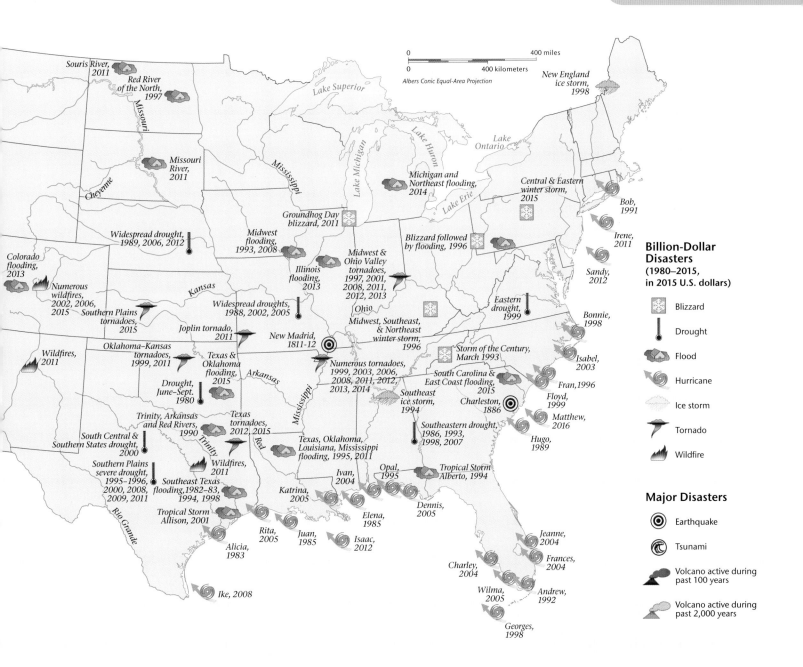

Souris River, 2011

Red River of the North, 1997

Missouri

Missouri River, 2011

Cheyenne

Widespread drought, 1989, 2006, 2012

Colorado flooding, 2013

Numerous wildfires, 2002, 2006, 2015

Kansas

Southern Plains tornadoes, 2015

Wildfires, 2011

Oklahoma–Kansas tornadoes, 1999, 2011

Joplin tornado, 2011

Texas & Oklahoma flooding, 2015

Arkansas

Drought, June–Sept. 1980

South Central & Southern States drought, 2000

Trinity, Arkansas and Red Rivers, 1990

Trinity

Red

Southern Plains severe drought, 1995–1996, 2000, 2008, 2009, 2011

Wildfires, 2011

Southeast Texas flooding, 1982–83, 1994, 1998

Tropical Storm Allison, 2001

Alicia, 1983

Rita, 2005

Katrina, 2005

Texas tornadoes, 2012, 2015

Texas, Oklahoma, Louisiana, Mississippi flooding, 1995, 2011

Mississippi

Juan, 1985

Ivan, 2004

Elena, 1985

Isaac, 2012

Ike, 2008

Rio Grande

Lake Superior

Lake Michigan

Lake Huron

Lake Erie

Lake Ontario

Michigan and Northeast flooding, 2014

Groundhog Day blizzard, 2011

Midwest flooding, 1993, 2008

Illinois flooding, 2013

Midwest & Ohio Valley tornadoes, 1997, 2001, 2008, 2011, 2012, 2013

Widespread droughts, 1988, 2002, 2005

Ohio

Midwest, Southeast, & Northeast winter storm, 1996

New Madrid, 1811-12

Numerous tornadoes, 1999, 2003, 2006, 2008, 2011, 2012, 2013, 2014

Southeast ice storm, 1994

Storm of the Century, March 1993

South Carolina & East Coast flooding, 2015

Charleston, 1886

Southeastern drought, 1986, 1993, 1998, 2007

Opal, 1995

Tropical Storm Alberto, 1994

Dennis, 2005

Charley, 2004

Wilma, 2005

Georges, 1998

Blizzard followed by flooding, 1996

Central & Eastern winter storm, 2015

New England ice storm, 1998

Bob, 1991

Irene, 2011

Sandy, 2012

Eastern drought, 1999

Bonnie, 1998

Isabel, 2003

Fran, 1996

Floyd, 1999

Matthew, 2016

Hugo, 1989

Jeanne, 2004

Frances, 2004

Andrew, 1992

Billion-Dollar Disasters
(1980–2015, in 2015 U.S. dollars)

- ▦ Blizzard
- | Drought
- ☁ Flood
- 🌀 Hurricane
- ☁ Ice storm
- 🌪 Tornado
- 🔥 Wildfire

Major Disasters

- ◎ Earthquake
- ◎ Tsunami
- 🌋 Volcano active during past 100 years
- 🌋 Volcano active during past 2,000 years

Scale:
0 — 400 miles
0 — 400 kilometers
Albers Conic Equal-Area Projection

TORNADO. Violently rotating column of air that, when it reaches the ground, is the most damaging of all atmospheric phenomena; most common in the central region of the country

WILDFIRE. Free-burning, uncontained fire in a forest or grassland; may result from lightning strikes or accidental or deliberate human activity in areas where conditions are dry

EARTHQUAKE. Shaking or vibration created by energy released by movement of Earth's crust along tectonic plate boundaries; can cause structural damage and loss of life

TSUNAMI. Series of unusually large ocean waves caused by an underwater earthquake, landslide, or volcanic eruption; very destructive in coastal areas

VOLCANO. Vent or opening in Earth's surface through which molten rock called lava, ash, and gases are released; often associated with tectonic plate boundaries

The Political United States

Like a giant patchwork quilt, the United States is made up of 50 states, each uniquely different but together making a national fabric held together by a Constitution and a federal government. State boundaries, outlined in various colors on the map, set apart internal political units within the country. The national capital—Washington, D.C.—is marked by a star in a double circle on the map. The capital of each state is marked by a star in a single circle.

9:00 AM

10:00 AM

7:00 AM
HAWAI'I-ALEUTIAN TIME

8:00 AM
ALASKA TIME

7:00 AM
HAWAI'I-ALEUTIAN TIME

TIME ZONES. Earth is divided into 24 time zones, each about 15 degrees of longitude wide, reflecting the distance Earth turns from west to east each hour. The U.S. is divided into six time zones, indicated by red dotted lines on these maps. When it is noon in Boston, what is the time in Seattle?

11:00 AM

12:00 PM

0 ———— 300 miles
0 ———— 300 kilometers
Albers Conic Equal-Area Projection

Lake of the Woods

Isle Royale

Lake Superior

Minot
Grand Forks
International Falls

NORTH DAKOTA
Bismarck Fargo
Duluth Superior
MINNESOTA
Marquette

MICHIGAN

MAINE
Bangor
Augusta

Lake Champlain
Burlington
VT.
Montpelier
N.H.
Concord
Portland

Aberdeen
SOUTH DAKOTA
Pierre
Rapid City
Minneapolis
St. Paul

WISCONSIN
Green Bay
Madison

Lake Michigan
Grand Rapids
Lansing

Lake Huron

Lake Ontario
Rochester
Syracuse Albany
NEW YORK
Buffalo Hartford
CONN.
MASS.
Boston
Cape Cod
Providence
RHODE ISLAND

NEBRASKA
Cedar Rapids
IOWA
Des Moines
Omaha
Grand Island
Lincoln

Milwaukee
Rockford
Chicago Gary

Davenport
Peoria
ILLINOIS
Springfield

Detroit

Lake Erie
Erie
PENNSYLVANIA
Pittsburgh
Harrisburg

Toledo Cleveland
OHIO
Columbus
Dayton
Cincinnati

Newark
New York
Trenton
NEW JERSEY
Philadelphia
Baltimore
Dover
DELAWARE

Long Island

S. Platte
Platte

Fort Wayne
INDIANA
Indianapolis

WEST VIRGINIA
Washington
D.C. MARYLAND
Annapolis
Chesapeake Bay

Kansas City
Topeka
Jefferson City
St. Louis

Ohio

Louisville
Frankfort
Evansville Lexington

Charleston

Richmond

KANSAS
Dodge City
Wichita

MISSOURI
Springfield

Wabash

KENTUCKY
Paducah

VIRGINIA
Roanoke
Norfolk
Virginia Beach

Arkansas

Greensboro
Raleigh
Cape Hatteras

Tulsa
OKLAHOMA
Oklahoma City
Amarillo
Lawton

Fort Smith
Memphis
ARKANSAS
Little Rock

Nashville
TENNESSEE
Chattanooga
Knoxville

NORTH CAROLINA
Charlotte
Greenville

Huntsville

Columbia
SOUTH CAROLINA

Red

Lubbock
Wichita Falls
Fort Worth
Dallas

Shreveport

MISSISSIPPI
Jackson

Birmingham
ALABAMA
Montgomery

Atlanta
GEORGIA
Macon
Columbus

Charleston
Savannah

Savannah

Midland
Abilene
Odessa
Waco

TEXAS
Austin
Beaumont
Houston
San Antonio

LOUISIANA
Red
Natchez
Baton Rouge
Lafayette
New Orleans

Biloxi
Mobile
Mobile Bay
Mississippi River Delta

Tallahassee
Apalachee Bay

FLORIDA
Gainesville

Jacksonville

Orlando
Cape Canaveral

Laredo
Corpus Christi

Rio Grande

Brownsville

Tampa
St. Petersburg

Lake Okeechobee

The Everglades

Fort Lauderdale
Miami

Florida Keys

Red River basin ceded by Great Britain, 1818
Ceded by Great Britain, 1842
Ceded by Great Britain, 1842

Oregon Country ceded by Great Britain, 1846

Louisiana Purchase from France, 1803

United States, 1783

Ceded by Mexico, 1848

Texas annexed by U.S., 1845

Western boundary of original 13 colonies, 1775

Alaska purchased from Russia, 1867

Gadsden Purchase from Mexico, 1853

Area acquired from Spain, 1810-1821

Hawai'i annexed in 1898

⊙ **WESTWARD EXPANSION.** The United States had its origins in 13 British colonies established along the Atlantic coast. After gaining independence in 1783, the young country began adding new territories—some by treaty, others by purchase or by war. The map traces the country's expansion and shows the date each territory was acquired.

Population

More than 324 million* and growing! The population of the United States topped the 300 million mark in 2006, and it continues to grow by more than 2 million people each year. Before the arrival of European settlers, the population consisted of Native Americans living in tribal groups scattered across the country. In the 16th and 17th centuries, Europeans, some with slaves from Africa, settled first along the eastern seaboard and later moved westward. In 1790 the U.S. population was not quite 4 million people. Today, New York City alone has a population more than double that number. The country's population is unevenly distributed. The map shows the number of people per square mile for each county in every state. The greatest densities are in the East and along the West Coast, especially around major cities. The most rapid growth is occurring in the South and the West—an area referred to as the Sunbelt—as well as in suburban areas around cities.

*August 2016 figure

ALASKA

0   400 miles
0   400 kilometers

Anchorage

HAWAI'I

Honolulu

0   150 miles
0   150 kilometers

COMMUTER RUSH HOUR. Crowds of people press toward trains in New York City's Grand Central Station. With more than three-quarters of the population living in urban areas, commuter transportation poses a major challenge to cities in the United States.

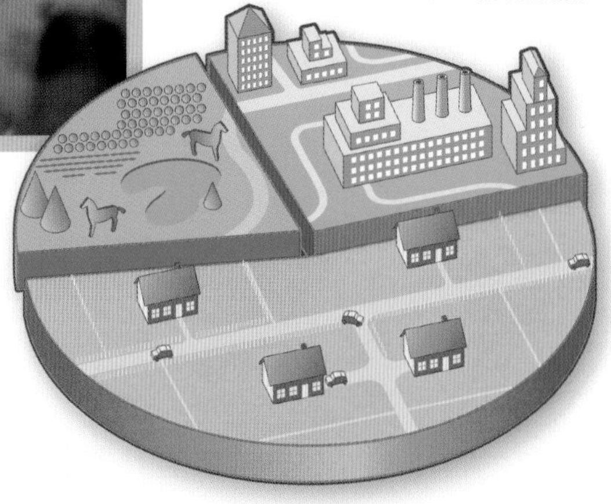

WHERE WE LIVE. The first U.S. census in 1790 revealed that only 5 percent of people lived in towns. As industry has grown and agriculture has become increasingly mechanized, people have left farms (green), moving to urban places (blue) and their surrounding suburbs (orange).

POPULATION

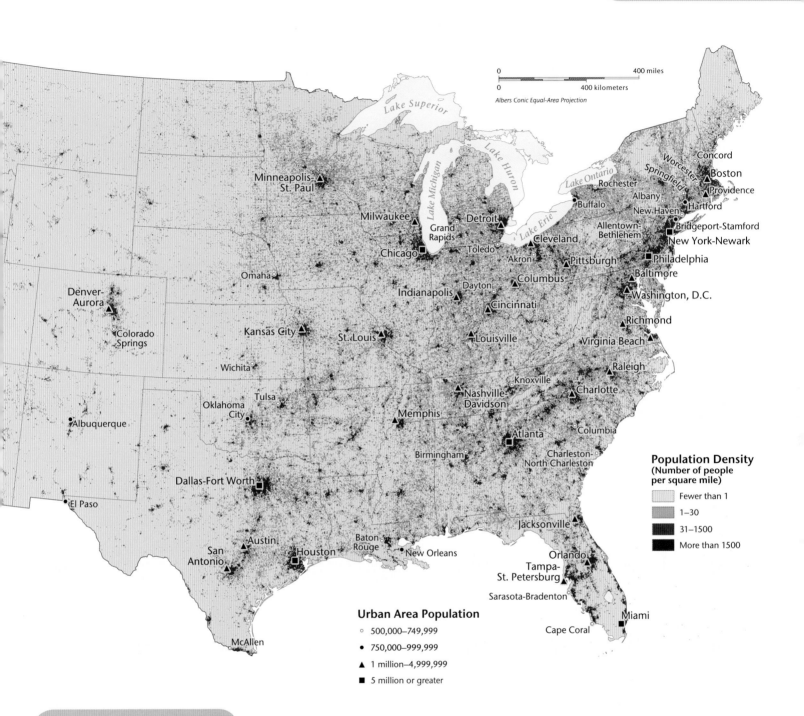

0   400 miles

0   400 kilometers

Albers Conic Equal-Area Projection

Population Density
(Number of people
per square mile)

	Fewer than 1
	1–30
	31–1500
	More than 1500

Urban Area Population

○   500,000–749,999

●   750,000–999,999

▲   1 million–4,999,999

■   5 million or greater

HOW OLD ARE WE?

Population pyramids show the distribution of population by sex and age groups, called cohorts. In 1960 the largest cohorts, born after World War II and known as Baby Boomers, were under 15 years of age. By 2000 Baby Boomers had reached middle age. By 2040 they will reach the top of the pyramid.

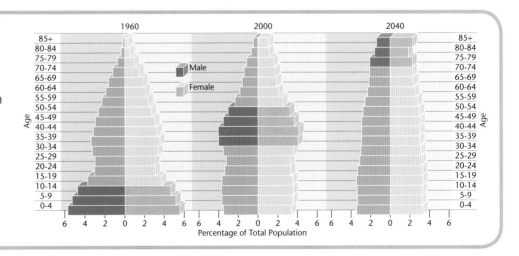

PEOPLE
ON THE MOVE

People on the Move

From earliest human history, the land of the United States has been a focus of migration. Native peoples arrived thousands of years ago. The first European settlers came in the 16th and 17th centuries, and slave ships brought people from Africa. Today, people are still on the move. Since the mid-20th century, most international migrants have come from Latin America—especially Mexico and countries of Central America and the Caribbean—and Asia, particularly China, the Philippines, and India. Although most of the population is still of European descent, certain regions have large minority concentrations, as shown on the map, that influence local cultural landscapes.

San Francisco
San Jose

Los Angeles

San Diego

Phoenix

ALASKA

0   400 miles
0   400 kilometers

HAWAI'I

0   150 miles
0   150 kilometers

◉ **BRIDGE OF HOPE.** Many Mexicans enter the U.S. (foreground) by bridges across the Rio Grande, such as this one between Nuevo Laredo, Mexico, and Laredo, Texas.

◉ **IMMIGRANT INFLUENCE.** With Hispanics making up more than 17 percent of the population, signs in Spanish are popping up everywhere—even at voting areas.

◉ **SUNBELT SPRAWL.** Spreading suburbs are becoming a common feature of the desert Southwest as people flock to the Sunbelt.

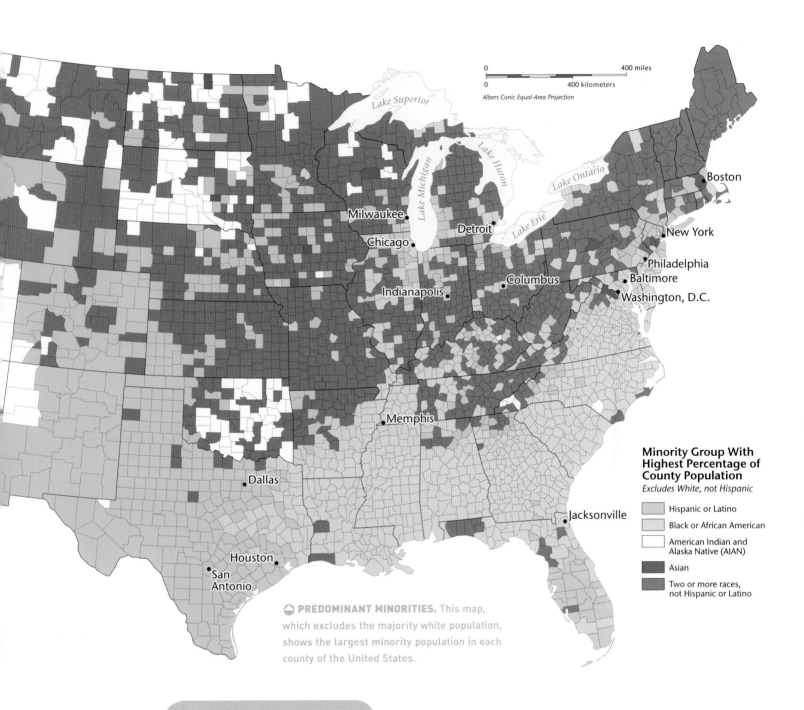

400 miles

400 kilometers

Albers Conic Equal-Area Projection

**Minority Group With
Highest Percentage of
County Population**
Excludes White, not Hispanic

Hispanic or Latino

Black or African American

American Indian and
Alaska Native (AIAN)

Asian

Two or more races,
not Hispanic or Latino

PREDOMINANT MINORITIES. This map,
which excludes the majority white population,
shows the largest minority population in each
county of the United States.

POPULATION SHIFT

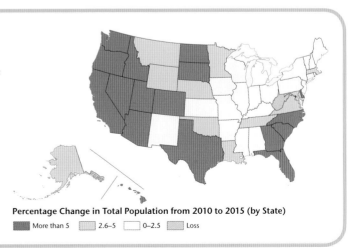

In the past half century, people have
begun moving from the historical
industrial and agricultural regions of
the Northeast and Midwest toward
the South and West, attracted by the
promise of jobs, generally lower
living costs, and a more relaxed way
of life. This continuing trend can be
seen in the population growth patterns shown in the map at right.

Percentage Change in Total Population from 2010 to 2015 (by State)

More than 5   2.6–5   0–2.5   Loss

Energy

People use energy every day in almost everything they do—from turning on a lamp, to using a computer, to riding a bus to school or work. Almost 40 percent of all energy consumption is used to create electricity, but another 27 percent goes to transportation. Energy sources fall into two main categories: nonrenewable and renewable. Nonrenewable energy resources include fossil fuels (petroleum, natural gas, and coal) and uranium (nuclear power). They have a limited supply that is not quickly replenished. Renewable energy includes wind, water, solar, geothermal, and biomass materials (wood, plant material, and garbage). These sources have an abundant supply that is constantly replenished. About 90 percent of all energy used in the United States comes from nonrenewable energy sources.

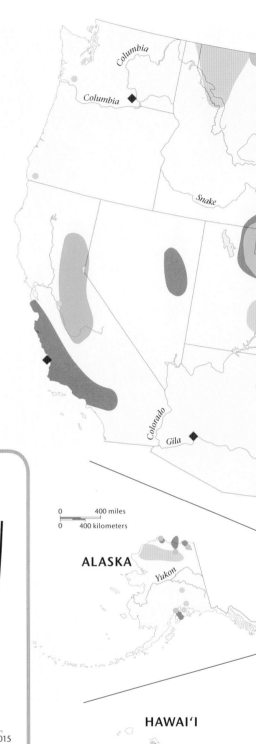

EARTHQUAKES & OIL PRODUCTION

Earthquake activity in the central U.S. has increased dramatically since 2009. Geophysicists—scientists who study forces at work within Earth, including earthquakes—have concluded that this increased earthquake activity results from drilling companies pumping wastewater—toxic water that occurs naturally in oil and natural gas deposits—back into the ground.

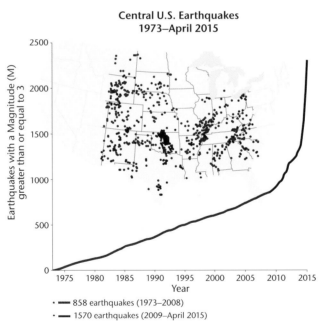

Central U.S. Earthquakes 1973–April 2015

Earthquakes with a Magnitude (M) greater than or equal to 3

Year

• 858 earthquakes (1973–2008)
• 1570 earthquakes (2009–April 2015)

From 1973–2008 there were 858 earthquakes of magnitude 3 or greater (blue dots on the map, above) in the central U.S. But from 2009 to early 2016 there were 2,310 earthquakes of magnitude 3 or greater (red dots), with most concentrated in central Oklahoma. During this time the amount of toxic wastewater pumped back into the ground doubled. Scientists believe that this injection of wastewater increases pressure on deep underground faults, triggering earthquakes. The state of Oklahoma has now imposed strict limits on underground wastewater disposal.

ENERGY

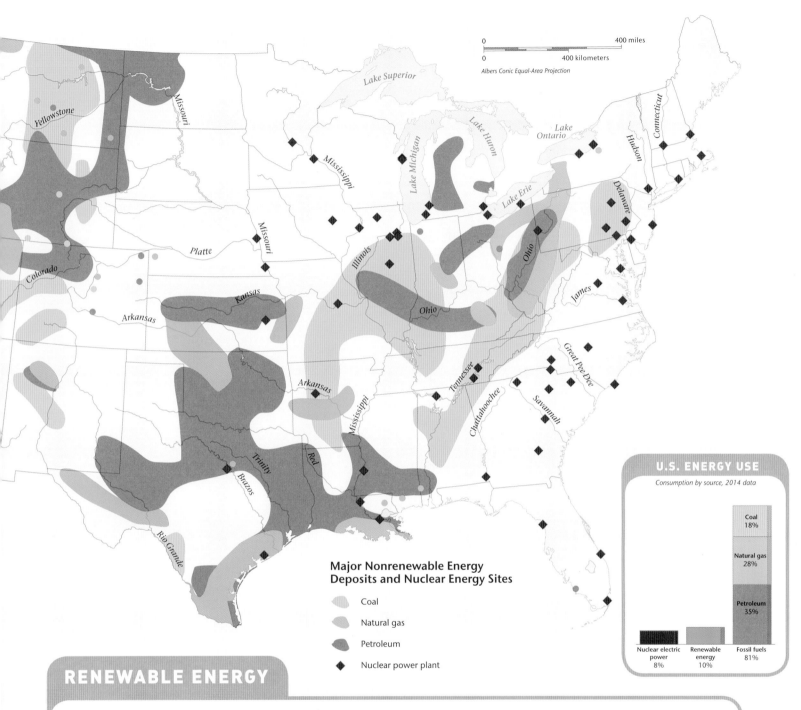

Lake Superior

Lake Huron

Lake Michigan

Lake Ontario

Lake Erie

Connecticut

Hudson

Delaware

James

Missouri

Yellowstone

Missouri

Platte

Colorado

Arkansas

Kansas

Illinois

Ohio

Ohio

Tennessee

Chattahoochee

Savannah

Great Pee Dee

Arkansas

Mississippi

Mississippi

Red

Trinity

Brazos

Rio Grande

0   400 miles

0   400 kilometers

Albers Conic Equal-Area Projection

Major Nonrenewable Energy Deposits and Nuclear Energy Sites

- Coal
- Natural gas
- Petroleum
- ◆ Nuclear power plant

U.S. ENERGY USE

Consumption by source, 2014 data

Coal 18%

Natural gas 28%

Petroleum 35%

Nuclear electric power 8%	Renewable energy 10%	Fossil fuels 81%

RENEWABLE ENERGY

Renewable energy comes from sources that are readily available and naturally replenished. In the United States about 10 percent of all energy consumed comes from renewable sources, including hydroelectric energy from moving water; geothermal energy from heat within Earth's core; solar energy from the sun; wind energy (left) from moving air; and biomass energy from burning organic matter such as wood, plant material, and garbage.

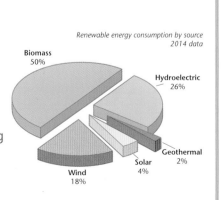

Renewable energy consumption by source 2014 data

Biomass 50%

Hydroelectric 26%

Geothermal 2%

Solar 4%

Wind 18%

THE NATIONAL CAPITAL

THE BASICS

Founding
July 16, 1790

Total area (land and water)
68 sq mi (177 sq km)

Land area
61 sq mi (158 sq km)

Population
672,228

Racial/ethnic groups
44.1% white; 48.3% African American; 4.2% Asian; 0.7% Native American; 10.6% Hispanic (any race)

Foreign born
14.0%

Urban population
100.0% (2010)

Population density
11,020.1 per sq mi
(4,254.6 per sq km)

GEO WHIZ

License plates in the District of Columbia bear the slogan "Taxation Without Representation," reflecting the fact that residents have no voting representative in either house of the U.S. Congress.

The flag of the District of Columbia, with its three red stars and two red stripes, is based on the shield in George Washington's family coat of arms.

In 1790 Benjamin Banneker, a free black, helped survey the land that would become the capital city.

The National Capital

Chosen as a compromise location between Northern and Southern interests and built on land ceded by Virginia and Maryland in the late 1700s, Washington, D.C., sits on a bank of the Potomac River. It is the seat of U.S. government and symbol of the country's history. Pierre L'Enfant, a French architect, was appointed by President George Washington to design the city, which is distinguished by a grid pattern cut by diagonal avenues. At the city's core is the National Mall, a broad park lined by monuments, museums, and stately government buildings.

AMERICAN BEAUTY ROSE

WOOD THRUSH

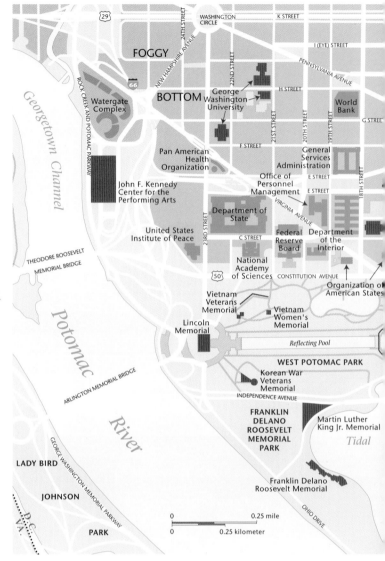

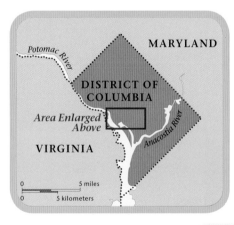

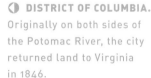 **DISTRICT OF COLUMBIA.** Originally on both sides of the Potomac River, the city returned land to Virginia in 1846.

GREAT LEADER. Abraham Lincoln, who was president during the Civil War and a strong opponent of slavery, is remembered in a monument that houses this seated statue at the west end of the National Mall.

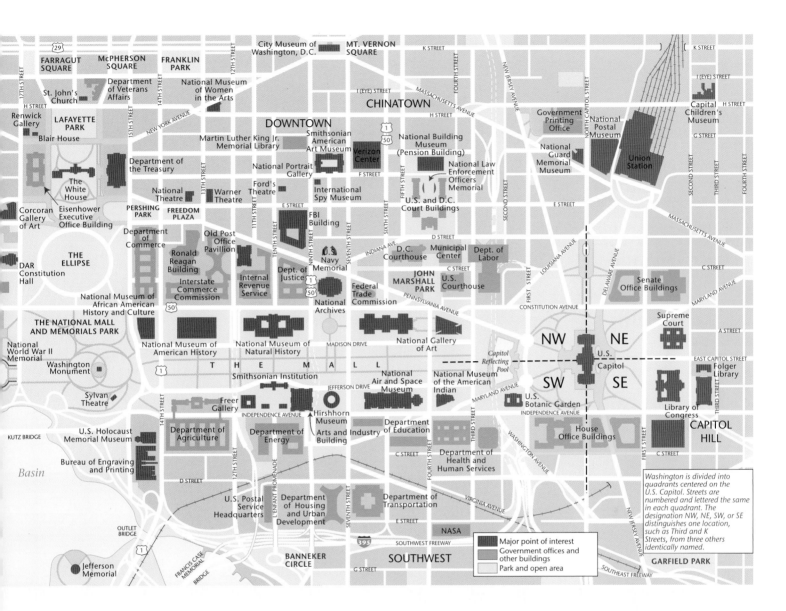

FARRAGUT SQUARE

McPHERSON SQUARE

FRANKLIN PARK

City Museum of Washington, D.C.

MT. VERNON SQUARE

K STREET

K STREET

St. John's Church

Department of Veterans Affairs

National Museum of Women in the Arts

I (EYE) STREET

CHINATOWN

I (EYE) STREET

Capital Children's Museum

Renwick Gallery

LAFAYETTE PARK

Blair House

DOWNTOWN

H STREET

Government Printing Office

National Postal Museum

G STREET

Martin Luther King Jr. Memorial Library

Smithsonian American Art Museum

National Building Museum (Pension Building)

National Guard Memorial Museum

Union Station

The White House

Department of the Treasury

National Portrait Gallery

Verizon Center

National Law Enforcement Officers Memorial

Corcoran Gallery of Art

Eisenhower Executive Office Building

National Theatre

Warner Theatre

Ford's Theatre

International Spy Museum

F STREET

U.S. and D.C. Court Buildings

E STREET

PERSHING PARK

FREEDOM PLAZA

FBI Building

DAR Constitution Hall

THE ELLIPSE

Department of Commerce

Old Post Office Pavilion

Dept. of Justice

Navy Memorial

D STREET

D.C. Courthouse

Municipal Center

Dept. of Labor

Ronald Reagan Building

Internal Revenue Service

National Archives

C STREET

JOHN MARSHALL PARK

U.S. Courthouse

C STREET

Senate Office Buildings

Interstate Commerce Commission

Federal Trade Commission

CONSTITUTION AVENUE

National Museum of African American History and Culture

THE NATIONAL MALL AND MEMORIALS PARK

National World War II Memorial

Washington Monument

National Museum of American History

National Museum of Natural History

MADISON DRIVE

National Gallery of Art

Capitol Reflecting Pool

NW | NE

Supreme Court

A STREET

EAST CAPITOL STREET

Folger Library

T H E   M A L L

Smithsonian Institution

JEFFERSON DRIVE

National Air and Space Museum

National Museum of the American Indian

U.S. Capitol

SW | SE

Library of Congress

CAPITOL HILL

Sylvan Theatre

Freer Gallery

INDEPENDENCE AVENUE

Hirshhorn Museum

U.S. Botanic Garden

INDEPENDENCE AVENUE

KUTZ BRIDGE

U.S. Holocaust Memorial Museum

Department of Agriculture

Department of Energy

Arts and Industry Building

Department of Education

Department of Health and Human Services

House Office Buildings

Bureau of Engraving and Printing

D STREET

C STREET

C STREET

Basin

U.S. Postal Service Headquarters

L'ENFANT PROMENADE

Department of Housing and Urban Development

Department of Transportation

E STREET

OUTLET BRIDGE

NASA

SOUTHWEST FREEWAY

SOUTHWEST

GARFIELD PARK

Jefferson Memorial

FRANCIS CASE MEMORIAL BRIDGE

BANNEKER CIRCLE

G STREET

SOUTHEAST FREEWAY

Washington is divided into quadrants centered on the U.S. Capitol. Streets are numbered and lettered the same in each quadrant. The designation NW, NE, SW, or SE distinguishes one location, such as Third and K Streets, from three others identically named.

■ Major point of interest
■ Government offices and other buildings
☐ Park and open area

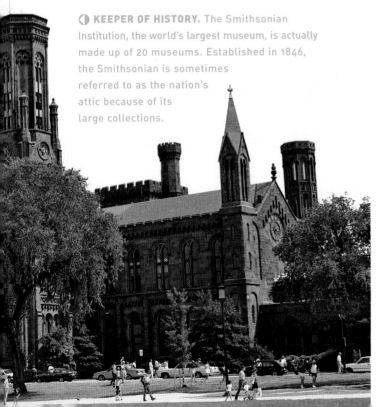

◖ KEEPER OF HISTORY. The Smithsonian Institution, the world's largest museum, is actually made up of 20 museums. Established in 1846, the Smithsonian is sometimes referred to as the nation's attic because of its large collections.

◯ NATIONAL ICON. The gleaming dome of the U.S. Capitol, home to the Senate and House of Representatives, is a familiar symbol of Washington's main business—the running of the country's government.

THE REGION

196,214 sq mi
(508,192 sq km)

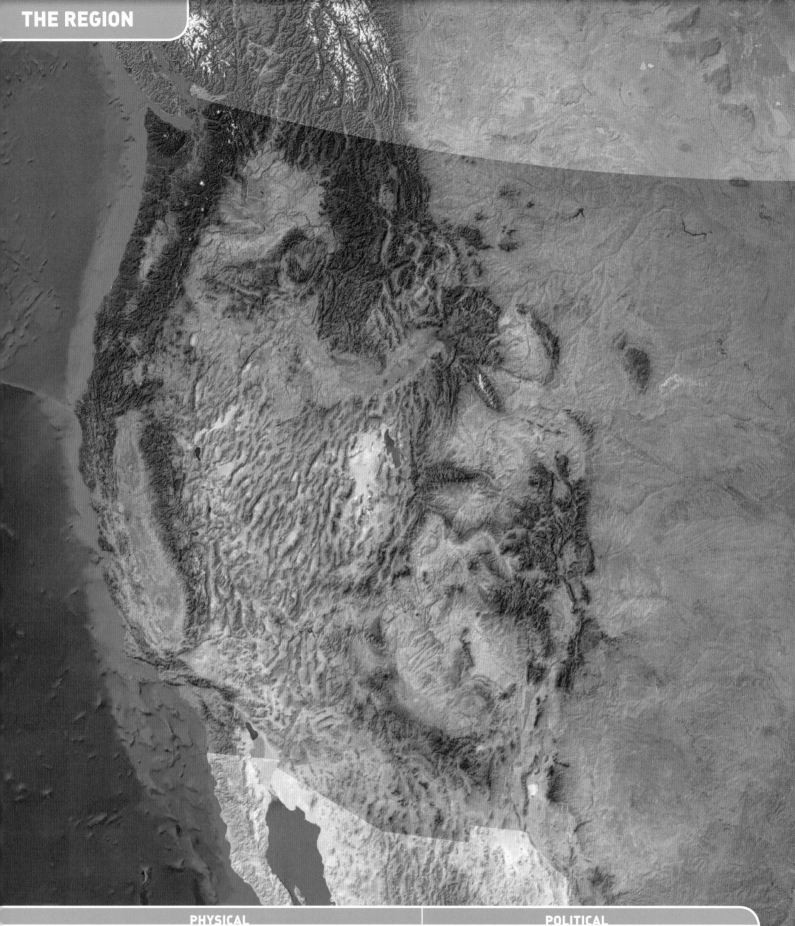

PHYSICAL

**Total area
(land and water)**
196,214 sq mi
(508,192 sq km)

Highest point
Mount Washington, NH
6,288 ft (1,917 m)

Lowest point
Sea level, shores of the
Atlantic Ocean

Longest rivers
St. Lawrence, Susquehanna,
Connecticut, Hudson

Largest lakes
Erie, Ontario, Champlain

Vegetation
Needleleaf, broadleaf, and
mixed forest

Climate
Continental to mild, with cool
to warm summers, cold winters,
and moderate precipitation
throughout the year

POLITICAL

Total population
59,645,340

States (11):
Connecticut, Delaware, Maine, Maryland,
Massachusetts, New Hampshire, New
Jersey, New York, Pennsylvania, Rhode
Island, Vermont

Largest state
New York: 54,555 sq mi (141,297 sq km)

Smallest state
Rhode Island: 1,545 sq mi (4,001 sq km)

Most populous state
New York: 19,795,791

Least populous state
Vermont: 626,042

Largest city proper
New York, NY: 8,550,405

The Northeast

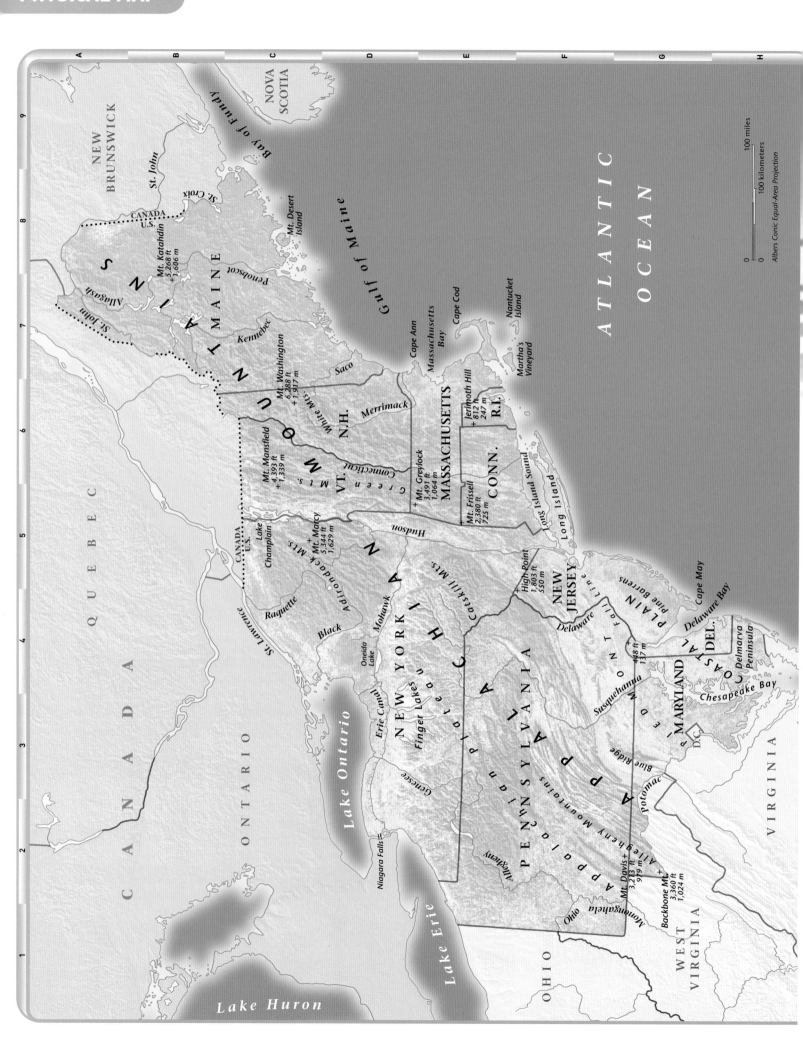

NEW BRUNSWICK

NOVA SCOTIA

CANADA
U.S.

Bay of Fundy

St. John

St. Croix

Mt. Katahdin
+5,268 ft
1,606 m

Allagash

St. John

MAINE

Penobscot

Mt. Desert Island

Kennebec

Saco

Gulf of Maine

QUEBEC

CANADA

APPALACHIAN MOUNTAINS

Mt. Washington
+6,288 ft
1,917 m

White Mts.

N.H.

Merrimack

Cape Ann

Massachusetts Bay

Cape Cod

Nantucket Island

Martha's Vineyard

ATLANTIC OCEAN

100 miles
100 kilometers
Albers Conic Equal-Area Projection

Mt. Mansfield
+4,393 ft
1,339 m

VT.

Green Mts.

Connecticut

Mt. Greylock
3,491 ft
1,064 m
+

MASSACHUSETTS

Jerimoth Hill
812 ft
247 m
+

R.I.

CONN.

Mt. Frissell
2,380 ft
725 m
+

Long Island Sound

Long Island

CANADA
U.S.

Lake Champlain

Adirondack Mts.

Mt. Marcy
+5,344 ft
1,629 m

Hudson

High Point
1,803 ft
550 m
+

NEW JERSEY

Cape May

Raquette

Black

Mohawk

Oneida Lake

St. Lawrence

NEW YORK

Finger Lakes

Erie Canal

Catskill Mts.

Appalachian Plateau

PENNSYLVANIA

Delaware

Piedmont

Pine Barrens

Delaware Bay

DEL.

Delmarva Peninsula

448 ft
137 m
+

COASTAL PLAIN

Fall Line

Susquehanna

MARYLAND

D.C.

Chesapeake Bay

Genesee

ONTARIO

Lake Ontario

Niagara Falls

Lake Erie

Allegheny

Blue Ridge

Potomac

Allegheny Mountains

Monongahela

Ohio

Mt. Davis
3,213 ft
979 m
+

Backbone Mt.
3,360 ft
1,024 m
+

WEST VIRGINIA

VIRGINIA

OHIO

Lake Huron

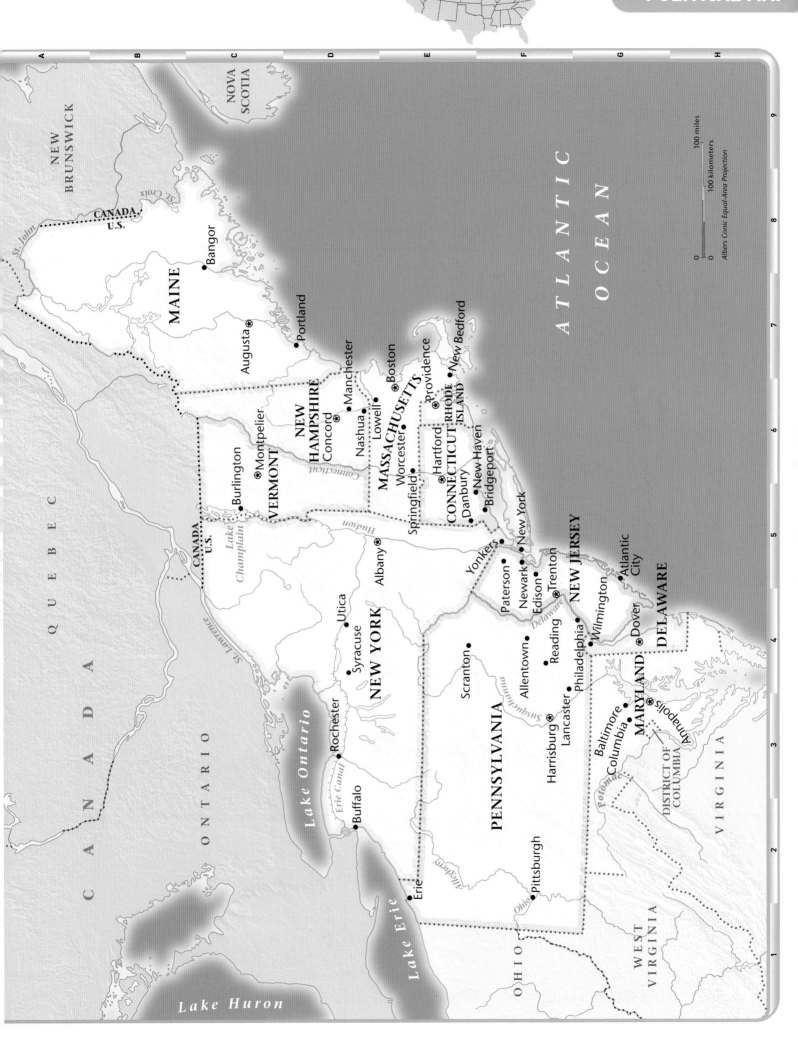

A B C D E F G H

NEW BRUNSWICK

NOVA SCOTIA

QUEBEC

CANADA

ONTARIO

CANADA U.S.

CANADA U.S.

MAINE

Bangor

Portland

Augusta ✴

St. Croix

St. John

Lake Champlain

St. Lawrence

Lake Ontario

Erie Canal

Rochester

Buffalo

Erie

Lake Erie

Lake Huron

OHIO

VERMONT

Burlington

Montpelier ✴

NEW HAMPSHIRE

Concord ✴

Manchester

Nashua

Lowell

Boston ✴

Worcester

Springfield

MASSACHUSETTS

Hartford ✴

Providence ✴

RHODE ISLAND

New Bedford

CONNECTICUT

Danbury

New Haven

Bridgeport

Connecticut

Hudson

Albany ✴

Utica

Syracuse

NEW YORK

Scranton

Yonkers

New York

Paterson

Newark

Edison

Trenton ✴

NEW JERSEY

Atlantic City

Allentown

Reading

Lancaster

Philadelphia

Harrisburg ✴

PENNSYLVANIA

Pittsburgh

Susquehanna

Allegheny

Ohio

Delaware

Wilmington

Dover ✴

DELAWARE

Baltimore

Columbia

MARYLAND

Annapolis ✴

DISTRICT OF COLUMBIA

Potomac

VIRGINIA

WEST VIRGINIA

ATLANTIC OCEAN

100 miles
100 kilometers
Albers Conic Equal-Area Projection
0
0

The Northeast

BIRTHPLACE OF A NATION

The United States had its beginnings in the Northeast region. Early European traders and settlers were quickly followed by immigrants from around the globe, making the region's population the most diverse in the country. The region includes the country's financial center, New York City, and its political capital, Washington, D.C. Although the region boasts tranquil mountains, lakes, and rivers, its teeming cities have always been the heart of the Northeast.

⬥ **DINNER DELICACY.** Lobsters, a favorite food for many people, turn bright red when cooked. These crustaceans live in the cold waters of the Atlantic Ocean and are caught using baited traps.

⬥ **MELTING POT.** From colonial times, the Northeast has been a gateway for immigration. These young girls, dressed in traditional saris and performing in an India Cultural Festival in New Jersey, reflect the rich diversity of the region.

◐ **DEFENDER OF FREEDOM.** Rising 548 feet (167 m) above Penn Square, Philadelphia's City Hall, with its statue of William Penn, is the country's largest municipal building. Penn was the founder of the Pennsylvania colony and a defender of equal rights for men and women.

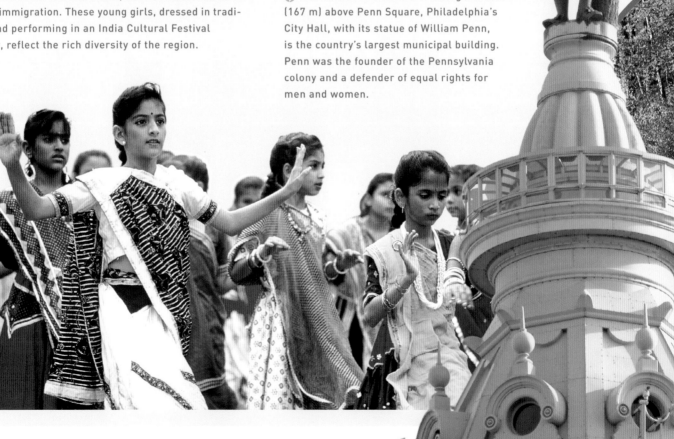

⬤ **DAWN'S EARLY LIGHT.** The lights of New York City's skyline sparkle against the early morning sky. The tall buildings of Lower Manhattan, reflected in the dark waters of the East River, are home to companies with influence that reaches around the world.

⬤ **STILL WATERS.** A father and son enjoy a quiet day of fishing on the smooth-as-glass waters of Lake Chocurua in New Hampshire's White Mountains. Deciduous trees turning red and gold will soon shed their leaves, and the hillsides will turn white with winter's snow, attracting skiers to the valley.

WHERE THE PICTURES ARE

Train station pp. 40-41
Moose p. 40
Tapping maple sugar p. 50
Skier pp. 50-51
Covered bridge p. 51
Hartford skyline p. 30
Lacrosse girls p. 31
Suburban mansions p. 42
Baseball game pp. 42-43
Statue of Liberty p. 44
Truck farmer p. 42
Grape harvesting p. 45
Niagara Falls p. 44

Church p. 41

Canoers on lake pp. 28-29
Lighthouse pp. 34-35
View from Cadillac Mt. p. 34
Puffins p. 35
Tobacco p. 30
Whales feeding p. 38
Mayflower II p. 38
Lobsters pp. 28-29
Cranberry harvest p. 39
Sailing p. 48
Newport Harbor pp. 48-49
Fossil hunter p. 48
New York skyline p. 29
Dancing girls p. 28
William Penn statue p. 28, Liberty Bell p. 46
Winterthur Mansion p. 32
Go Hens! p. 32
Ferris Wheel p. 42
Boardwalk scene pp. 32-33
Wild ponies p. 37

Pittsburgh p. 46
Amish barn p. 47
Baltimore skyline p. 36
Blue crab p. 36

THE BASICS

Statehood
January 9, 1788; 5th state

Total area (land and water)
5,543 sq mi (14,357 sq km)

Land area
4,842 sq mi (12,542 sq km)

Population
3,590,886

Capital
Hartford
Population 124,006

Largest city
Bridgeport
Population 147,629

Racial/ethnic groups
80.8% white; 11.6% African
American; 4.6% Asian; 0.5%
Native American; 15.4% Hispanic
origin (any race)

Foreign born
13.6%

Urban population
88.0% (2010)

Population density
741.6 per sq mi (286.3 per sq km)

GEO WHIZ

The sperm whale, Connecticut's
state animal, has a brain larger
than that of any other creature
known to have lived on Earth.

The first hamburgers in U.S.
history were served by Louis
Lassen at his New Haven lunch
wagon in 1895.

The nuclear-powered U.S.S.
Virginia, the first of a class
of technologically advanced
submarines, was built at
Groton, home of the U.S. Naval
Submarine Base.

Connecticut

As early as 1614 Dutch explorers founded trading posts along the coast of Connecticut, but the first permanent European settlements were established in 1635 by English Puritans from nearby Massachusetts. The Connecticut Fundamental Orders, which in 1639 established a democratic system of government in the colony, were an important model for the writing of the U.S. Constitution in 1787. This earned the state its nickname—the Constitution State. Even in colonial times Connecticut was an important industrial center, producing goods that competed with factories in England. During the Revolutionary War, Connecticut produced military goods for the colonial army. Today, Connecticut industries produce jet aircraft engines, helicopters, and nuclear submarines. Connecticut is home to many international corporations, but it is best known as the "insurance state." Following independence, businessmen offered to insure ship cargoes in exchange for a share of the profits. Soon after, other types of insurance were offered. Now, Connecticut is home to more than 100 insurance companies.

MOUNTAIN LAUREL
ROBIN

LEAFY HARVEST. Tents protect shade tobacco, the state's leading agricultural export by value. Leaves from the plants, which are grown in the Connecticut River Valley, are used for premium cigar wrappers.

BRIGHT CITY LIGHTS. Established as a fort in the early 1600s, Hartford was one of the earliest cities of colonial America. Today, this modern state capital is a center of economic growth and cultural diversity.

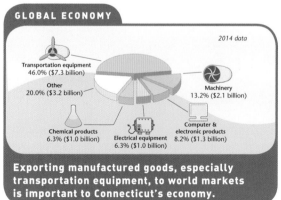

GLOBAL ECONOMY

2014 data

Transportation equipment
46.0% ($7.3 billion)

Other
20.0% ($3.2 billion)

Machinery
13.2% ($2.1 billion)

Chemical products
6.3% ($1.0 billion)

Electrical equipment
6.3% ($1.0 billion)

Computer & electronic products
8.2% ($1.3 billion)

Exporting manufactured goods, especially transportation equipment, to world markets is important to Connecticut's economy.

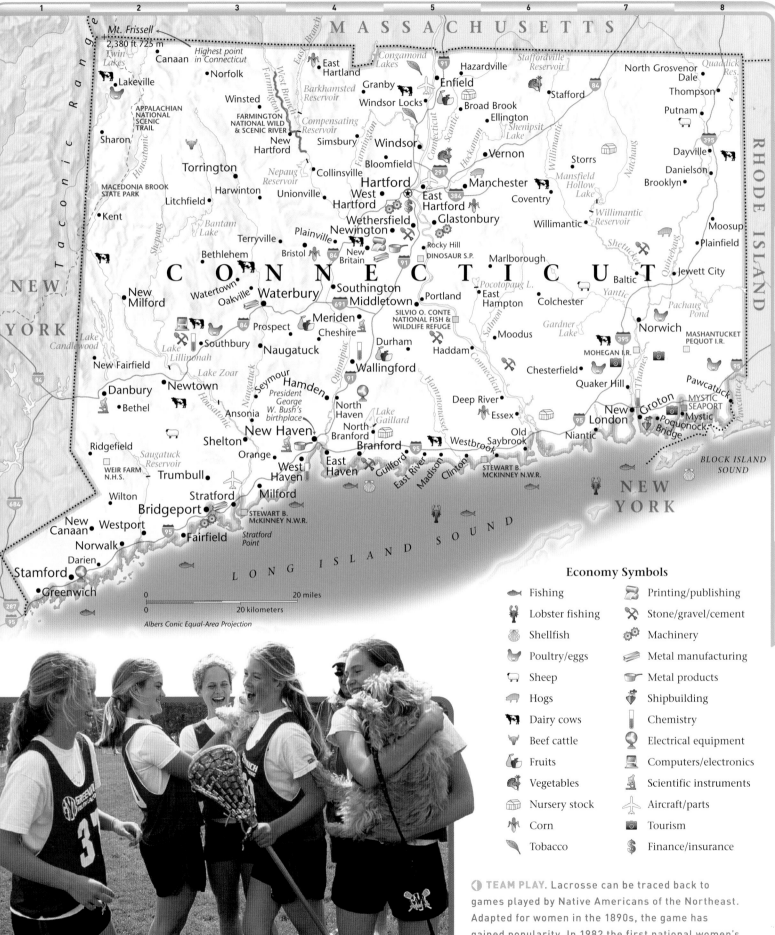

M A S S A C H U S E T T S

Mt. Frissell
2,380 ft 725 m
Highest point in Connecticut

Twin Lakes
Canaan
Lakeville
Norfolk
East Hartland
Congamond Lakes
Hazardville
Staffordville Reservoir
North Grosvenor Dale
Quaddick Res.
Thompson

Winsted
Granby
Enfield
Stafford
Putnam

Barkhamsted Reservoir
Windsor Locks
Broad Brook
Ellington

APPALACHIAN NATIONAL SCENIC TRAIL
Sharon
FARMINGTON NATIONAL WILD & SCENIC RIVER
Compensating Reservoir
New Hartford
Simsbury
Windsor
Vernon
Shenipsit Lake
Storrs
Dayville
Danielson

Torrington
Nepaug Reservoir
Collinsville
Bloomfield
Mansfield Hollow Lake
Brooklyn

MACEDONIA BROOK STATE PARK
Litchfield
Harwinton
Unionville
Hartford
West Hartford
Manchester
Coventry
Willimantic Reservoir
Moosup

Kent
Bantam Lake
Plainville
Wethersfield
Newington
East Hartford
Glastonbury
Willimantic
Plainfield

Terryville
Bristol
New Britain
Rocky Hill
DINOSAUR S.P.
Marlborough
Baltic
Jewett City

C O N N E Bethlehem **C T I C U T**
Watertown
Oakville
Waterbury
Southington
Middletown
Portland
East Hampton
Pocotopaug L.
Colchester
Yantic
Pachaug Pond

New Milford
Prospect
Meriden
Cheshire
Durham
Haddam
Salmon
Moodus
Gardner Lake
Norwich
MASHANTUCKET PEQUOT I.R.

Lake Candlewood
Southbury
Naugatuck
Chesterfield
MOHEGAN I.R.
Quaker Hill

Lake Lillinonah
Wallingford
Silvio O. Conte National Fish & Wildlife Refuge

New Fairfield
Lake Zoar
Seymour
Hamden
Quinnipiac
Deep River
Pawcatuck

Danbury
Newtown
President George W. Bush's birthplace
North Haven
Lake Gaillard
Essex
New London
Groton
MYSTIC SEAPORT

Bethel
Ansonia
North Branford
Westbrook
Niantic
Mystic
Poquonock Bridge

Ridgefield
Shelton
New Haven
Branford
Old Saybrook

WEIR FARM N.H.S.
Saugatuck Reservoir
Orange
East Haven
Guilford
East River
Madison
Clinton
STEWART B. McKINNEY N.W.R.
BLOCK ISLAND SOUND

Trumbull
West Haven
Milford
Stratford Point

Wilton
Stratford
STEWART B. McKINNEY N.W.R.

Bridgeport
N E W Y O R K

New Canaan
Westport
Fairfield

Norwalk
Darien

Stamford
Greenwich

L O N G   I S L A N D   S O U N D

0   20 miles
0   20 kilometers

Albers Conic Equal-Area Projection

N E W Y O R K
R H O D E I S L A N D
Taconic Range
Housatonic
Farmington
West Branch Farmington
East Branch
Connecticut
Scantic
Hockanum
Willimantic
Natchaug
Shetucket
Quinebaug
Shepaug
Naugatuck
Housatonic
Hammonasset
Connecticut
Thames

Economy Symbols

Fishing		Printing/publishing	
Lobster fishing		Stone/gravel/cement	
Shellfish		Machinery	
Poultry/eggs		Metal manufacturing	
Sheep		Metal products	
Hogs		Shipbuilding	
Dairy cows		Chemistry	
Beef cattle		Electrical equipment	
Fruits		Computers/electronics	
Vegetables		Scientific instruments	
Nursery stock		Aircraft/parts	
Corn		Tourism	
Tobacco		Finance/insurance	

TEAM PLAY. Lacrosse can be traced back to games played by Native Americans of the Northeast. Adapted for women in the 1890s, the game has gained popularity. In 1982 the first national women's lacrosse championship was held in New Jersey.

DECEMBER 7, 1787

THE BASICS

Statehood
December 7, 1787; 1st state

Total area (land and water)
2,489 sq mi (6,446 sq km)

Land area
1,949 sq mi (5,047 sq km)

Population
945,934

Capital
Dover
Population 37,355 (2014)

Largest city
Wilmington
Population 71,948

Racial/ethnic groups
70.4% white; 22.4% African
American; 3.9% Asian; 0.7%
Native American; 9.0% Hispanic
origin (any race)

Foreign born
8.4%

Urban population
83.3% (2010)

Population density
485.3 per sq mi (187.4 per sq km)

GEO WHIZ

Each year contestants bring
their pumpkins and launch-
ing machines to the Punkin
Chunkin World Championship in
Bridgeville to see who can
catapult their big, orange
squash the farthest.

The Delaware Estuary is
one of the most important
shorebird migration sites in
the Western Hemisphere.

The first steam railroad to
provide regular service began
operations in New Castle in 1831.

Delaware

Second smallest among the states in the area, Delaware has played a big role in the history of the United States. The Delaware River Valley was explored at various times by the Spanish, Portuguese, and Dutch, but the Swedes established the first per-manent European settlement in 1638. In 1655 the colony fell under Dutch author-ity, but in 1682 the land was annexed by William Penn and the Pennsylvania colony. In 1787 Delaware was the first state to ratify the new U.S. Constitution. Delaware's Atlantic coast beaches are popular with tourists. Its fertile farmland, mainly in the south, produces soybeans, corn, dairy products, and poultry. But the state's real economic power is located in the north, around Wilmington, where factories employ thousands of workers to process food products and produce machinery and chemicals. Industry has been a source of wealth, but it also poses a danger to the environment. Protecting the environment is a high priority for Delaware.

PEACH BLOSSOM
BLUE HEN CHICKEN

⬤ **TEAM SPIRIT.** Enthusiastic fans and the University of Delaware band support the "Fightin' Blue Hens." Located in Newark, the university traces its roots to 1743.

⬤ **PAST GRANDEUR.** Built in 1837 in the fashion of a Brit-ish country house, Winterthur was expanded from 12 to 196 rooms by the du Ponts, chemical industry tycoons. In 1951 the house was opened to the public as a museum for the family's extensive collection of antiques and Americana.

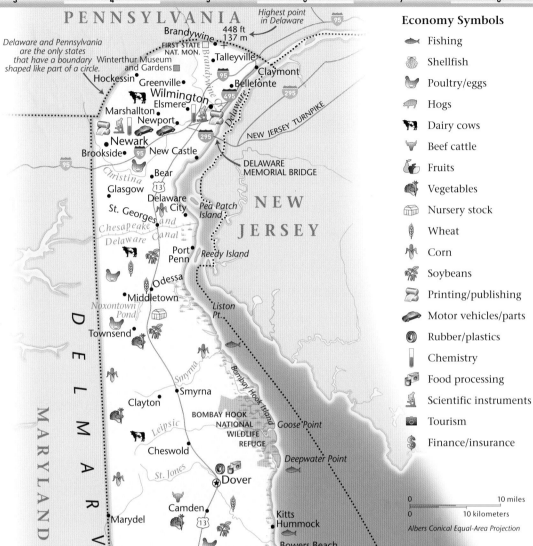

PENNSYLVANIA

NEW JERSEY

MARYLAND

D E L M A R V A   P E N I N S U L A

DELAWARE

Delaware Bay

ATLANTIC

OCEAN

Highest point in Delaware
448 ft 137 m

Delaware and Pennsylvania are the only states that have a boundary shaped like part of a circle.

Economy Symbols

- Fishing
- Shellfish
- Poultry/eggs
- Hogs
- Dairy cows
- Beef cattle
- Fruits
- Vegetables
- Nursery stock
- Wheat
- Corn
- Soybeans
- Printing/publishing
- Motor vehicles/parts
- Rubber/plastics
- Chemistry
- Food processing
- Scientific instruments
- Tourism
- Finance/insurance

0 ——— 10 miles
0 ——— 10 kilometers
Albers Conical Equal-Area Projection

Map labels: Brandywine, Talleyville, FIRST STATE NAT. MON., Winterthur Museum and Gardens, Hockessin, Greenville, Claymont, Bellefonte, Wilmington, Elsmere, Marshallton, Newport, Newark, Brookside, New Castle, DELAWARE MEMORIAL BRIDGE, NEW JERSEY TURNPIKE, Bear, Glasgow, Delaware City, St. Georges, Pea Patch Island, Chesapeake and Delaware Canal, Port Penn, Reedy Island, Odessa, Middletown, Noxontown Pond, Townsend, Liston Pt., Smyrna, Clayton, BOMBAY HOOK NATIONAL WILDLIFE REFUGE, Bombay Hook Island, Goose Point, Leipsic, Cheswold, Deepwater Point, St. Jones, Dover, Camden, Kitts Hummock, Marydel, Bowers Beach, Felton, Frederica, Harrington, Houston, Milford, Lincoln, Slaughter Beach, PRIME HOOK NATIONAL WILDLIFE REFUGE, Greenwood, Ellendale, Broadkill Beach, Cape Henlopen, Bridgeville, Milton, Lewes, Lewes & Rehoboth Canal, Harbeson, Midway, Rehoboth Beach, Georgetown, Rehoboth Bay, Dewey Beach, Seaford, Blades, Laurel, Oak Orchard, Indian River Bay, Indian River Inlet, Millsboro, Dagsboro, Ocean View, Bethany Beach, Frankford, Assawoman Canal, Cypress Swamp, Selbyville, Delmar, Fenwick Island, Marshyhope Creek, Nanticoke, Choptank

Christina, Delaware (river), Smyrna (river)

🐬 **SEASIDE RETREAT.** Originally established in 1873 as a church campground, Rehoboth Beach is still a popular getaway destination on Delaware's Atlantic coastline. A concrete dolphin overlooks the town's boardwalk, a popular promenade that separates shops and restaurants from the beach. The boardwalk has been destroyed on several occasions by storms.

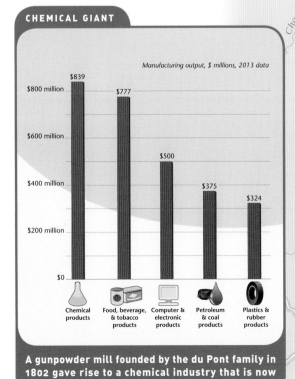

CHEMICAL GIANT

Manufacturing output, $ millions, 2013 data

Product	Output
Chemical products	$839
Food, beverage, & tobacco products	$777
Computer & electronic products	$500
Petroleum & coal products	$375
Plastics & rubber products	$324

A gunpowder mill founded by the du Pont family in 1802 gave rise to a chemical industry that is now the state's leading industry and employer.

THE BASICS

Statehood
March 15, 1820; 23rd state

Total area (land and water)
35,380 sq mi (91,633 sq km)

Land area
30,843 sq mi (79.883 sq km)

Population
1,329,328

Capital
Augusta
Population 18,705 (2014)

Largest city
Portland
Population 66,881

Racial/ethnic groups
94.9% white; 1.4% African American; 1.2% Asian; 0.7% Native American; 1.6% Hispanic origin (any race)

Foreign born
3.4%

Urban population
38.7% (2010)

Population density
43.1 per sq mi (16.6 per sq km)

GEO WHIZ

With world shark populations declining, some conservation-minded deep-sea fishermen in Maine have turned the idea of a shark tournament upside down. They still compete to see who can catch the biggest fish, but they tag and release the sharks.

Forests cover more than 85 percent of Maine. No wonder it is called the Pine Tree State.

Glaciers formed during the last ice age carved hundreds of inlets out of Maine's shoreline and created some 2,000 islands off the coast.

Maine

Maine's story begins long before the arrival of European settlers in the 1600s. Evidence of native people dates to at least 3000 B.C., and Leif Erikson and his Viking sailors may have explored Maine's coastline 500 years before Columbus crossed the Atlantic. English settlements were established along the southern coast in the 1620s, and in 1677 the territory of Maine came under control of Massachusetts. Following the Revolutionary War, the people of Maine pressed for separation from Massachusetts, and in 1820 Maine entered the Union as a nonslave state under the terms of the Missouri Compromise. Most of Maine's population is concentrated in towns along the coast. Famous for its rugged beauty, the coast is the focus of the tourist industry. Cold offshore waters contribute to a lively fishing industry, and timber from the state's mountainous interior supports wood product and paper businesses. Maine, a leader in environmental awareness, seeks a balance between economic growth and environmental protection.

WHITE PINE CONE AND TASSEL

CHICKADEE

🌐 **ACADIA NATIONAL PARK,** established in 1929, attracts thousands of tourists each year. The park includes Cadillac Mountain, the highest point along the North Atlantic coast and the site from which the earliest sunrises in the United States can be viewed from October 7 through March 6.

BLUEBERRY LEADER

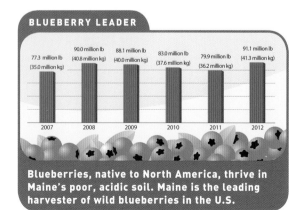

2007	2008	2009	2010	2011	2012
77.3 million lb (35.0 million kg)	90.0 million lb (40.8 million kg)	88.1 million lb (40.0 million kg)	83.0 million lb (37.6 million kg)	79.9 million lb (36.2 million kg)	91.1 million lb (41.3 million kg)

Blueberries, native to North America, thrive in Maine's poor, acidic soil. Maine is the leading harvester of wild blueberries in the U.S.

THE PINE TREE STATE
MAINE

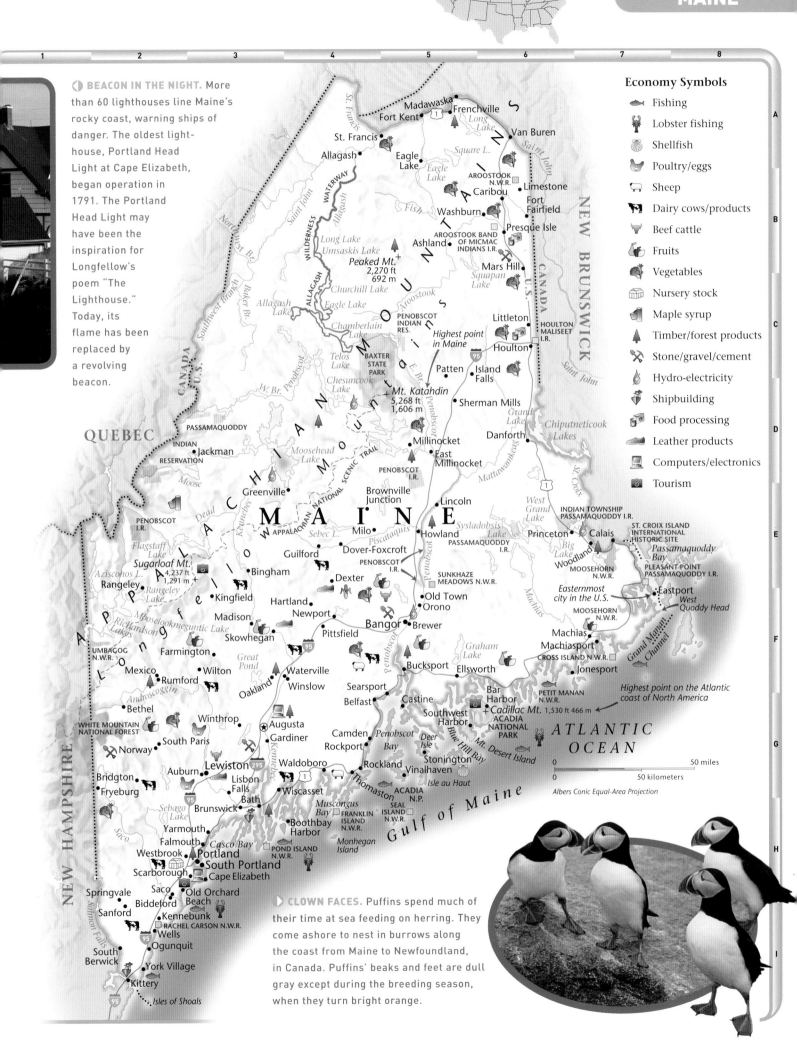

◖ **BEACON IN THE NIGHT.** More than 60 lighthouses line Maine's rocky coast, warning ships of danger. The oldest lighthouse, Portland Head Light at Cape Elizabeth, began operation in 1791. The Portland Head Light may have been the inspiration for Longfellow's poem "The Lighthouse." Today, its flame has been replaced by a revolving beacon.

Economy Symbols

- Fishing
- Lobster fishing
- Shellfish
- Poultry/eggs
- Sheep
- Dairy cows/products
- Beef cattle
- Fruits
- Vegetables
- Nursery stock
- Maple syrup
- Timber/forest products
- Stone/gravel/cement
- Hydro-electricity
- Shipbuilding
- Food processing
- Leather products
- Computers/electronics
- Tourism

QUEBEC

NEW BRUNSWICK

CANADA
U.S.

NEW HAMPSHIRE

MAINE

APPALACHIAN MOUNTAINS

St. Francis
Madawaska
Fort Kent
Frenchville
Van Buren
St. Francis
Allagash
Eagle Lake
Square L.
Long Lake
Saint John
AROOSTOOK N.W.R.
Caribou
Limestone
Washburn
Fort Fairfield
Ashland
AROOSTOOK BAND OF MICMAC INDIANS I.R.
Presque Isle
Mars Hill
Squapan Lake
Long Lake
Umsaskis Lake
Peaked Mt. 2,270 ft 692 m
Churchill Lake
Littleton
HOULTON MALISEET I.R.
Eagle Lake
PENOBSCOT INDIAN RES.
Houlton
Chamberlain Lake
Highest point in Maine
Telos Lake
BAXTER STATE PARK
Patten
Island Falls
Chesuncook Lake
Mt. Katahdin 5,268 ft 1,606 m
Sherman Mills
Grand Lake
Chiputneticook Lakes
Danforth
Millinocket
East Millinocket
PENOBSCOT I.R.
Jackman
Moosehead Lake
Brownville Junction
Lincoln
West Grand Lake
INDIAN TOWNSHIP PASSAMAQUODDY I.R.
Greenville
Sebec L.
Milo
Howland
Sysladobsis Lake
Princeton
Calais
ST. CROIX ISLAND INTERNATIONAL HISTORIC SITE
Guilford
Dover-Foxcroft
Piscataquis
PASSAMAQUODDY I.R.
Big Lake
Woodland
Passamaquoddy Bay
Sugarloaf Mt. 4,237 ft 1,291 m
Bingham
PENOBSCOT I.R.
SUNKHAZE MEADOWS N.W.R.
MOOSEHORN N.W.R.
PLEASANT POINT PASSAMAQUODDY I.R.
Rangeley
Kingfield
Dexter
Old Town
Orono
Easternmost city in the U.S.
Eastport
West Quoddy Head
Madison
Hartland
Newport
Bangor
Brewer
MOOSEHORN N.W.R.
Skowhegan
Pittsfield
Machias
Machiasport
Farmington
Graham Lake
Bucksport
Ellsworth
CROSS ISLAND N.W.R.
Jonesport
Mexico
Wilton
Waterville
Winslow
Searsport
Belfast
Castine
Bar Harbor
PETIT MANAN N.W.R.
Highest point on the Atlantic coast of North America
Rumford
Oakland
Southwest Harbor
Cadillac Mt. 1,530 ft 466 m
Bethel
Great Pond
Camden
Rockport
Penobscot Bay
Deer Isle
ACADIA NATIONAL PARK
ATLANTIC OCEAN
Winthrop
Augusta
Gardiner
Stonington
Vinalhaven
Mt. Desert Island
Norway
South Paris
Rockland
Thomaston
Isle au Haut
Auburn
Lewiston
Waldoboro
ACADIA N.P.
SEAL ISLAND N.W.R.
Bridgton
Lisbon Falls
Wiscasset
Muscongus Bay
FRANKLIN ISLAND N.W.R.
Fryeburg
Brunswick
Boothbay Harbor
Monhegan Island
Yarmouth
POND ISLAND N.W.R.
Falmouth
Casco Bay
Gulf of Maine
Westbrook
Portland
South Portland
Scarborough
Cape Elizabeth
Springvale
Saco
Old Orchard Beach
Biddeford
Sanford
Kennebunk
RACHEL CARSON N.W.R.
Wells
Ogunquit
South Berwick
York Village
Kittery
Isles of Shoals

50 miles
50 kilometers
Albers Conic Equal-Area Projection

▷ **CLOWN FACES.** Puffins spend much of their time at sea feeding on herring. They come ashore to nest in burrows along the coast from Maine to Newfoundland, in Canada. Puffins' beaks and feet are dull gray except during the breeding season, when they turn bright orange.

THE BASICS

Statehood
April 28, 1788; 7th state

Total area (land and water)
12,406 sq mi (32,131 sq km)

Land area
9,707 sq mi (25,142 sq km)

Population
6,006,401

Capital
Annapolis
Population 38,856

Largest city
Baltimore
Population 621,849

Racial/ethnic groups
59.6% white; 30.5% African American; 6.5% Asian; 0.6% Native American; 9.5% Hispanic origin (any race)

Foreign born
14.0 %

Urban population
87.2% (2010)

Population density
618.8 per sq mi (238.9 per sq km)

GEO WHIZ

The Naval Support Facility Thurmont, better known as Camp David, is the mountain retreat of American presidents. It is part of Catoctin Mountain Park in north-central Maryland.

Residents on Smith Island, in the lower Chesapeake Bay, are being robbed of their land by rising sea levels and of their traditional livelihood by dwindling blue crab harvests. They fear a major Atlantic hurricane could wipe out their island home.

The name of Baltimore's professional football team—the Ravens—may have been inspired by the title of a poem by Edgar Allan Poe, who lived in Baltimore in the mid-1800s and whose grave is in that city.

Maryland

Native Americans, who raised crops and harvested oysters from the nearby waters of Chesapeake Bay, lived on the land that would become Maryland long before early European settlers arrived. In 1608 Captain John Smith explored the waters of the bay, and in 1634 English settlers established the colony of Maryland. In 1788 Maryland became the seventh state to ratify the new U.S. Constitution. Chesapeake Bay, the largest estuary in the United States, almost splits Maryland into two parts. East of the bay lies the flat coastal plain, and to the west the land rises through the hilly piedmont and mountainous panhandle. Chesapeake Bay, the state's economic and environmental focal point, supports a busy seafood industry. It is also a major transportation artery, linking Baltimore and other Maryland ports to the Atlantic Ocean. Most of the people of Maryland live in an urban corridor between Baltimore and Washington, D.C., where jobs in government, research, and high-tech businesses provide employment.

BLACK-EYED SUSAN

NORTHERN (BALTIMORE) ORIOLE

⚫ **GATEWAY CITY.** Since the early 1700s, Baltimore, near the upper Chesapeake Bay, has been a major seaport and focus of trade, industry, and immigration. Today, the Inner Harbor is not only a modern working port but also the city's vibrant cultural center.

◀ **COLORFUL CRUSTACEAN.** Blue crabs, found in Maryland's Chesapeake Bay waters, were a staple in the diet of Native Americans. They have been harvested commercially since the mid-1800s, and the tasty meat is a popular menu item—especially in crab cakes—in seafood restaurants throughout the area.

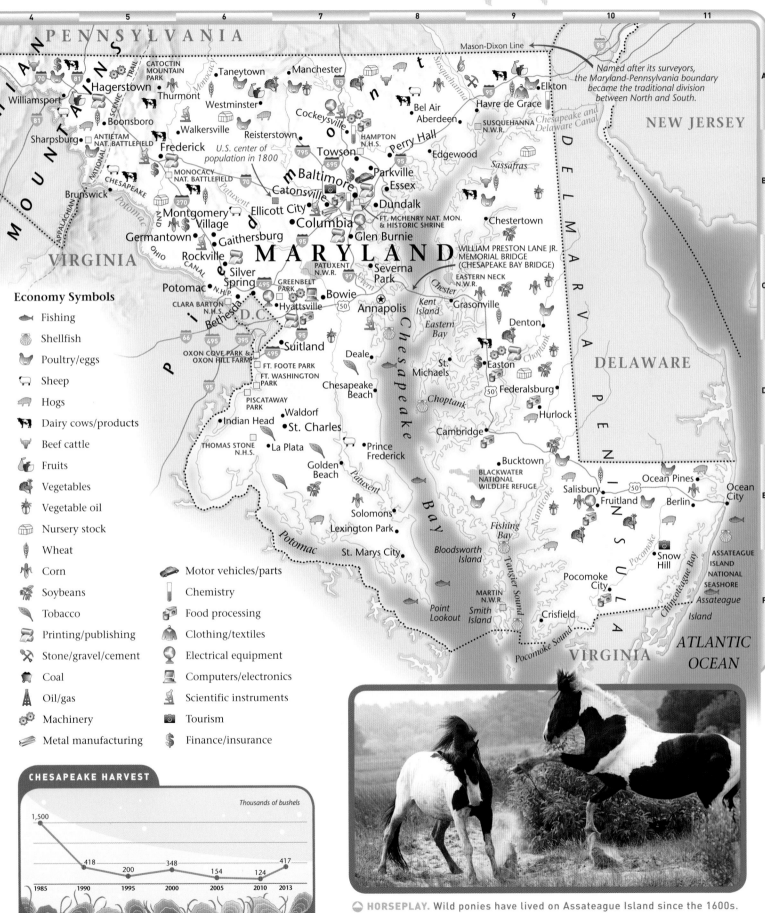

Named after its surveyors, the Maryland-Pennsylvania boundary became the traditional division between North and South.

Economy Symbols

- Fishing
- Shellfish
- Poultry/eggs
- Sheep
- Hogs
- Dairy cows/products
- Beef cattle
- Fruits
- Vegetables
- Vegetable oil
- Nursery stock
- Wheat
- Corn
- Soybeans
- Tobacco
- Printing/publishing
- Stone/gravel/cement
- Coal
- Oil/gas
- Machinery
- Metal manufacturing
- Motor vehicles/parts
- Chemistry
- Food processing
- Clothing/textiles
- Electrical equipment
- Computers/electronics
- Scientific instruments
- Tourism
- Finance/insurance

CHESAPEAKE HARVEST

Thousands of bushels

1,500 (1985)
418 (1990)
200 (1995)
348 (2000)
154 (2005)
124 (2010)
417 (2013)

Maryland's oyster harvest fell dramatically due to overharvesting, pollution, and disease, but it is now making a comeback.

HORSEPLAY. Wild ponies have lived on Assateague Island since the 1600s. Some believe the original ponies were survivors from a Spanish galleon that sank offshore. Today, more than 300 ponies live on this Atlantic barrier island shared by Maryland and Virginia.

THE BASICS

Statehood
February 6, 1788; 6th state

Total area (land and water)
10,554 sq mi (27,336 sq km)

Land area
7,800 sq mi (20,202 sq km)

Population
6,794,422

Capital
Boston
Population 667,137

Largest city
Boston
Population 667,137

Racial/ethnic groups
82.1% white; 8.4% African American; 6.6% Asian; 0.5% Native American; 11.2% Hispanic origin (any race)

Foreign born
15.0%

Urban population
92.0% (2010)

Population density
871.1 per sq mi
(336.3 per sq km)

GEO WHIZ

In 1717 the pirate ship *Whydah*, under the command of Captain Samuel Bellamy (also known as Black Sam), went down in a storm off Cape Cod. Treasure and artifacts recovered from the ship are on display at the Whydah Museum, in Provincetown.

Massachusetts is the birthplace of several famous inventors, including Eli Whitney, Samuel Morse, and Benjamin Franklin.

The country's first lighthouse was built on Little Brewster Island in Boston Harbor in 1716. It was automated in 1998 and opened to the public in 1999.

Stellwagen Bank National Marine Sanctuary helps make Cape Cod one of the world's best spots for whale-watching.

Massachusetts

The earliest human inhabitants of Massachusetts were Native Americans who arrived more than 10,000 years ago. The first Europeans to visit Massachusetts may have been Norsemen around A.D. 1000, and later fishermen came from France and Spain. But the first permanent European settlement was established in 1620, when people aboard the sailing ship *Mayflower* landed near Plymouth on the coast of Massachusetts. The Puritans arrived soon after, and by 1630 they had established settlements at Salem and Boston. By 1640 more than 16,000 people, most seeking religious freedom, had settled in Massachusetts. The early economy of Massachusetts was based on shipping, fishing, and whaling. By the 19th century, industry, taking advantage of abundant water power, had a firm foothold. Factory jobs attracted thousands of immigrants, mainly from Europe. In the late 20th century, Massachusetts experienced a boom in high-tech jobs, drawing on the state's skilled labor force and its 114 colleges and universities.

⚓ **REMINDER OF TIMES PAST.** Shrouded in morning mist, this replica of the *Mayflower* docked in Plymouth Harbor is a reminder of Massachusetts's early history.

CHICKADEE

MAYFLOWER

◐ **LEVIATHANS OF THE DEEP.** In the 19th century, Massachusetts was an important center for the whaling industry, with more than 300 registered whaling ships. Today, humpback whales swim in the protected waters of a marine sanctuary in Massachusetts Bay.

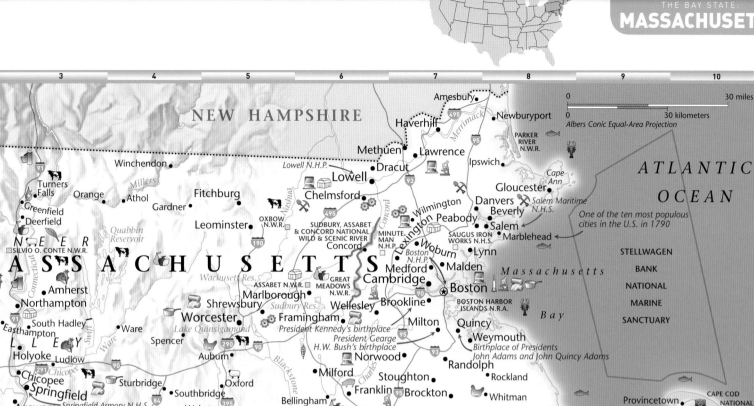

NEW HAMPSHIRE

ATLANTIC OCEAN

MASSACHUSETTS

One of the ten most populous cities in the U.S. in 1790

STELLWAGEN BANK NATIONAL MARINE SANCTUARY

Massachusetts *Bay*

CONNECTICUT

RHODE ISLAND

President Kennedy's birthplace
President George H.W. Bush's birthplace
Birthplace of Presidents John Adams and John Quincy Adams

Cape Cod Bay

CAPE COD NATIONAL SEASHORE

Cape Cod Canal

Buzzards Bay

Nantucket Sound

Rhode Island Sound

Vineyard Sound

Martha's Vineyard

Nantucket Island

Economy Symbols

- Fishing
- Lobster fishing
- Shellfish
- Poultry/eggs
- Sheep
- Hogs
- Dairy cows/products
- Beef cattle
- Fruits
- Vegetables
- Nursery stock
- Wheat
- Tobacco
- Maple syrup
- Printing/publishing
- Stone/gravel/cement
- Hydro-electricity
- Machinery
- Metal products
- Computers/electronics
- Scientific instruments
- Aerospace
- Tourism

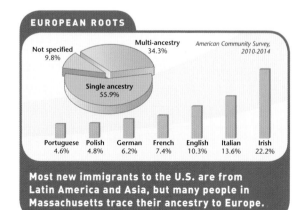

BIG BUSINESS. Cranberries, grown in fields called bogs, are the state's largest agricultural crop. These tiny berries, one of only three fruits native to North America, are consumed mainly in the form of juice or as a tasty accompaniment to holiday dishes. Workers flood fields to make harvesting the floating berries easier.

EUROPEAN ROOTS

American Community Survey, 2010-2014

Not specified 9.8%
Multi-ancestry 34.3%
Single ancestry 55.9%

Portuguese	Polish	German	French	English	Italian	Irish
4.6%	4.8%	6.2%	7.4%	10.3%	13.6%	22.2%

Most new immigrants to the U.S. are from Latin America and Asia, but many people in Massachusetts trace their ancestry to Europe.

New Hampshire

The territory that would become the state of New Hampshire, the ninth state to approve the U.S. Constitution in 1788, began as a fishing colony established along the short 18-mile (29-km)-long coastline in 1623. New Hampshire was named a royal colony in 1679, but as the Revolutionary War approached, it was the first colony to declare its independence from English rule. In the early 19th century, life in New Hampshire followed two very different paths. Near the coast, villages and towns grew up around sawmills, shipyards, and warehouses. But in the forested, mountainous interior, people lived on small, isolated farms, and towns provided only basic services. Today, modern industries such as computer and electronic component manufacturing and other high-tech companies, together with biotech and medical research, have brought prosperity to the state. In addition, the state's natural beauty attracts tourists year-round to hike on forest trails, swim in pristine lakes, and ski on snow-covered mountain slopes.

THE BASICS

Statehood
June 21, 1788; 9th state

Total area (land and water)
9,349 sq mi (24,214 sq km)

Land area
8,953 sq mi (23,187 sq km)

Population
1,330,608

Capital
Concord
Population 42,444 (2014)

Largest city
Manchester
Population 110,229

Racial/ethnic groups
93.9% white; 1.5% African American; 2.6% Asian; 0.3% Native American; 3.4% Hispanic origin (any race)

Foreign born
5.6%

Urban population
60.3% (2010)

Population density
148.6 per sq mi
(57.4 per sq km)

GEO WHIZ

The Granite State boasts more than 200 different kinds of rocks and minerals, making it a great destination for collectors.

The first potato grown in the United States was planted in 1719 in Londonderry on the Common Field, better known as the Commons.

Ben Kilham's unique way of rehabilitating abandoned black bear cubs he finds in the New Hampshire woods has earned him the nickname Bear Man by residents of Lyme.

LUMBERING GIANT.
Averaging 6 feet (2 m) tall at the shoulders, moose are the largest of North America's deer. Moose are found throughout New Hampshire.

PURPLE FINCH
PURPLE LILAC

ROARING WINDS

F4 "devastating tornado"
207-260 mph
(333-418 km/h)

Category 5 Hurricane wind speeds greater than 155 mph (249 km/h)

Mt. Washington record:
231 miles an hour
(371 km/h)
April 1934

Mount Washington holds the record for the highest surface wind speed in the U.S., comparable to winds in Category 5 hurricanes and F4 tornadoes.

ALL ABOARD. Tourists traveling by train through the White Mountains enjoy the cool autumn weather and the colorful fall foliage of the deciduous trees that cover the mountains.

AUTUMN PEACE. A white steepled church sits nestled among trees in a village near New Hampshire's White Mountains. Such traditional churches, common in the New England landscape, are a reminder of early settlers' search for religious freedom.

Economy Symbols

- Fishing
- Lobster fishing
- Shellfish
- Sheep
- Dairy cows/products
- Beef cattle
- Fruits
- Nursery stock
- Corn
- Maple syrup
- Timber/forest products
- Stone/gravel/cements
- Hydro-electricity
- Machinery
- Metal products
- Computers/electronics
- Scientific instruments
- Tourism

QUEBEC

CANADA
U.S.

Third L.
First Connecticut Lake
Second Lake
Lake Francis

SILVIO O. CONTE N.W.R.
Colebrook

Blue Mt.
3,723 ft
1,135 m

UMBAGOG N.W.R.
Umbagog L.

North Stratford

Groveton

Mt. Cabot
4,160 ft 1,268 m

WHITE MOUNTAIN NATIONAL FOREST

Lancaster

Berlin

Gorham

Highest point in New Hampshire

Whitefield

Littleton

Franconia

Mt. Washington
6,288 ft 1,917 m

Presidential Range

Mt. Lafayette
5,249 ft
1,600 m

Haverhill Bath Bridge
Lisbon
FRANCONIA NOTCH S.P.

CRAWFORD NOTCH S.P.

WILDCAT BROOK NATIONAL WILD & SCENIC RIVER

Woodsville

Oldest covered bridge in the U.S. (1829)

Lincoln

North Conway

WHITE MOUNTAIN NATIONAL FOREST

Haverhill

VERMONT

Orford

Warren

Conway

Conway Lake

MAINE

NEW HAMPSHIRE

Baker

Squam Lake

Bearcamp

Center Sandwich

Ossipee Lake

Center Ossipee

Hanover

APPALACHIAN

Enfield

Canaan

Newfound Lake

Ashland

Meredith

Lake Wentworth

Wolfeboro

Lebanon

Mascoma Lake

Bristol

Winnipesaukee

Sanbornville

| 0 | 20 miles |
| 0 | 20 kilometers |

Albers Conic Equal-Area Projection

SAINT-GAUDENS N.H.S.

Winnisquam Lake

Laconia

Merrymeeting Lake

New London

Franklin

Tilton

Crystal Lake

Alton Bay

Claremont

Newport

Sugar

JOHN HAY N.W.R.

Northfield

Farmington

Milton

Sunapee Lake

MT. SUNAPEE S.P.

Mt. Sunapee
2,743 ft
836 m

Suncook Lakes

Canterbury

Rochester

Somersworth

Charlestown

President Pierce's birthplace

Contoocook

Pittsfield

Dover

Henniker

Concord

Durham

GREAT BAY N.W.R.

North Walpole

Highland Lake

Hillsboro

Suncook

Bow Lake

LAMPREY NATIONAL WILD & SCENIC RIVER

Newmarket

Walpole

Antrim

Contoocook

Raymond

Portsmouth

Surry Mt. Lake

Nubanusit Lake

Manchester

Massabesic Lake

Great Bay

Rye

Isles of Shoals

Keene

Monadnock Mt.
3,165 ft
965 m

Peterborough

Londonderry

East Derry

Exeter

Kingston

Hampton

PISGAH S.P.

Ashuelot

WAPACK N.W.R.

Wilton

Merrimack

Derry

Atkinson

Plaistow

ATLANTIC OCEAN

Hinsdale

Troy

Jaffrey

Milford

Salem

Winchester

Greenville

New Ipswich

Nashua

MASSACHUSETTS

APPALACHIAN

WHITE MOUNTAINS

NATIONAL SCENIC TRAIL

Connecticut
Ammonoosuc
Androscoggin
Upper Ammonoosuc
Moore Reservoir
Ellis
Saco
Ossipee
Saco
Pemigewasset
Merrimack
Suncook
Cocheco
Salmon Falls
Piscataqua
Lamprey
Southegan
Merrimack
Contoocook

THE GARDEN STATE:
NEW JERSEY

THE BASICS

Statehood
December 18, 1787; 3rd state

Total area (land and water)
8,723 sq mi (22,591 sq km)

Land area
7,354 sq mi (19,047 sq km)

Population
8,958,013

Capital
Trenton
Population 84,225

Largest city
Newark
Population 281,944

Racial/ethnic groups
72.6% white; 14.8% African American; 9.7% Asian; 0.6% Native American; 19.7% Hispanic origin (any race)

Foreign born
21.5%

Urban population
94.7% (2010)

Population density
1,218.1 per sq mi
(470.3 per sq km)

GEO WHIZ

Site of a one-time trash heap, the Meadowlands, a swampy lowland along the Hackensack River, is now home to a major sports complex.

In 1930 New Jerseyite Charles Darrow developed the game Monopoly. He named Boardwalk and other streets in the game after those in Atlantic City.

Hadrosaurus, the first dinosaur skeleton excavated in North America, was named in honor of Haddonfield, its discovery site.

New Jersey

◐ **HOLD ON!** New Jersey's Atlantic coast is lined with sandy beaches that attract vacationers from near and far. Amusement parks, such as this one in Wildwood, add to the fun.

Long before Europeans settled in New Jersey, the region was home to hunting and farming communities of Delaware Indians. The Dutch set up a trading post in northern New Jersey in 1618, calling it New Netherland, but yielded the land in 1664 to the English, who named it New Jersey after the English Channel Isle of Jersey. New Jersey saw more than 90 battles during the Revolutionary War. It became the third U.S. state in 1787 and the first to sign the Bill of Rights. In the 19th century, southern New Jersey remained largely agricultural, while the northern part of the state rapidly industrialized. Today, highways and railroads link the state to urban centers along the Atlantic seaboard. More than 9,000 farms grow fruits and vegetables for nearby urban markets. Industries as well as services and trade are thriving. Beaches along the Atlantic coast attract thousands of tourists each year.

AMERICAN GOLDFINCH
VIOLET

◐ **HEADED TO MARKET.** New Jersey is a leading producer of fresh fruits and vegetables. These organic vegetables are headed for urban markets in the Northeast.

◐ **SUBURBAN SPRAWL.** With almost 95 percent of the state's population living in urban areas, housing developments with close-set, look-alike houses are a common characteristic of the suburban landscape. Residents commute to jobs in the city.

⬤ **PLAY BALL!** Fans pack the seats at Newark's Bears and Eagles Riverfront Stadium to watch a minor league baseball game. Built in 1999, the stadium is a part of Newark's plan to revitalize the downtown area, drawing people into the city.

Economy Symbols

🐟	Fishing	🌽	Corn
🦪	Shellfish	🌱	Soybeans
🦃	Poultry/eggs	📰	Printing/publishing
🐑	Sheep	⚒	Stone/gravel/cement
🐖	Hogs	⚙	Machinery
🐄	Dairy cows/products	🧪	Chemistry
🍎	Fruits	📷	Food processing
🥬	Vegetables	💻	Computers/electronics
🏠	Nursery stock	🚀	Aerospace
🌾	Wheat	📷	Tourism

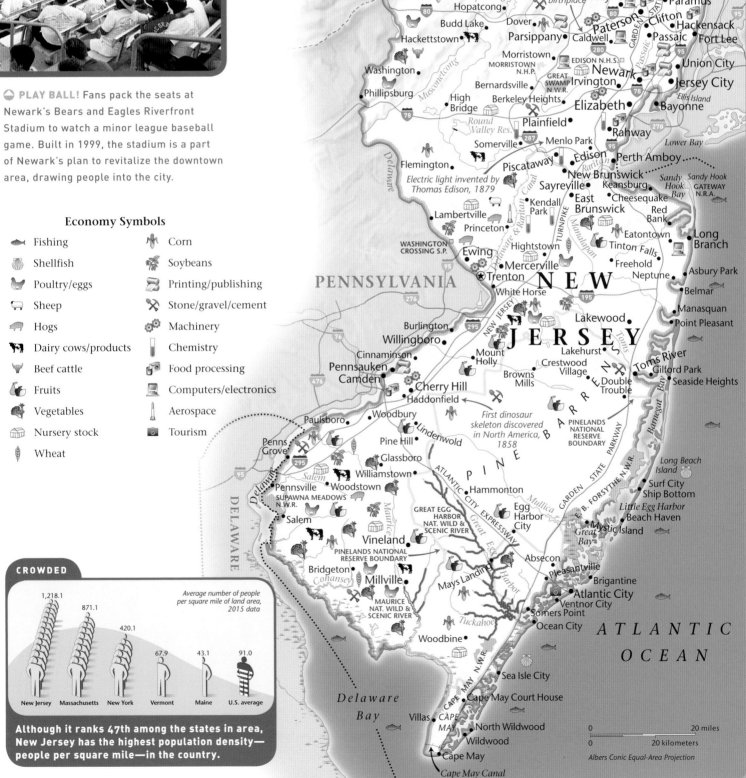

CROWDED

Average number of people per square mile of land area, 2015 data

1,218.1	871.1	420.1	67.9	43.1	91.0
New Jersey	Massachusetts	New York	Vermont	Maine	U.S. average

Although it ranks 47th among the states in area, New Jersey has the highest population density—people per square mile—in the country.

Albers Conic Equal-Area Projection

THE BASICS

Statehood
July 26, 1788; 11th state

Total area (land and water)
54,555 sq mi (141,297 sq km)

Land area
47,126 sq mi (122,057 sq km)

Population
19,795,791

Capital
Albany
Population (98,469)

Largest city
New York City
Population (8,550,405)

Racial/ethnic groups
70.1% white; 17.6% African American; 8.8% Asian; 1.0% Native American; 18.8% Hispanic origin (any race)

Foreign born
22.3%

Urban population
87.9% (2010)

Population density
362.9 per sq mi
(140.1 per sq km)

GEO WHIZ

Each year at Halloween, the Headless Horseman rides again through the countryside of Sleepy Hollow, as residents reenact Washington Irving's *The Legend of Sleepy Hollow.*

The Erie Canal, built in the 1820s between Albany and Buffalo, opened the Midwest to development by linking the Hudson River and the Great Lakes.

Cooperstown, home of the National Baseball Hall of Fame, takes its name from a town established in the late 1700s by the father of famed American author James Fenimore Cooper.

New York

When Englishman Henry Hudson explored New York's Hudson River Valley in 1609, the territory was already inhabited by large tribes of Native Americans, including the powerful Iroquois. In 1624 a Dutch trading company established the New Netherland colony, but after just 40 years the colony was taken over by the English and renamed for England's Duke of York. In 1788 New York became the 11th state. The state can be divided into two parts. The powerful port city of New York, center of trade and commerce and gateway to immigrants, is the largest city in the United States. Its metropolitan area, which extends into the surrounding states of Connecticut, New Jersey, and Pennsylvania, has more than 20 million people. Cities such as Buffalo and Rochester are industrial centers, and Ithaca and Syracuse boast major universities. Agriculture is also important, and the state is a major producer of dairy products, fruits, and vegetables.

⬢ **LADY LIBERTY.** Standing in New York Harbor, the Statue of Liberty, a gift from the people of France, is a symbol of freedom and democracy.

EASTERN BLUEBIRD
ROSE

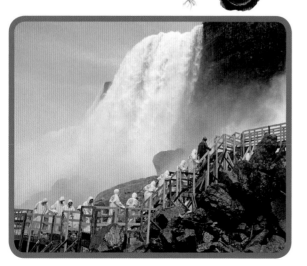

◖ **NATURAL WONDER.** Each year more than eight million tourists visit Niagara Falls on the U.S.-Canada border. Visitors in rain slickers trek through the mists below Bridal Veil Falls on the American side.

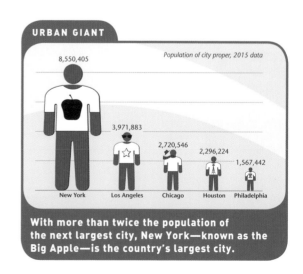

URBAN GIANT

Population of city proper, 2015 data

8,550,405	3,971,883	2,720,546	2,296,224	1,567,442
New York	Los Angeles	Chicago	Houston	Philadelphia

With more than twice the population of the next largest city, New York—known as the Big Apple—is the country's largest city.

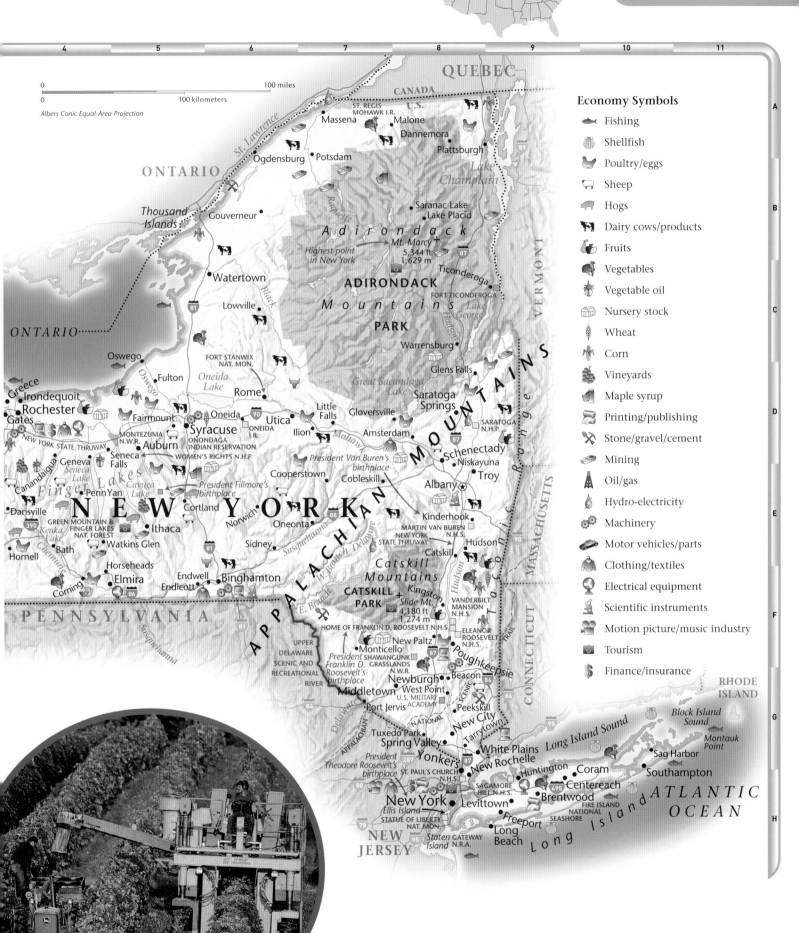

Economy Symbols

- Fishing
- Shellfish
- Poultry/eggs
- Sheep
- Hogs
- Dairy cows/products
- Fruits
- Vegetables
- Vegetable oil
- Nursery stock
- Wheat
- Corn
- Vineyards
- Maple syrup
- Printing/publishing
- Stone/gravel/cement
- Mining
- Oil/gas
- Hydro-electricity
- Machinery
- Motor vehicles/parts
- Clothing/textiles
- Electrical equipment
- Scientific instruments
- Motion picture/music industry
- Tourism
- Finance/insurance

0 — 100 miles
0 — 100 kilometers
Albers Conic Equal-Area Projection

QUEBEC
CANADA
U.S.

ONTARIO

St. Lawrence

Thousand Islands

ONTARIO

Massena
Malone
Dannemora
St. Regis Mohawk I.R.
Ogdensburg
Potsdam
Plattsburgh
Lake Champlain

Gouverneur

Adirondack
Saranac Lake
Lake Placid
Mt. Marcy
5,344 ft
1,629 m
Highest point in New York

Watertown

ADIRONDACK

Mountains

Ticonderoga
FORT TICONDEROGA
Lake George

Lowville

PARK

Warrensburg

Oswego
Oneida Lake
Rome
Fort Stanwix Nat. Mon.

Glens Falls

Hudson

Greece
Irondequoit
Rochester
Gates
Fulton
Fairmount
Oneida
Syracuse
Auburn
Utica
Little Falls
Ilion
Gloversville
Saratoga Springs
SARATOGA N.H.P.

ONONDAGA INDIAN RESERVATION
WOMEN'S RIGHTS N.H.P.
MONTEZUMA N.W.R.
ONEIDA I.R.

Amsterdam
Mohawk
Schenectady
Niskayuna
Troy

Geneva
Seneca Falls
President Van Buren's birthplace

Canandaigua
Penn Yan
President Fillmore's birthplace
Cooperstown
Cobleskill
Albany
NEW YORK STATE THRUWAY

Dansville
Ithaca
Cortland
Norwich
Oneonta
Kinderhook
Martin Van Buren N.H.S.

GREEN MOUNTAIN & FINGER LAKES NAT. FOREST
NEW YORK STATE THRUWAY

Bath
Watkins Glen
Hudson

Hornell
Horseheads
Sidney
Catskill

Elmira
Endwell
Binghamton
Catskill Mountains

Corning
Endicott

PENNSYLVANIA

Susquehanna

Slide Mt.
4,180 ft
1,274 m
Kingston
CATSKILL PARK
VANDERBILT MANSION N.H.S.

HOME OF FRANKLIN D. ROOSEVELT N.H.S.
ELEANOR ROOSEVELT N.H.S.

New Paltz
Poughkeepsie

UPPER DELAWARE SCENIC AND RECREATIONAL RIVER

Monticello
President Franklin D. Roosevelt's birthplace
SHAWANGUNK GRASSLANDS N.W.R.
Newburgh
Beacon

Middletown
West Point
U.S. Military Academy

Port Jervis
Peekskill
New City

Delaware

Tuxedo Park
Spring Valley
Yonkers
Tarrytown
White Plains
New Rochelle

President Theodore Roosevelt's birthplace
ST. PAUL'S CHURCH N.H.S.

New York
Levittown
SAGAMORE HILL N.H.S.
Huntington
Coram
Centereach
Brentwood
FIRE ISLAND NATIONAL SEASHORE

Ellis Island
STATUE OF LIBERTY NAT. MON.
Freeport
Long Beach

NEW JERSEY
Staten Island
GATEWAY N.R.A.

Long Island Sound
Block Island Sound
Montauk Point
Sag Harbor
Southampton

RHODE ISLAND

VERMONT
MASSACHUSETTS
CONNECTICUT

Long Island
ATLANTIC OCEAN

SWEET HARVEST. The Finger Lakes region, with its unique combination of soils and climate conditions, is well suited to growing wine grapes. With more than 10,000 acres (4,047 ha) of vineyards, it is the center of New York's wine industry, producing varieties for both domestic and export markets.

Pennsylvania

Pennsylvania, the 12th of England's 13 American colonies, was established in 1682 by Quaker William Penn and 360 settlers seeking religious freedom and fair government. The colony enjoyed abundant natural resources—dense woodlands, fertile soils, industrial minerals, and water power—that soon attracted Germans, Scotch-Irish, and other immigrants. Pennsylvania played a central role in the move for independence from Britain, and Philadelphia served as the new country's capital from 1790 to 1800. In the 19th century Philadelphia, in the east, and Pittsburgh, in the west, became booming centers of industrial growth. Philadelphia produced ships, locomotives, and textiles, while the iron and steel industry fueled Pittsburgh's growth. Jobs in industry as well as agriculture attracted immigrants from around the world. Today, Pennsylvania's economy has shifted toward information technology, health care, financial services, and tourism, but coal and steel production continue to play a role in the state's economy.

THE BASICS

Statehood
December 12, 1787; 2nd state

Total area (land and water)
46,054 sq mi (119,280 sq km)

Land area
44,743 sq mi (115,883 sq km)

Population
12,802,503

Capital
Harrisburg
Population 49,082 (2014)

Largest city
Philadelphia
Population 1,567,442

Racial/ethnic groups
82.6% white; 11.7% African American; 3.4% Asian; 0.4% Native American; 6.8% Hispanic origin (any race)

Foreign born
6.0%

Urban population
78.7% (2010)

Population density
286.1 per sq mi
(110.5 per sq km)

GEO WHIZ

The Martin Guitar Company in Nazareth has been handcrafting guitars for musicians all over the world for more than 150 years.

For more than a century streets in Philadelphia have been transformed on New Year's Day for the annual Mummers Parade.

🔔 **LET FREEDOM RING.** The Liberty Bell, cast in 1753 by Pennsylvania craftsmen, hangs in Philadelphia. Because of a crack, it is no longer rung.

MOUNTAIN LAUREL

RUFFED GROUSE

◖ **RIVER TOWN.** Pittsburgh, one of the largest inland ports in the United States, was established in 1758 where the Monongahela and Allegheny Rivers meet to form the Ohio River. Once a booming steel town, Pittsburgh is now a center of finance, medicine, and education.

MAKING COINS

Circulating coin production, 2015 data

4.7 billion — PENNIES

753 million — NICKELS

1.5 billion — DIMES

1.4 billion — QUARTERS

The 1792 Coinage Act established the first U.S. mint in Philadelphia. It is still one of the country's main coin-producing facilities.

LAKE ERIE

Erie
Millcreek
Meadville
Pymatuning Reservoir
Titusville
Greenville
Oil City
Sharon
Grove City
New Castle
Butler
Beaver Falls
OHIO RIVER N.W.R.
McCandless
Aliquippa
Plum
Pittsburgh
Penn Hills
McKeesport
Jeannette
Washington
Monessen
Waynesburg
Uniontown
FRIENDSHIP HILL N.H.S.
FT. NECESSITY NATIONAL BATTLEFIELD

OHIO

ERIE NATIONAL WILDLIFE REFUGE

Monongahela *Cheat*

WEST VIRGINIA

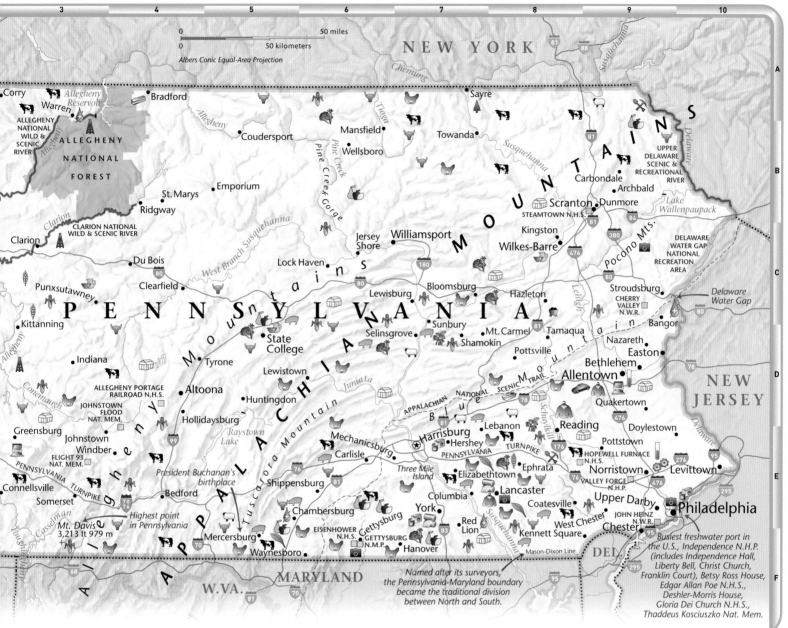

Economy Symbols

- Poultry/eggs
- Sheep
- Hogs
- Dairy cows/products
- Beef cattle
- Fruits
- Vegetables
- Nursery stock
- Corn
- Soybeans
- Tobacco
- Vineyards
- Timber/forest products
- Printing/publishing
- Stone/gravel/cement
- Mining
- Coal
- Oil/gas
- Hydro-electricity
- Machinery
- Metal manufacturing
- Railroad equipment
- Motor vehicles/parts
- Rubber/plastics
- Chemistry
- Food processing
- Glass/clay products
- Computers/electronics
- Tourism
- Finance/insurance

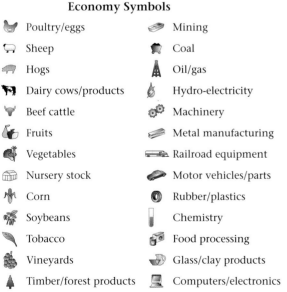

TEAMWORK. Amish people in Lancaster County work together to erect a barn. The Amish, who came to Pennsylvania in the early 1700s from Switzerland and Germany, live in traditional farming communities and shun modern technology.

THE BASICS

Statehood
May 29, 1790; 13th state

Total area (land and water)
1,545 sq mi (4,001 sq km)

Land area
1,034 sq mi (2,678 sq km)

Population
1,056,298

Capital
Providence
Population 179,207

Largest city
Providence
Population 179,207

Racial/ethnic groups
84.8% white; 7.9% African
American; 3.6% Asian; 1.0%
Native American; 14.4% Hispanic
origin (any race)

Foreign born
13.1%

Urban population
90.7% (2010)

Population density
1,021.6 per sq mi
(394.4 per sq km)

GEO WHIZ

Pawtucket is one of several
communities in Rhode Island
that have become home to a
growing number of people from
Cape Verde, in West Africa.

Wild coyotes are living
and thriving on islands
in Narragansett Bay.
Researchers have outfitted
some with GPS tracking
collars so that their
numbers and whereabouts
can be studied online—
even by schoolkids.

VIOLET
RHODE ISLAND RED

Rhode Island

In 1524 Italian navigator Giovanni Verrazzano was the first European explorer to visit Rhode Island, but place-names such as Quonochontaug and Narragansett tell of an earlier Native American population. In 1636 Roger Williams, seeking greater religious freedom, left Massachusetts and established the first European settlement in what was to become the colony of Rhode Island. In the years following the Revolutionary War, Rhode Island pressed for fairness in trade, taxes, and representation in Congress as well as greater freedom of worship, before becoming the 13th state. By the 19th century Rhode Island had become an important center of trade and textile factories, attracting many immigrants from Europe. In addition to its commercial activities, Rhode Island's coastline became a popular vacation retreat for the wealthy. Today, Rhode Island, like many other states, has seen its economy shift toward high-tech jobs and service industries. It is also promoting its scenic coastline and bays as well as its rich history to attract tourists.

CLUES TO THE PAST.
Fossils embedded in rocks left behind 10,000 years ago by retreating glaciers tell of Block Island's past.

SETTING SAIL. Newport Harbor invites sailors of all ages. From 1930 to 1983 the prestigious America's Cup Yacht Race took place in the waters off Newport. Today, the town provides moorings for boats of all types.

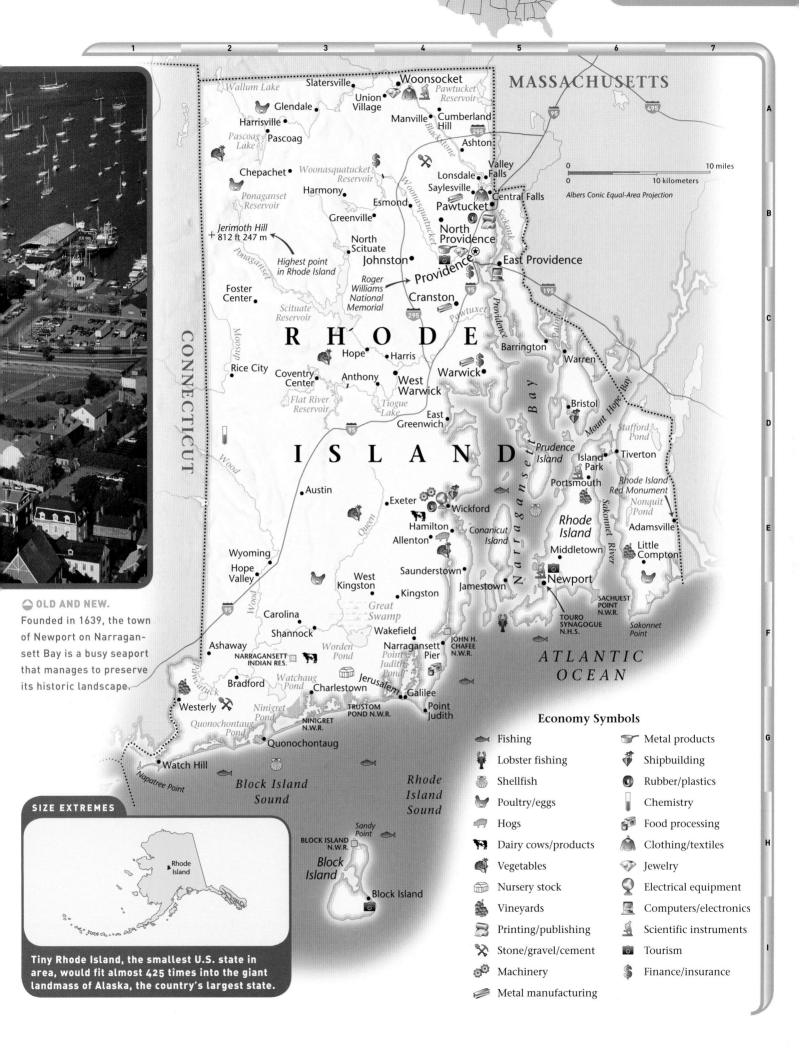

MASSACHUSETTS

CONNECTICUT

R H O D E

I S L A N D

Wallum Lake
Slatersville
Woonsocket
Pawtucket Reservoir
Union Village
Glendale
Manville
Cumberland Hill
Harrisville
Ashton
Pascoag Lake
Pascoag
Valley Falls
Lonsdale
Chepachet
Woonasquatucket Reservoir
Saylesville
Central Falls
Harmony
Esmond
Pawtucket
Ponaganset Reservoir
Greenville
North Providence
Jerimoth Hill
+ 812 ft 247 m
Highest point in Rhode Island
North Scituate
Johnston
Providence
East Providence
Foster Center
Roger Williams National Memorial
Cranston
Scituate Reservoir
Pawtuxet
Barrington
Warren
Hope
Harris
Warwick
Rice City
Coventry Center
Anthony
West Warwick
Bristol
Flat River Reservoir
Tiogue Lake
East Greenwich
Stafford Pond
Prudence Island
Island Park
Tiverton
Rhode Island Red Monument
Nonquit Pond
Austin
Portsmouth
Adamsville
Exeter
Wickford
Rhode Island
Little Compton
Hamilton
Conanicut Island
Middletown
Allenton
Wyoming
Saunderstown
Hope Valley
West Kingston
Kingston
Jamestown
Newport
Carolina
Great Swamp
Wakefield
SACHUEST POINT N.W.R.
Shannock
TOURO SYNAGOGUE N.H.S.
Sakonnet Point
Ashaway
NARRAGANSETT INDIAN RES.
Worden Pond
Narragansett Pier
JOHN H. CHAFEE N.W.R.
ATLANTIC OCEAN
Point Judith Pond
Bradford
Watchaug Pond
Jerusalem
Charlestown
Galilee
Westerly
Ninigret Pond
TRUSTOM POND N.W.R.
Point Judith
NINIGRET N.W.R.
Quonochontaug Pond
Watch Hill
Napatree Point
Block Island Sound
Rhode Island Sound
Quonochontaug

Narragansett Bay
Mount Hope Bay
Sakonnet River

Wood River
Moosup River
Ponaganset River
Blackstone River
Woonasquatucket River
Providence River
Palmer River
Seekonk River
Queen River
Pawcatuck River

Sandy Point
BLOCK ISLAND N.W.R.
Block Island
Block Island

0 ___ 10 miles
0 ___ 10 kilometers
Albers Conic Equal-Area Projection

⬤ OLD AND NEW.
Founded in 1639, the town of Newport on Narragansett Bay is a busy seaport that manages to preserve its historic landscape.

SIZE EXTREMES

Rhode Island
Rhode Island

Tiny Rhode Island, the smallest U.S. state in area, would fit almost 425 times into the giant landmass of Alaska, the country's largest state.

Economy Symbols

🐟	Fishing	🍲	Metal products
🦞	Lobster fishing	⚒	Shipbuilding
🐚	Shellfish	◉	Rubber/plastics
🐔	Poultry/eggs	🧪	Chemistry
🐖	Hogs	📦	Food processing
🐄	Dairy cows/products	👜	Clothing/textiles
🥬	Vegetables	💎	Jewelry
🏡	Nursery stock	🌐	Electrical equipment
🍇	Vineyards	💻	Computers/electronics
📖	Printing/publishing	🔬	Scientific instruments
⚒	Stone/gravel/cement	📷	Tourism
⚙	Machinery	$	Finance/insurance
📜	Metal manufacturing		

THE BASICS

Statehood
March 4, 1791; 14th state

Total area (land and water)
9,616 sq mi (24,906 sq km)

Land area
9,217 sq mi (23,871 sq km)

Population
626,042

Capital
Montpelier
Population 7,671 (2014)

Largest city
Burlington
Population 42,211

Racial/ethnic groups
94.8% white; 1.3% African American; 1.6% Asian; 0.4% Native American; 1.8% Hispanic origin (any race)

Foreign born
4.1%

Urban population
38.9% (2010)

Population density
67.9 per sq mi (26.2 per sq km)

GEO WHIZ

The tombstones of President Harry S. Truman, industrialist John D. Rockefeller, Sr., songwriter Stephen Foster, and fast-food-chain founder Col. Harland Sanders are all made of granite from Barre.

Burlington is the home of Ben & Jerry's ice cream. The company gives its leftovers to local farmers, who feed it to their hogs.

From 1777 until it became a state in 1791, Vermont was an independent country.

Vermont is the only state in New England that does not border the Atlantic Ocean.

Vermont

When French explorer Jacques Cartier arrived in Vermont in 1535, Native Americans living in woodland villages had been there for hundreds of years. Settled first by the French in 1666 and then by the English in 1724, the territory of Vermont became an area of conflict between these colonial powers. The French finally withdrew, but conflict continued between New York and New Hampshire, both of which wanted to take over Vermont. The people of Vermont declared their independence in 1777, and Vermont became the 14th U.S. state in 1791. Vermont's name, which means "green mountain," comes from the extensive forests that cover much of the state and provide the basis for furniture and pulp industries. Vermont also boasts the world's largest deep-hole granite quarry and the largest underground marble quarry. Both produce valuable building materials. Tourism and recreation are also important. Lakes, rivers, and mountain trails are popular summer attractions, and snow-covered mountains lure skiers throughout the winter.

◔ **LIQUID GOLD.** In spring sap from maple trees is collected in buckets by drilling a hole in the tree trunk—called "tapping." The sap is boiled to remove water, then filtered, and finally bottled.

RED CLOVER
HERMIT THRUSH

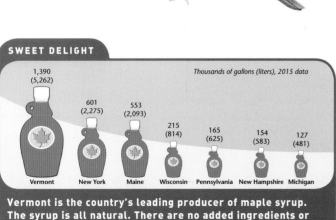

SWEET DELIGHT

Thousands of gallons (liters), 2015 data

1,390 (5,262)	601 (2,275)	553 (2,093)	215 (814)	165 (625)	154 (583)	127 (481)
Vermont	New York	Maine	Wisconsin	Pennsylvania	New Hampshire	Michigan

Vermont is the country's leading producer of maple syrup. The syrup is all natural. There are no added ingredients or preservatives, just boiled sap collected from maple trees.

◔ **WINTER WONDERLAND.** One of the snowiest places in the Northeast, Jay Peak averages 355 inches (900 cm) of snow each year. With 76 trails, the mountain, near Vermont's border with Canada, attracts beginner and expert skiers from near and far.

THE GREAT MOUNTAIN STATE:
VERMONT

Economy Symbols

- 🐔 Poultry/eggs
- 🐑 Sheep
- 🐄 Dairy cows/products
- 🐂 Beef cattle
- 🍇 Fruits
- 🥬 Vegetables
- 🏠 Nursery stock
- 🌽 Corn
- 🍁 Maple syrup
- 🌲 Timber/forest products
- 🗞 Printing/publishing
- ✖ Stone/gravel/cement
- 💧 Hydro-electricity
- 🥘 Metal products
- 📷 Food processing
- 💻 Computers/electronics
- 📷 Tourism

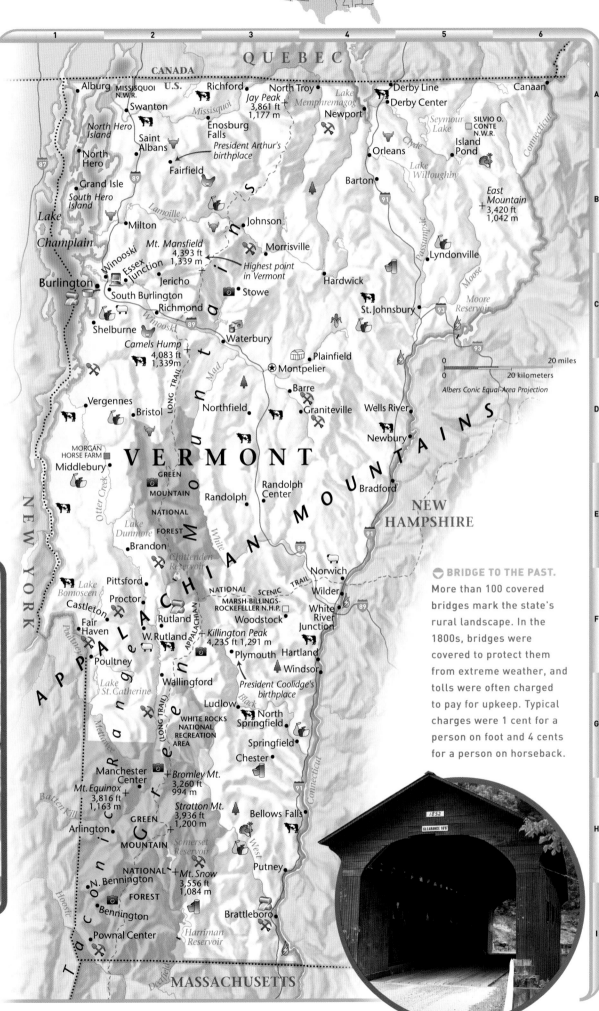

🌉 **BRIDGE TO THE PAST.**
More than 100 covered
bridges mark the state's
rural landscape. In the
1800s, bridges were
covered to protect them
from extreme weather, and
tolls were often charged
to pay for upkeep. Typical
charges were 1 cent for a
person on foot and 4 cents
for a person on horseback.

THE REGION

Total area
(land and water)
566,988 sq mi
(1,468,492 sq km)

Highest point
Mount Mitchell, NC
6,684 ft (2,037 m)

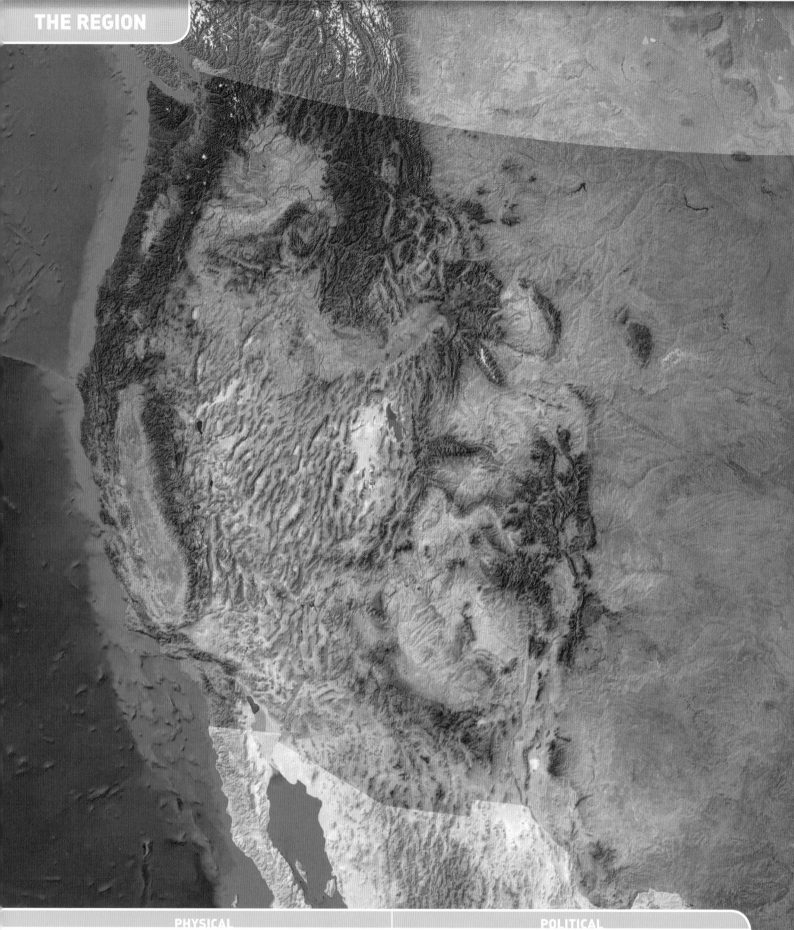

PHYSICAL

Total area
(land and water)
566,988 sq mi
(1,468,492 sq km)

Highest point
Mount Mitchell, NC
6,684 ft (2,037 m)

Lowest point
New Orleans, LA
8 ft (2 m) below sea level

Longest rivers
Mississippi, Arkansas,
Red, Ohio

Largest lakes
Okeechobee, Pontchartrain,
Kentucky (reservoir)

Vegetation
Needleleaf, broadleaf, and
mixed forest

Climate
Continental to mild, ranging
from cool summers in the
north to humid, subtropical
conditions in the south

POLITICAL

Total population
82,177,832

States (12):
Alabama, Arkansas, Florida, Georgia,
Kentucky, Louisiana, Mississippi, North
Carolina, South Carolina, Tennessee,
Virginia, West Virginia

Largest state
Florida: 65,758 sq mi (170,312 sq km)

Smallest state
West Virginia: 24,230 sq mi (62,756 sq km)

Most populous state
Florida: 20,271,272

Least populous state
West Virginia: 1,844,128

Largest city proper
Jacksonville, FL: 868,031

The Southeast

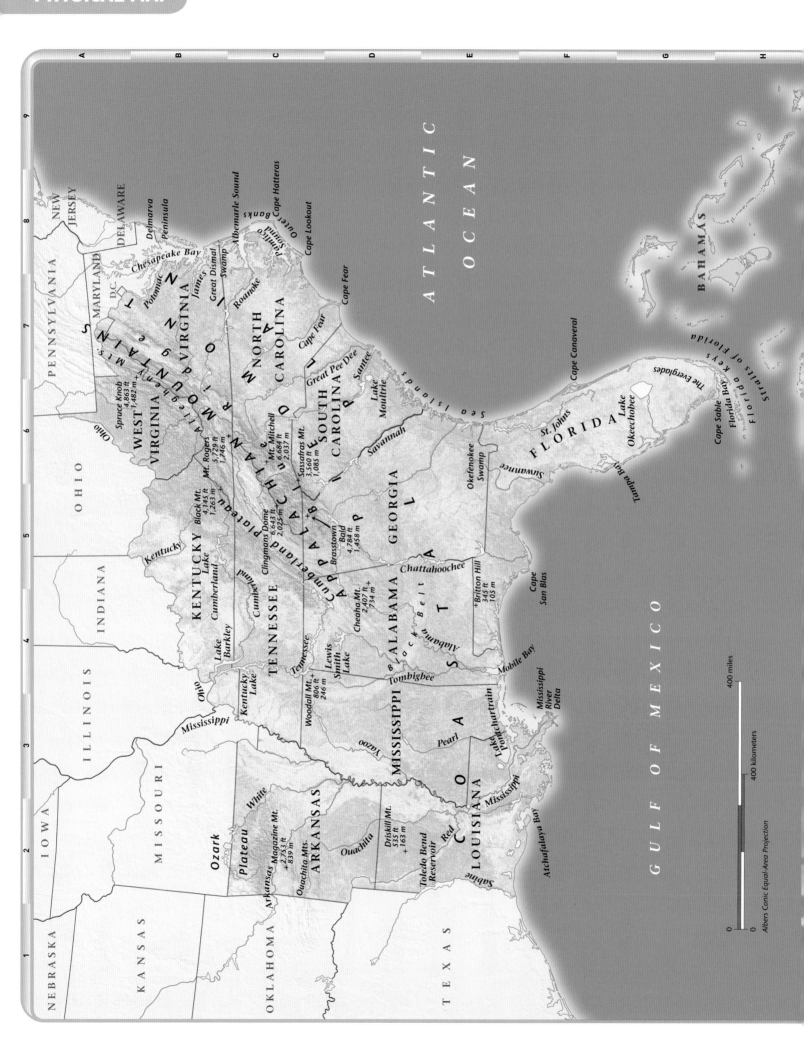

A B C D E F G H

9 8 7 6 5 4 3 2 1

NEW JERSEY
DELAWARE
PENNSYLVANIA
MARYLAND
D.C.
Delmarva Peninsula
Chesapeake Bay
Potomac
James
Great Dismal Swamp
VIRGINIA
WEST VIRGINIA
Roanoke
Albemarle Sound
Pamlico Sound
Outer Banks
Cape Hatteras
Cape Lookout
NORTH CAROLINA
Spruce Knob 4,863 ft 1,482 m
Mt. Rogers 5,729 ft 1,746 m
OHIO
Ohio
Allegheny Mts.
Cape Fear
Cape Fear
ATLANTIC OCEAN

BAHAMAS

INDIANA
ILLINOIS
Kentucky Lake
KENTUCKY
Black Mt. 4,145 ft 1,263 m
Cumberland Plateau
Clingmans Dome 6,643 ft 2,025 m
APPALACHIAN MOUNTAINS
Mt. Mitchell 6,684 ft 2,037 m
Sassafras Mt. 3,560 ft 1,085 m
SOUTH CAROLINA
Great Pee Dee
Santee
Lake Moultrie
Savannah
Sea Islands
Strait of Florida
Florida Keys
Straits of Florida

Ohio
Lake Barkley
Kentucky Lake
TENNESSEE
Tennessee
Cumberland
Brasstown Bald 4,784 ft 1,458 m
GEORGIA
Chattahoochee
Okefenokee Swamp
St. Johns
Suwannee
FLORIDA
Lake Okeechobee
The Everglades
Cape Sable
Florida Bay
Cape Canaveral

MISSOURI
White
Ozark Plateau
Magazine Mt. 2,753 ft 839 m
Arkansas
ARKANSAS
Ouachita Mts.
Ouachita
Driskill Mt. 535 ft 163 m
Lewis Smith Lake
Woodall Mt. 806 ft 246 m
MISSISSIPPI
Cheaha Mt. 2,407 ft 734 m
ALABAMA
Black Belt
Alabama
Tombigbee
Mobile Bay
+Britton Hill 345 ft 105 m
Cape San Blas
Tampa Bay

IOWA
NEBRASKA
KANSAS
OKLAHOMA
TEXAS
Yazoo
Mississippi
Pearl
COASTAL
LOUISIANA
Red
Toledo Bend Reservoir
Sabine
Atchafalaya Bay
Mississippi
Lake Pontchartrain
Mississippi River Delta
GULF OF MEXICO

400 miles
400 kilometers
0 0
Albers Conic Equal-Area Projection

A B C D E F G H

9 8 7 6 5 4 3 2 1

NEW JERSEY

DELAWARE

PENNSYLVANIA

MARYLAND

D.C.

Arlington

VIRGINIA

Richmond ⊛

Chesapeake Bay

Lynchburg

Norfolk

Virginia Beach

Potomac

James

OHIO

Parkersburg

WEST VIRGINIA

Charleston ⊛

Huntington

Roanoke

Ohio

Roanoke

Raleigh ⊛

Greensboro

Winston-Salem

NORTH CAROLINA

Fayetteville

Wilmington

Cape Fear

ATLANTIC OCEAN

Charlotte

Greenville

Great Pee Dee

SOUTH CAROLINA

Columbia ⊛

Charleston

Myrtle Beach

Santee

INDIANA

Frankfort ⊛

Lexington

Louisville

KENTUCKY

Bowling Green

Kentucky

Knoxville

Nashville

Clarksville

TENNESSEE

Chattanooga

Rome

Athens

Atlanta

GEORGIA

Macon

Columbus

Albany

Savannah

Savannah

Chattahoochee

Tallahassee ⊛

Jacksonville

Gainesville

FLORIDA

Orlando

St. Johns

Suwannee

Tampa

St. Petersburg

Cape Coral

Fort Lauderdale

Miami

Key West

Straits of Florida

BAHAMAS

CUBA

ILLINOIS

Paducah

Ohio

Tennessee

Huntsville

Birmingham

Tuscaloosa

ALABAMA

Montgomery ⊛

Mobile

Alabama

GULF OF MEXICO

MISSOURI

Memphis

Mississippi

Tupelo

Greenville

MISSISSIPPI

Jackson ⊛

Vicksburg

Yazoo

Pearl

Hattiesburg

Gulfport

Baton Rouge

New Orleans

Jonesboro

Little Rock ⊛

ARKANSAS

White

Arkansas

Ouachita

Fayetteville

Fort Smith

Texarkana

Shreveport

LOUISIANA

Red

Alexandria

Lafayette

Mississippi

KANSAS

OKLAHOMA

TEXAS

NEBRASKA

400 miles

400 kilometers

0

0

Albers Conic Equal-Area Projection

ABOUT THE SOUTHEAST

◐ **OPEN WIDE.** An American alligator in Florida's Big Cypress Swamp shows off sharp teeth. These large reptiles live mainly in freshwater swamps and marshes in coastal areas of the Southeast. Adult males average 14 feet (4 m) in length.

The Southeast

TRADITION MEETS TECHNOLOGY

F rom deeply weathered mountains in West Virginia to warm, humid wetlands in south Florida and the Mississippi River's sprawling delta in southern Louisiana, the Southeast is marked by great physical diversity. The region's historical roots are in agriculture— especially cotton and tobacco. The Civil War brought economic and political upheaval in the mid-19th century, but today the Southeast is part of the Sunbelt, where 5 of the top 20 metropolitan areas of the United States are found and where high-tech industries are redefining the way people earn a living and the way the region is connected to the global economy.

◐ **ENCHANTED KINGDOM.** Fireworks light up the night sky above Cinderella's Castle at Walt Disney World near Orlando, Florida. The park, which accounts for 6 percent of all jobs in central Florida, attracts millions of tourists from around the world each year.

⬤ **SOCIAL CONSCIENCE.** Members of the Big Nine Social Aid and Pleasure Club of New Orleans's Lower Ninth Ward march in a parade through a neighborhood devastated by Hurricane Katrina. Such clubs, which date back to late-19th-century benevolent societies, bring support and hope to communities in need.

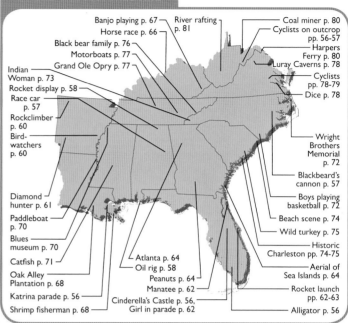

WHERE THE PICTURES ARE

Banjo playing p. 67
River rafting p. 81
Coal miner p. 80
Cyclists on outcrop pp. 56-57
Horse race p. 66
Harpers Ferry p. 80
Black bear family p. 76
Luray Caverns p. 78
Motorboats p. 77
Cyclists pp. 78-79
Indian Woman p. 73
Grand Ole Opry p. 77
Dice p. 78
Rocket display p. 58
Race car p. 57
Rockclimber p. 60
Wright Brothers Memorial p. 72
Bird-watchers p. 60
Blackbeard's cannon p. 57
Boys playing basketball p. 72
Beach scene p. 74
Diamond hunter p. 61
Wild turkey p. 75
Paddleboat p. 70
Historic Charleston pp. 74-75
Blues museum p. 70
Atlanta p. 64
Catfish p. 71
Oil rig p. 58
Aerial of Sea Islands p. 64
Oak Alley Plantation p. 68
Peanuts p. 64
Rocket launch pp. 62-63
Katrina parade p. 56
Manatee p. 62
Shrimp fisherman p. 68
Cinderella's Castle p. 56, Girl in parade p. 62
Alligator p. 56

VIEW FROM ABOVE. Cyclists look out from a rocky ledge across West Virginia's Germany Valley. The area took its name from German immigrants who moved there in the mid-1700s from North Carolina and Pennsylvania and established farming villages.

CAR STARS. For more than 50 years, auto racing has been a leading sport in the U.S., especially in the Southeast. The International Motorsports Hall of Fame, located adjacent to the Talladega Superspeedway in Alabama, features racing cars, motorcycles, and vintage cars.

PIRATE'S DEFENSE. This 4.5-foot (1.4-m) cast-iron cannon was recovered from the wreck of the *Queen Anne's Revenge* off North Carolina's coast. The vessel, which probably belonged to Blackbeard, the notorious pirate, grounded on a sandbar and sank in 1718 near Cape Lookout.

THE BASICS

Statehood
December 14, 1819; 22nd state

Total area (land and water)
52,420 sq mi (135,767 sq km)

Land area
50,645 sq mi (131,171 sq km)

Population
4,858,979

Capital
Montgomery
Population 200,602

Largest city
Birmingham
Population 212,461

Racial/ethnic groups
69.5% white; 26.8% African American; 1.4% Asian; 0.7% Native American; 4.2% Hispanic (any race)

Foreign born
3.5%

Urban population
59.0% (2010)

Population density
95.9 per sq mi (37.0 per sq km)

GEO WHIZ

Condoleezza Rice, the first African-American woman to serve as U.S. secretary of state, and Rosa Parks, whose refusal to give up her seat on a Montgomery bus earned her the title "mother of the modern-day civil rights movement," were both born in Alabama: Rice in Birmingham and Parks in Tuskegee.

Russell Cave, near Bridgeport, was home to prehistoric peoples for more than 10,000 years. In 1961 a national monument was established on land donated by the National Geographic Society. Today, visitors can take guided tours of the cave and see the kinds of tools and weapons its early inhabitants used.

In 2004 Hurricane Ivan, one of the worst storms to batter Alabama's Gulf coast since 1900, struck Orange Beach.

Alabama

Alabama has a colorful story. The French established the first permanent European settlement at Mobile Bay in 1702, but different groups—British, Native Americans, and U.S. settlers—struggled over control of the land for more than 100 years. In 1819 Alabama became the 22nd state, but in 1861 it joined the Confederacy. During the Civil War, Montgomery was the capital of the secessionist South for a time. After the war Alabama struggled to rebuild its agriculture-based economy. By 1900 the state was producing more than one million bales of cotton annually. In the mid-20th century Alabama was at the center of the civil rights movement, which pressed for equal rights for all people regardless of race or social status. Martin Luther King, Jr., and Rosa Parks were among the key players. Modern industries, including the NASA space program, have given the state's economy a big boost. In 2002 assembly plants built by automakers from Asia created thousands of new jobs.

◆ **UNDERWATER RESOURCE.** A massive drill descends from an offshore oil rig to tap petroleum deposits beneath the water of the Gulf of Mexico off Alabama's shore.

NORTHERN FLICKER

CAMELLIA

ON THE ROAD

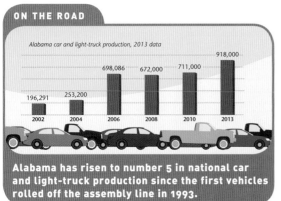

Alabama car and light-truck production, 2013 data

					918,000
		698,086	672,000	711,000	
196,291	253,200				
2002	2004	2006	2008	2010	2013

Alabama has risen to number 5 in national car and light-truck production since the first vehicles rolled off the assembly line in 1993.

◆ **ROCKET POWER.** A giant Saturn V moon rocket dominates a display of rockets in front of the U.S. Space and Rocket Center at NASA's Marshall Space Flight Center in Huntsville. Since it opened in 1970, almost 16 million people have visited the center.

Economy Symbols

- Fishing
- Shellfish
- Poultry/eggs
- Hogs
- Dairy cows/products
- Beef cattle
- Fruits
- Vegetables
- Vegetable oil
- Peanuts
- Nursery stock
- Wheat
- Corn
- Soybeans
- Cotton
- Timber/forest products
- Printing/publishing
- Stone/gravel/cement
- Mining
- Coal
- Oil/gas
- Hydro-electricity
- Metal manufacturing
- Metal products
- Shipbuilding
- Motor vehicles/parts
- Rubber/plastics
- Chemistry
- Food processing
- Clothing/textiles
- Glass/clay products
- Electrical equipment
- Computers/electronics
- Aircraft/parts
- Aerospace
- Tourism
- Finance/insurance

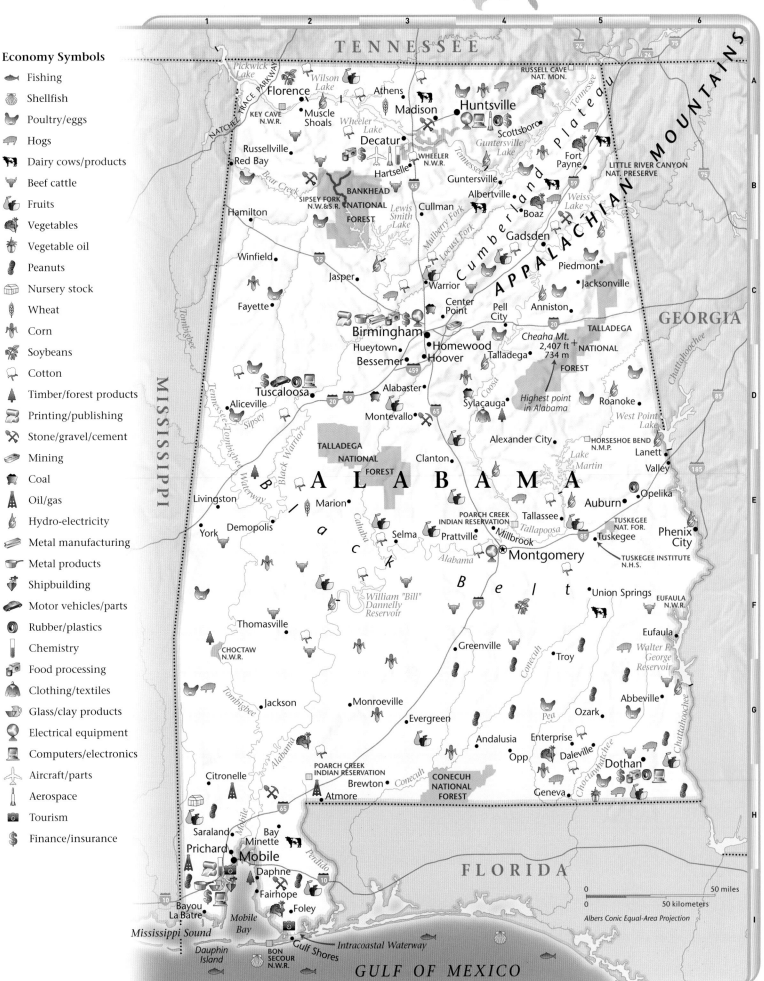

TENNESSEE

Pickwick Lake
Wilson Lake
Florence
Athens
Madison
Huntsville
RUSSELL CAVE NAT. MON.
KEY CAVE N.W.R.
Muscle Shoals
Wheeler Lake
Scottsboro
Decatur
Guntersville Lake
Fort Payne
Russellville
Red Bay
Hartselle
WHEELER N.W.R.
Guntersville
LITTLE RIVER CANYON NAT. PRESERVE
Bear Creek
Albertville
Weiss Lake
Hamilton
BANKHEAD NATIONAL FOREST
SIPSEY FORK N.W.&S.R.
Lewis Smith Lake
Cullman
Boaz
Mulberry Fork
Gadsden
Locust Fork
Winfield
Jasper
Piedmont
Warrior
Jacksonville
Fayette
Center Point
Pell City
Anniston
TALLADEGA NATIONAL FOREST
Birmingham
Cheaha Mt. 2,407 ft 734 m
Hueytown
Homewood
Talladega
Highest point in Alabama
Roanoke
Bessemer
Hoover
Coosa
Tuscaloosa
Aliceville
Alabaster
Sylacauga
Sipsey
Montevallo
Black Warrior
TALLADEGA NATIONAL FOREST
Clanton
Alexander City
Lake Martin
HORSESHOE BEND N.M.P.
Lanett
Livingston
Marion
Cahaba
West Point Lake
Valley
Demopolis
POORCH CREEK INDIAN RESERVATION
Tallassee
Auburn
York
Selma
Prattville
Tallapoosa
TUSKEGEE NAT. FOR.
Opelika
William "Bill" Dannelly Reservoir
Millbrook
Tuskegee
Phenix City
Alabama
Montgomery
TUSKEGEE INSTITUTE N.H.S.
Union Springs
EUFAULA N.W.R.
Thomasville
Conecuh
Eufaula
CHOCTAW N.W.R.
Greenville
Troy
Walter F. George Reservoir
Jackson
Monroeville
Pea
Ozark
Abbeville
Evergreen
Andalusia
Enterprise
Citronelle
POORCH CREEK INDIAN RESERVATION
Brewton
Conecuh
Opp
Daleville
Dothan
Atmore
CONECUH NATIONAL FOREST
Geneva
Saraland
Bay Minette
Prichard
Mobile
Perdido
Daphne
Fairhope
Bayou La Batre
Foley
Mississippi Sound
Mobile Bay
Gulf Shores
Intracoastal Waterway
Dauphin Island
BON SECOUR N.W.R.

MISSISSIPPI

A L A B A M A

Black Belt

GEORGIA

FLORIDA

GULF OF MEXICO

0   50 miles
0   50 kilometers
Albers Conic Equal-Area Projection

THE BASICS

Statehood
June 15, 1836; 25th state

Total area (land and water)
53,179 sq mi (137,732 sq km)

Land area
52,035 sq mi (134,771 sq km)

Population
2,978,204

Capital
Little Rock
Population 197,992

Largest city
Little Rock
Population 197,992

Racial/ethnic groups
79.5% white; 15.7% African American; 1.6% Asian; 1.0% Native American; 7.2% Hispanic (any race)

Foreign born
4.5%

Urban population
56.2% (2010)

Population density
57.2 per sq mi (22.1 per sq km)

GEO WHIZ

In 1924 Arkansas's Crater of Diamonds State Park yielded the largest natural diamond ever found in the United States—a 40.23-carat whopper named "Uncle Sam."

Stuttgart has been the site of the annual World Championship Duck Calling Contest since 1936, when the winner received a hunting coat valued at $6.60. Today, the prize package is worth more than $15,000.

Texarkana is divided by the Arkansas-Texas border. It has two governments, one for each state.

Arkansas

The land that is Arkansas was explored by the Spanish in 1541 and later by the French, but it came under U.S. control with the Louisiana Purchase in 1803. As settlers arrived, Native Americans were pushed out, and cotton fields spread across the fertile valleys of the Arkansas and Mississippi Rivers. Arkansas became the 25th state in 1836, but joined the Confederacy in 1861. Following the war Arkansas faced hard times, and many people moved away in search of jobs. Today, agriculture remains an important part of the economy. Rice has replaced cotton as the state's main crop, and poultry and grain production are also important. Natural gas, in the northwestern part of the state, and petroleum, along the southern border with Louisiana, are key mining products in Arkansas. The state is headquarters for Walmart, the world's largest retail chain, and tourism is growing as visitors are attracted to the natural beauty of the Ozark and Ouachita Mountains.

APPLE BLOSSOM
MOCKINGBIRD

🔘 **HOLD ON!** A rock climber clings to a sandstone cliff in northwest Arkansas, where the Ozark and Ouachita Mountains make up the Interior Highlands of the United States. The Ouachita are folded mountains, but the Ozarks are really a deeply eroded plateau.

SUPERSTORE

$343,624,000   *Retail sales, 2014 data*

$103,033,000 $79,694,000 $74,203,000 $72,671,000 $72,618,000

| Walmart (AR)* | Kroger (OH) | Costco (WA) | Home Depot (GA) | Walgreens (IL) | Target (MN) |

*( ) = state where store headquarters is located

Founded in 1962 in Bentonville, retail giant Walmart, with more than 5,200 stores nationwide, leads the country in annual revenue.

◑ **BIRD-WATCHERS.** Biologists and volunteers scan the treetops for a rare ivory-billed woodpecker in the White River National Wildlife Refuge. Established in 1935 along the White River near where it joins the Mississippi, the refuge provides a protected habitat for migratory birds.

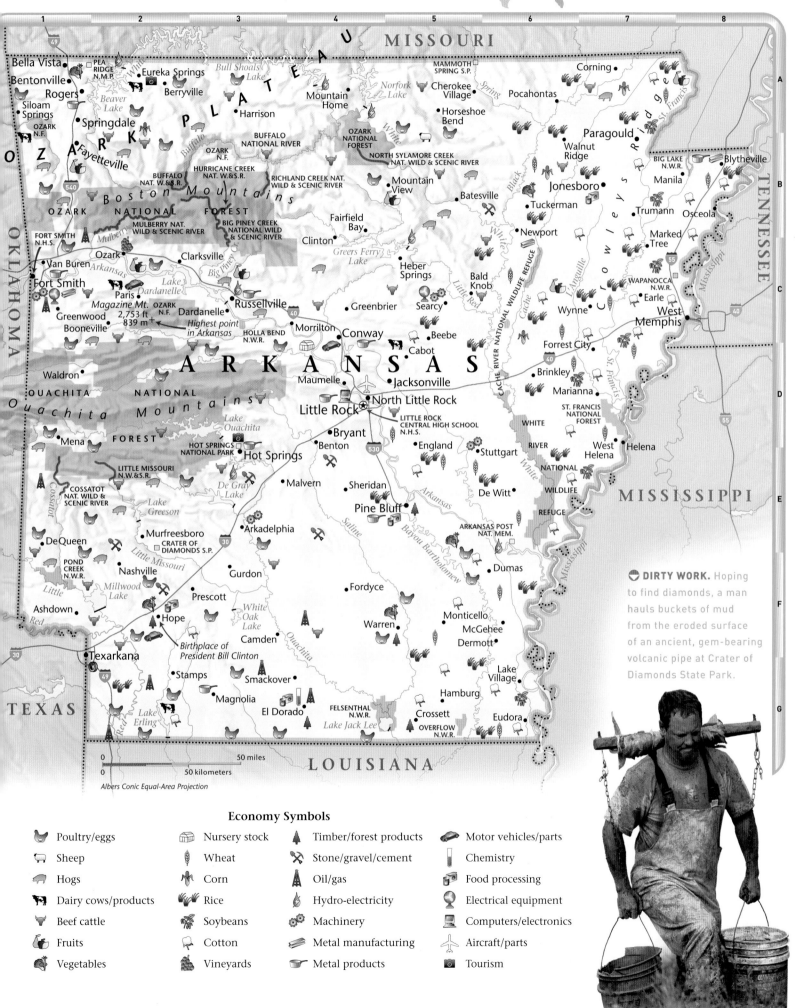

MISSOURI

OKLAHOMA

TENNESSEE

MISSISSIPPI

TEXAS

LOUISIANA

OZARK PLATEAU

Bella Vista
Bentonville
Rogers
Siloam Springs
OZARK N.F.
Springdale
Fayetteville
Waldron

PEA RIDGE N.M.P.
Eureka Springs
Berryville
Beaver Lake
Harrison
Bull Shoals Lake

Buffalo
OZARK N.F.
BUFFALO NATIONAL FOREST
HURRICANE CREEK NAT. W.&S.R.
BUFFALO NAT. W.&S.R.
MULBERRY NAT. WILD & SCENIC RIVER
BIG PINEY CREEK NATIONAL WILD & SCENIC RIVER

Boston Mountains

OZARK NATIONAL FOREST

Fort Smith N.H.S.
Ozark
Van Buren
Fort Smith
Paris
Magazine Mt. 2,753 ft 839 m+
Highest point in Arkansas
Greenwood
Booneville
OZARK N.F.
Dardanelle
Lake Dardanelle
Clarksville
Russellville
Big Piney
Arkansas
HOLLA BEND N.W.R.
Morrilton
Conway

Mountain Home
Norfork Lake
MAMMOTH SPRING S.P.
Cherokee Village
Horseshoe Bend
OZARK NATIONAL FOREST
NORTH SYLAMORE CREEK NAT. WILD & SCENIC RIVER
RICHLAND CREEK NAT. WILD & SCENIC RIVER
Mountain View
Fairfield Bay
Clinton
Greers Ferry Lake
Heber Springs
Batesville
Newport
Bald Knob
Greenbrier
Searcy
Beebe

Corning
Pocahontas
Spring
Paragould
Walnut Ridge
Jonesboro
Tuckerman
St. Francis
Crowleys Ridge
BIG LAKE N.W.R.
Blytheville
Manila
Trumann
Osceola
Marked Tree
Black
White
Little Red
L'Anguille
Cache
WAPANOCCA N.W.R.
Earle
Wynne
West Memphis
CACHE RIVER NATIONAL WILDLIFE REFUGE

ARKANSAS

NATIONAL

Ouachita Mountains

FOREST

OUACHITA NATIONAL FOREST
Mena
Cossatot
COSSATOT NAT. WILD & SCENIC RIVER
LITTLE MISSOURI N.W.&S.R.
Lake Ouachita
HOT SPRINGS NATIONAL PARK
Hot Springs
De Gray Lake
Lake Greeson
Murfreesboro
CRATER OF DIAMONDS S.P.
Arkadelphia
Little Missouri
DeQueen
POND CREEK N.W.R.
Nashville
Millwood Lake
Little
Red
Ashdown
Gurdon
Prescott
White Oak Lake
Hope
Birthplace of President Bill Clinton
Texarkana
Stamps
Camden
Smackover
Magnolia
El Dorado
Lake Erling
Red
FELSENTHAL N.W.R.
Lake Jack Lee

Maumelle
Little Rock
North Little Rock
Bryant
Benton
LITTLE ROCK CENTRAL HIGH SCHOOL N.H.S.
Jacksonville
Cabot
England
Sheridan
Saline
Pine Bluff
Fordyce
Warren
Monticello
McGehee
Dermott
Hamburg
Crossett
OVERFLOW N.W.R.

Stuttgart
De Witt
WHITE RIVER NATIONAL WILDLIFE REFUGE
Arkansas
Bayou Bartholomew
ARKANSAS POST NAT. MEM.
Dumas
Ouachita
Mississippi
Forrest City
Brinkley
Marianna
ST. FRANCIS NATIONAL FOREST
West Helena
Helena
Lake Village
Eudora

0 50 miles
0 50 kilometers
Albers Conic Equal-Area Projection

DIRTY WORK.
Hoping to find diamonds, a man hauls buckets of mud from the eroded surface of an ancient, gem-bearing volcanic pipe at Crater of Diamonds State Park.

Economy Symbols

Poultry/eggs	Nursery stock	Timber/forest products	Motor vehicles/parts
Sheep	Wheat	Stone/gravel/cement	Chemistry
Hogs	Corn	Oil/gas	Food processing
Dairy cows/products	Rice	Hydro-electricity	Electrical equipment
Beef cattle	Soybeans	Machinery	Computers/electronics
Fruits	Cotton	Metal manufacturing	Aircraft/parts
Vegetables	Vineyards	Metal products	Tourism

THE SUNSHINE STATE:
FLORIDA

BASICS

Statehood
March 3, 1845; 27th state

Total area (land and water)
65,758 sq mi (170,312 sq km)

Land area
53,625 sq mi (138,887 sq km)

Population
20,271,272

Capital
Tallahassee
Population 189,907

Largest city
Jacksonville
Population 868,031

Racial/ethnic groups
77.7% white; 16.8% African American; 2.8% Asian; 0.5% Native American; 24.5% Hispanic (any race)

Foreign born
19.4%

Urban population
91.2% (2010)

Population density
308.3 per sq mi (119.0 per sq km)

GEO WHIZ

Key West, the southernmost point in the continental U.S., is just 90 miles (145 km) from the island country of Cuba.

In 1937 Amelia Earhart and her navigator took off from Miami with the goal of making an around-the-world flight, but disappeared over the Pacific Ocean and were never seen again. You can read all about this famous flying ace in NG's children's book *Sky Pioneer*, by Corinne Szabo.

Everglades National Park, the largest subtropical wilderness in the United States, is home to rare and endangered species such as the Florida panther and the West Indian manatee.

Lightning strikes occur more often in Florida than in any other state in the United States.

Florida

Florida is home to St. Augustine, the country's oldest permanent European settlement, established by the Spanish in 1565. But native peoples had called Florida home long before then. Florida became a U.S. territory in 1821 and a state in 1845. The state's turbulent early history included the Civil War and three wars with Native Americans over control of the land. Railroads opened Florida to migration from the northern states as early as the 1890s. The mild climate and sandy beaches attracted people seeking to escape cold winters in the north. This trend continues, and today the area attracts both tourists and retirees. South Florida has a large Hispanic population that has migrated from all over Latin America—especially from nearby Cuba. Florida is working to solve many challenges: competition between city-dwellers and farmers for limited water resources; the annual risk of tropical storms; and the need to preserve its natural environment, including the vast Everglades wetland.

CULTURAL PRIDE. A young girl marches in Orlando's Puerto Rican Parade, a celebration of the music, dance, and culture of this U.S. island territory.

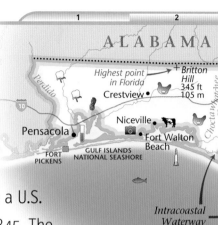

ALABAMA

Highest point in Florida — Britton Hill 345 ft 105 m
Crestview
Pensacola
Niceville
Fort Walton Beach
FORT PICKENS
GULF ISLANDS NATIONAL SEASHORE
Perdido
Choctawhatchee
Intracoastal Waterway

LIFTOFF! A NASA rocket rises amid clouds of steam from John F. Kennedy Space Center on Florida's Atlantic coast. The center has been the launch site for many U.S. space exploration projects.

ORANGE BLOSSOM
MOCKINGBIRD

JUICY HARVEST

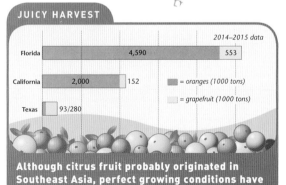

2014–2015 data

	oranges (1000 tons)	grapefruit (1000 tons)
Florida	4,590	553
California	2,000	152
Texas	93	280

= oranges (1000 tons)
= grapefruit (1000 tons)

Although citrus fruit probably originated in Southeast Asia, perfect growing conditions have made Florida the leading producer in the U.S.

GENTLE GIANT. The manatee, which is closely related to the elephant, is Florida's state marine mammal. Averaging 10 feet (3 m) in length and 1,000 pounds (454 kg), these endangered animals live on a diet of sea grasses.

GEORGIA

ATLANTIC OCEAN

FLORIDA

GULF OF MEXICO

Marianna
Panama City
Tallahassee
Perry
Live Oak
Lake City
Jacksonville
Fernandina Beach
Jacksonville Beach

OKEFENOKEE NATIONAL WILDLIFE REFUGE

TIMUCUAN ECOLOGICAL AND HISTORIC PRESERVE
FORT CAROLINE NAT. MEM.

OSCEOLA NAT. FOREST
ST. MARKS N.W.R.
APALACHICOLA NATIONAL FOREST
ST. VINCENT N.W.R.

Gainesville
Palatka
St. Augustine
Palm Coast
Ormond Beach
Daytona Beach
New Smyrna Beach

CASTILLO DE SAN MARCOS NAT. MON.
FORT MATANZAS NAT. MON.

Oldest permanent European settlement in the U.S., est. 1565

Ocala
The Villages
Homosassa Springs
Leesburg
Apopka
Winter Garden
Orlando
Sanford
De Land
Deltona
Titusville
John F. Kennedy Space Center
Cape Canaveral
Merritt Island
Melbourne
Palm Bay

Lake George
Lake Woodruff N.W.R.
OCALA NATIONAL FOREST
CANAVERAL NATIONAL SEASHORE
MERRITT ISLAND N.W.R.

Spring Hill
Bayonet Point
Tarpon Springs
Clearwater
Tampa
St. Petersburg
Walt Disney World
Kissimmee
Poinciana
Lakeland
Winter Haven
Haines City
Vero Beach
Fort Pierce
Port St. Lucie

LOWER SUWANNEE NATIONAL WILDLIFE REFUGE
CEDAR KEYS N.W.R.
CRYSTAL RIVER N.W.R.
CHASSAHOWITZKA N.W.R.
PINELLAS N.W.R.
EGMONT KEY N.W.R.
DE SOTO NAT. MEM.
TAMPA I.R.
FLORIDA'S TURNPIKE
PELICAN ISLAND N.W.R.
FORT PIERCE I.R.

Bradenton
Sarasota
Venice
Port Charlotte
Punta Gorda
Cape Coral
Fort Myers
Lehigh Acres
Bonita Springs
Golden Gate
Naples

Arcadia
Sebring
Lake Okeechobee
Belle Glade
West Palm Beach
Jupiter
Delray Beach
Boca Raton
Coral Springs
Coconut Creek I.R.
Fort Lauderdale
Hollywood
Hialeah
Miami
Kendall
Miami Beach

ISLAND BAY N.W.R.
Charlotte Harbor
J. N. "DING" DARLING N.W.R.
Sanibel Island
Immokalee
BRIGHTON SEMINOLE I.R.
BIG CYPRESS SEMINOLE I.R.
IMMOKALEE I.R.
ARTHUR R. MARSHALL LOXAHATCHEE N.W.R.
HOBE SOUND N.W.R.
LOXAHATCHEE NAT. WILD & SCENIC RIVER
MICCOSUKEE INDIAN RES.
SEMINOLE I.R.

Big Cypress Swamp
BIG CYPRESS NATIONAL PRESERVE
The Everglades
EVERGLADES NATIONAL PARK
Ten Thousand Islands
Cape Sable
Florida Bay
Biscayne Bay
BISCAYNE N.P.
Homestead
Key Largo

Largest subtropical wilderness in the United States

FLORIDA KEYS NATIONAL MARINE SANCTUARY
DRY TORTUGAS NATIONAL PARK
GREAT WHITE HERON N.W.R.
KEY WEST N.W.R.
NAT. KEY DEER REFUGE
Marathon
Key West

FLORIDA KEYS
STRAITS OF FLORIDA

Southernmost incorporated place in the continental United States

St. Marys R.
St. Johns R.
Suwannee R.
Ochlockonee R.
Apalachicola R.
Lake Seminole
Peace R.
Kissimmee R.
Caloosahatchee R.
St. Lucie Canal
Indian R.

Tampa Bay

0   100 miles
0   100 kilometers
Albers Conic Equal-Area Projection

Economy Symbols

Fishing
Lobster fishing
Shellfish
Poultry/eggs
Hogs
Dairy cows
Beef cattle
Fruits
Vegetables
Peanuts
Nursery stock
Corn
Rice
Sugarcane
Cotton

Tobacco
Timber/forest products
Printing/publishing
Hydro-electricity
Metal products
Shipbuilding
Chemistry
Food processing
Electrical equipment
Computers/electronics
Scientific instruments
Aerospace
Tourism
Finance/insurance

THE EMPIRE STATE OF THE SOUTH:
GEORGIA

BASICS

Statehood
January 2, 1788; 4th state

**Total area
(land and water)**
59,425 sq mi
(153,910 sq km)

Land area
57,513 sq mi
(148,959 sq km)

Population
1,056,298

Capital
Atlanta
Population 463,878

Largest city
Atlanta
Population 463,878

Racial/ethnic groups
61.6% white; 31.7% African
American; 4.0% Asian; 0.5%
Native American; 9.4% Hispanic
(any race)

Foreign born
9.7%

Urban population
75.1% (2010)

Population density
171.9 per sq mi (66.4 per sq km)

GEO WHIZ

The Okefenokee Swamp, the largest swamp in North America, has meat-eating plants that capture small animals for food. The swamp was also the setting for the adventures of Pogo the Possum, Albert the Alligator, and other characters created by cartoonist Walt Kelly.

The Georgia Aquarium in Atlanta, the largest in the Western Hemisphere, features thousands of sea creatures in 10 million gallons (37.9 million liters) of water.

Confederate war heroes Robert E. Lee, Stonewall Jackson, and Jefferson Davis are carved into the granite face of Stone Mountain near Atlanta.

Georgia

When Spanish explorers arrived in the mid-1500s in what would become Georgia, they found the land already occupied by Cherokee, Creek, and other native people. Georgia was the frontier separating Spanish Florida and English South Carolina, but in 1733 James Oglethorpe founded a new colony on the site of present-day Savannah. Georgia became the fourth state in 1788 and built an economy based on agriculture and slave labor. The state suffered widespread destruction during the Civil War and endured a long period of poverty in the years that followed. Modern-day Georgia is part of the fast-changing Sunbelt region. Agriculture—especially poultry, cotton, and forest products—remains important. Atlanta has emerged as a regional center of banking, telecommunications, and transportation, and Savannah is a major container port near the Atlantic coast, linking the state to the global economy. Historic sites, sports, and beaches draw thousands of tourists to the state every year.

🔊 **CASH CROP.** Peanuts are a big moneymaker in Georgia, where almost half the U.S. crop is grown—about half of which is used to make peanut butter.

🔊 **LIGHT SHOW.** Busy interstate traffic appears as ribbons of light below Atlanta's nighttime skyline. Atlanta is a center of economic growth, leading all cities in the region with 18 Fortune 500 companies headquartered within the metropolitan area.

CHEROKEE ROSE
BROWN THRASHER

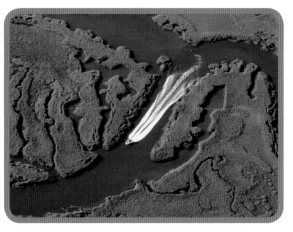

◑ **PAST MEETS PRESENT.** Georgia's 100-mile (160-km) coastline is laced with barrier islands, wetlands, and winding streams. In the 19th century plantations grew Sea Island cotton here. Today, tourists are attracted to the area's natural beauty and beaches.

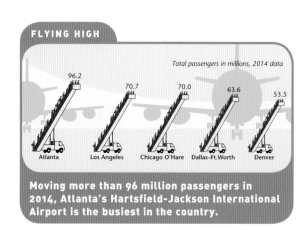

FLYING HIGH

Total passengers in millions, 2014 data

96.2	70.7	70.0	63.6	53.5
Atlanta	Los Angeles	Chicago O'Hare	Dallas–Ft. Worth	Denver

Moving more than 96 million passengers in 2014, Atlanta's Hartsfield-Jackson International Airport is the busiest in the country.

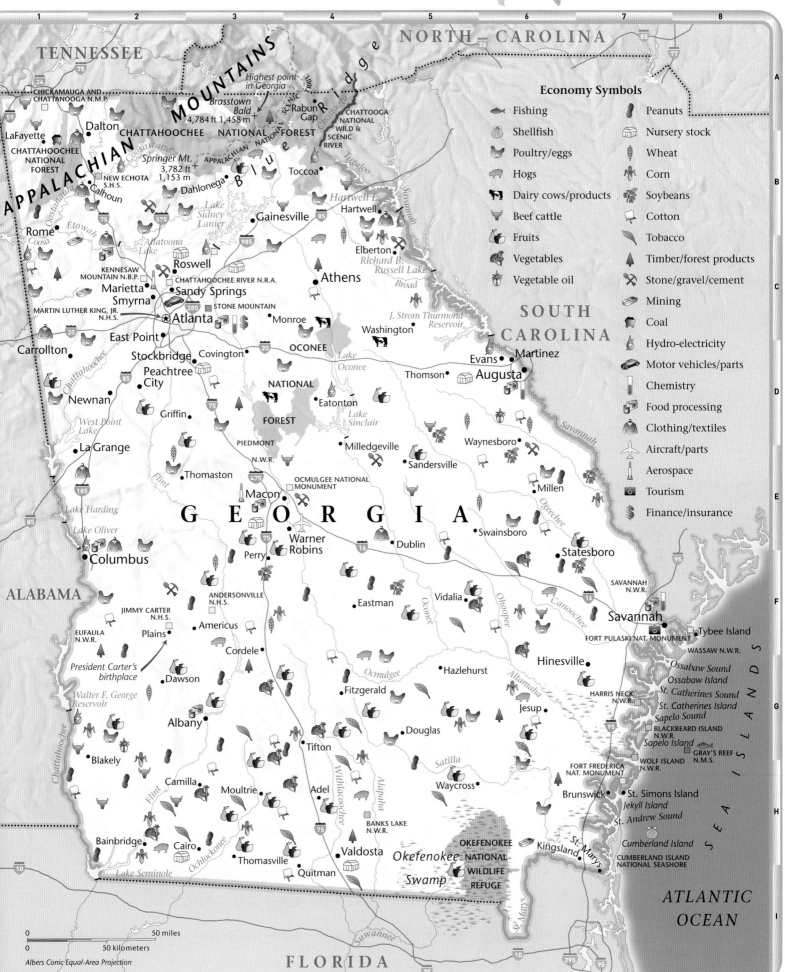

Economy Symbols

- Fishing
- Shellfish
- Poultry/eggs
- Hogs
- Dairy cows/products
- Beef cattle
- Fruits
- Vegetables
- Vegetable oil
- Peanuts
- Nursery stock
- Wheat
- Corn
- Soybeans
- Cotton
- Tobacco
- Timber/forest products
- Stone/gravel/cement
- Mining
- Coal
- Hydro-electricity
- Motor vehicles/parts
- Chemistry
- Food processing
- Clothing/textiles
- Aircraft/parts
- Aerospace
- Tourism
- Finance/insurance

TENNESSEE

NORTH CAROLINA

SOUTH CAROLINA

ALABAMA

GEORGIA

FLORIDA

ATLANTIC OCEAN

SEA ISLANDS

APPALACHIAN MOUNTAINS

CHICKAMAUGA AND CHATTANOOGA N.M.P.
LaFayette
Dalton
CHATTAHOOCHEE NATIONAL FOREST
Rome
Calhoun
NEW ECHOTA S.H.S.
Dahlonega
Springer Mt. 3,782 ft 1,153 m
Brasstown Bald 4,784 ft 1,458 m
Highest point in Georgia
Rabun Gap
CHATTOOGA NATIONAL WILD & SCENIC RIVER
Toccoa
CHATTAHOOCHEE NATIONAL FOREST
Blue Ridge
APPALACHIAN NATIONAL SCENIC TRAIL
Coosawattee
Lake Sidney Lanier
Gainesville
Hartwell L.
Hartwell
Elberton
Richard B. Russell Lake
Roswell
KENNESAW MOUNTAIN N.B.P.
CHATTAHOOCHEE RIVER N.R.A.
Marietta
Smyrna
Sandy Springs
MARTIN LUTHER KING, JR. N.H.S.
Atlanta
East Point
STONE MOUNTAIN
Monroe
Athens
Washington
J. Strom Thurmond Reservoir
Broad
Carrollton
Stockbridge
Covington
OCONEE
Lake Oconee
Evans
Martinez
Thomson
Augusta
Newnan
Peachtree City
Griffin
NATIONAL FOREST
Eatonton
Lake Sinclair
La Grange
Thomaston
PIEDMONT N.W.R.
Milledgeville
Sandersville
Waynesboro
West Point Lake
Lake Harding
Lake Oliver
Macon
OCMULGEE NATIONAL MONUMENT
Warner Robins
Perry
Dublin
Millen
Swainsboro
Statesboro
Columbus
SAVANNAH N.W.R.
Savannah
ANDERSONVILLE N.H.S.
Eastman
Vidalia
FORT PULASKI NAT. MONUMENT
Tybee Island
JIMMY CARTER N.H.S.
Americus
Hinesville
WASSAW N.W.R.
EUFAULA N.W.R.
Plains
President Carter's birthplace
Cordele
Hazlehurst
Ossabaw Sound
Ossabaw Island
Walter F. George Reservoir
Dawson
Fitzgerald
Jesup
St. Catherines Sound
St. Catherines Island
Sapelo Sound
Albany
Douglas
HARRIS NECK N.W.R.
BLACKBEARD ISLAND N.W.R.
Sapelo Island
Blakely
Tifton
GRAY'S REEF N.M.S.
WOLF ISLAND N.W.R.
Satilla
Waycross
FORT FREDERICA NAT. MONUMENT
Camilla
Moultrie
Adel
Brunswick
St. Simons Island
Bainbridge
Cairo
Valdosta
BANKS LAKE N.W.R.
Waycross
Jekyll Island
St. Andrew Sound
Thomasville
Quitman
OKEFENOKEE NATIONAL WILDLIFE REFUGE
Okefenokee Swamp
Kingsland
Cumberland Island
CUMBERLAND ISLAND NATIONAL SEASHORE
St. Marys

0 ———— 50 miles
0 ———— 50 kilometers
Albers Conic Equal-Area Projection

BASICS

Statehood
June 1, 1792; 15th state

Total area (land and water)
40,408 sq mi (104,656 sq km)

Land area
39,486 sq mi (102,269 sq km)

Population
4,425,092

Capital
Frankfort
Population 27,557 (2014)

Largest city
Louisville/Jefferson County
Population 615,366

Racial/ethnic groups
88.1% white; 8.3% African
American; 1.4% Asian; 0.3%
Native American; 3.4% Hispanic
(any race)

Foreign born
3.3%

Urban population
58.4% (2010)

Population density
112.1 per sq mi (43.3 per sq km)

GEO WHIZ

A favorite Kentucky dessert is
Derby Pie, a rich chocolate-and-
walnut pastry that was first created by George Kern, manager of
the Melrose Inn, in Prospect, in
the 1950s. It became so popular
that the name was registered
with the U.S. Patent Office and
the Commonwealth of Kentucky.

Pleasant Hill, near Lexington,
was the site of a Shaker
religious community. It is now
a National Historic Site with a
living history museum.

The song "Happy Birthday to
You," one of the most popular
songs in the English language,
was the creation of two Louisville
sisters in 1893.

Post-it notes are manufactured
exclusively in Cynthiana. Millions
of self-stick notes in 27 sizes
and 57 colors are produced
each year.

Kentucky

The original inhabitants of the area known today as Kentucky were Native American, but a treaty with the Cherokee, signed in 1775, opened the territory to settlers—including the legendary Daniel Boone—from the soon-to-be-independent eastern colonies. In 1776 Kentucky became a western county of the state of Virginia. In 1792 it became the 15th state. Eastern Kentucky is a part of Appalachia, a region rich in soft, bituminous coal but burdened with the environmental problems that often accompany the mining industry. The region is known for crafts and music that can be traced back to Scotch-Irish immigrants who settled there. In central Kentucky, the Bluegrass region produces some of the finest thoroughbred horses in the world, and the Kentucky Derby, held in Louisville, is a part of racing's coveted Triple Crown. In western Kentucky, coal found near the surface is strip mined, leaving scars on the landscape, but federal laws now require that the land be restored after mining.

GOLDENROD
CARDINAL

BENEATH THE SURFACE

Mammoth Cave System, KY	367 miles (591 km)
Jewel Cave, SD	140 miles (225 km)
Wind Cave, SD	125 miles (201 km)
Lechuguilla Cave, NM	121 miles (195 km)
Fisher Ridge Cave System, KY	110 miles (177 km)

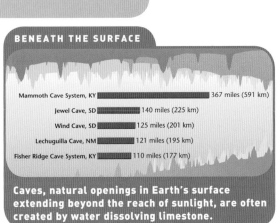

Caves, natural openings in Earth's surface extending beyond the reach of sunlight, are often created by water dissolving limestone.

THEY'RE OFF! Riders and horses press for the finish line at Churchill Downs, in Louisville. Kentucky is a major breeder of thoroughbred race horses, and horses are the leading source of farm income in the state.

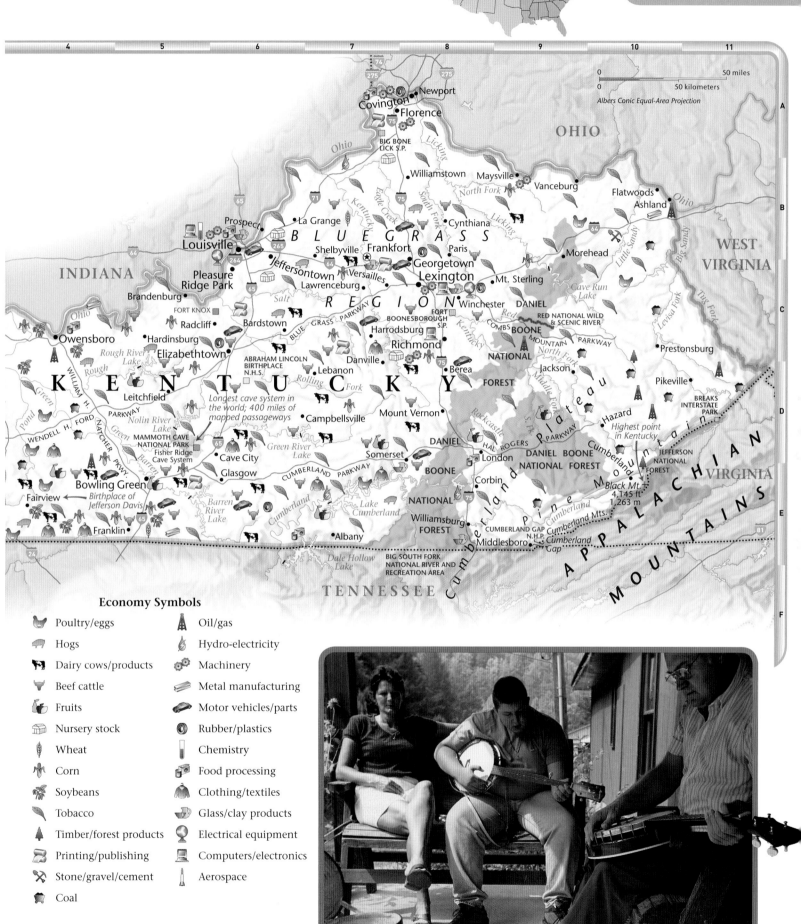

OHIO

Newport
Covington
Florence

BIG BONE
LICK S.P.

Williamstown   Maysville
Vanceburg

Flatwoods
Ashland

INDIANA

Prospect
Louisville
La Grange

B L U E G R A S S

Cynthiana

WEST
VIRGINIA

Pleasure
Ridge Park
Jeffersontown
Shelbyville   Frankfort
Versailles   Georgetown
Lawrenceburg   Lexington

Paris

Morehead

R E G I O N

Mt. Sterling

Cave Run
Lake

DANIEL

Brandenburg

Salt

FORT KNOX

BLUE   GRASS   PARKWAY

Winchester

RED NATIONAL WILD
& SCENIC RIVER

Prestonsburg

Radcliff
Bardstown

FORT
BOONESBOROUGH
S.P.

Harrodsburg

BOONE

Owensboro
Hardinsburg
Elizabethtown

Rough River
Lake

ABRAHAM LINCOLN
BIRTHPLACE
N.H.S.

Richmond

NATIONAL

Pikeville

K E N T U C K Y

Lebanon

Danville
Berea

FOREST

Jackson

Leitchfield

Longest cave system in
the world; 400 miles of
mapped passageways

Rolling   Fork

Hazard

BREAKS
INTERSTATE
PARK

Nolin River
Lake

Campbellsville

Mount Vernon

Highest point
in Kentucky

VIRGINIA

MAMMOTH CAVE
NATIONAL PARK
Fisher Ridge
Cave System

Green River
Lake

DANIEL

JEFFERSON
NATIONAL
FOREST

Cave City
Glasgow

Somerset

London

BOONE

Corbin

DANIEL BOONE
NATIONAL FOREST

Black Mt.
4,145 ft
1,263 m

Fairview

Bowling Green

CUMBERLAND   PARKWAY

Birthplace of
Jefferson Davis

Barren
River
Lake

Lake
Cumberland

NATIONAL

Williamsburg

CUMBERLAND GAP
N.H.P.

Franklin

Albany

FOREST

Middlesboro

APPALACHIAN   MOUNTAINS

Dale Hollow
Lake

BIG SOUTH FORK
NATIONAL RIVER AND
RECREATION AREA

TENNESSEE

Economy Symbols

- Poultry/eggs
- Hogs
- Dairy cows/products
- Beef cattle
- Fruits
- Nursery stock
- Wheat
- Corn
- Soybeans
- Tobacco
- Timber/forest products
- Printing/publishing
- Stone/gravel/cement
- Coal

- Oil/gas
- Hydro-electricity
- Machinery
- Metal manufacturing
- Motor vehicles/parts
- Rubber/plastics
- Chemistry
- Food processing
- Clothing/textiles
- Glass/clay products
- Electrical equipment
- Computers/electronics
- Aerospace

▶ STRUMMING A TUNE. Music is an important part of Kentucky's cultural heritage, especially in remote mountain areas where a banjo can become the focus of a family gathering.

Louisiana

BASICS

Statehood
April 30, 1812; 18th state

Total area (land and water)
52,378 sq mi (135,659 sq km)

Land area
43,204 sq mi (111,898 sq km)

Population
4,670,724

Capital
Baton Rouge
Population 228,590

Largest city
New Orleans
Population 389,617

Racial/ethnic groups
63.2% white; 32.5% African American; 1.8% Asian; 0.8% Native American; 5.0% Hispanic (any race)

Foreign born
3.9%

Urban population
73.2% (2010)

Population density
108.2 per sq mi (41.7 per sq km)

GEO WHIZ

The brown pelican, the state bird of Louisiana, was placed on the endangered species list in 1970. The species made a remarkable recovery, largely due to a ban of the pesticide DDT by the federal government, and was removed from the endangered list in 2009.

The magnolia, Louisiana's state flower, is the oldest flowering plant in the world. Some species are believed to be 100 million years old.

Cajuns, people whose French-speaking ancestors were exiled by the British from Acadia, in what is now Canada, live primarily in the bayou region of Louisiana. Their distinctive music and spicy food have become popular throughout the country.

🔺 **TASTY HARVEST.** Louisiana produces more than half of all shrimp caught in the U.S. Most comes from Barataria-Terrebonne, an estuary at the mouth of the Mississippi River.

MAGNOLIA
BROWN PELICAN

Louisiana's Native American heritage is evident in place-names such as Natchitoches and Opelousas. Spanish sailors explored the area in 1528, but the French, traveling down the Mississippi River, established permanent settlements in the mid-17th century and named the region for King Louis XIV. The United States gained possession of the territory as part of the Louisiana Purchase in 1803, and Louisiana became the 18th state in 1812. New Orleans and the Port of South Louisiana, located near the delta of the Mississippi River, are Louisiana's main ports. Trade from the interior of the United States moves through these ports and out to world markets. Oil and gas are drilled in the Mississippi Delta area and in the Gulf of Mexico. The explosion of an off-shore oil rig in 2010 brought serious environmental damage to coastal areas still recovering from Hurricane Katrina, a massive storm that roared in off the Gulf in 2005, flooding towns, breaking through levees, and changing the lives of everyone in southern Louisiana.

◖ **AVENUE TO THE PAST.** Stately live oaks, believed to be 300 years old, frame Oak Alley Plantation on the banks of the Mississippi River west of New Orleans. Built in 1839, the house has been restored to its former grandeur and is open to the public for tours and private events.

THE PELICAN STATE:
LOUISIANA

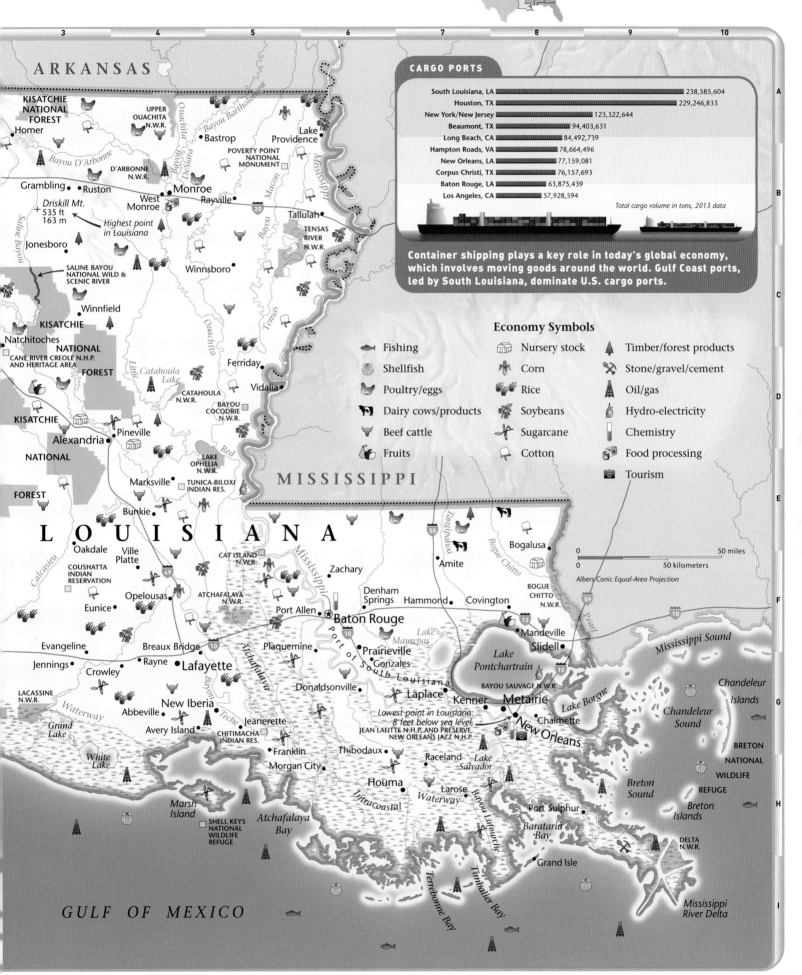

BASICS

Statehood
December 10, 1817; 20th state

Total area (land and water)
48,432 sq mi (125,438 sq km)

Land area
46,923 sq mi (121,531 sq km)

Population
2,992,333

Capital
Jackson
Population 170,674

Largest city
Jackson
Population 170,674

Racial/ethnic groups
59.5% white; 37.6% African American; 1.1% Asian; 0.6% Native American; 3.1% Hispanic (any race)

Foreign born
2.2%

Urban population
49.4% (2010)

Population density
607.8 per sq mi (234.7 per sq km)

GEO WHIZ

The Windsor Ruins, located near Port Gibson, are 23 monolithic columns that once made up the largest antebellum mansion in the state. The mansion survived the Civil War but was destroyed by a fire in 1890.

The Marine Life Oceanarium in Gulfport was almost completely destroyed by Hurricane Katrina in 2005. Eight of its 14 bottle-nose dolphins were swept into the Gulf of Mexico by a 40-foot (12-m) wave. These animals and two sea lions named Splash and Elliot were eventually rescued. Others were not so lucky.

Greenville is the birthplace of Jim Henson, creator of Kermit the Frog, Miss Piggy, Big Bird, and other famous Muppets.

Mississippi

Mississippi is named for the river that forms its western boundary. The name comes from the Chippewa words *mici zibi*, meaning "great river." Indeed it is a great river, draining much of the interior United States and providing a trade artery to the world. Explored by the Spanish in 1540 and claimed by the French in 1699, the territory of Mississippi passed to the United States in 1783 and became the 20th state in 1817. For more than a hundred years following statehood, Mississippi was the center of U.S. cotton production and trade. The fertile soils and mild climate of the delta region in northwestern Mississippi provided a perfect environment for cotton, a crop that depended on slave labor. When the Civil War broke out, it took a heavy toll on the state. Today, poverty, especially in rural areas, is a major challenge for the state where agriculture—poultry, cotton, soybeans, and rice—is still the base of the economy.

SINGING THE BLUES. The Gateway to the Blues Museum in Tunica traces the blues, a uniquely American music form, to Mississippi's cotton fields where West Africans, brought on slave ships, toiled in the 1800s.

MOCKINGBIRD
MAGNOLIA

GONE FISHIN'

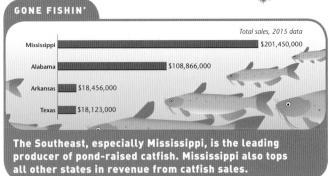

Total sales, 2015 data

Mississippi	$201,450,000
Alabama	$108,866,000
Arkansas	$18,456,000
Texas	$18,123,000

The Southeast, especially Mississippi, is the leading producer of pond-raised catfish. Mississippi also tops all other states in revenue from catfish sales.

DELTA QUEEN

BIG WHEEL TURNING. Now popular with tourists, paddlewheel boats made the Mississippi River a major artery for trade and travel in the 19th century.

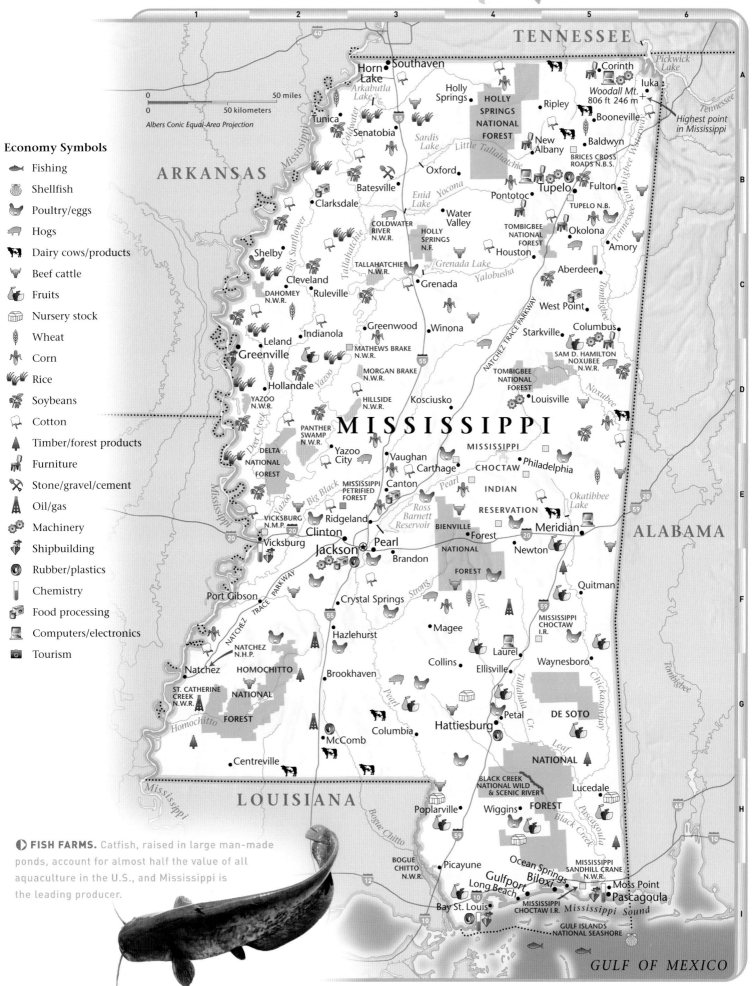

Economy Symbols

- Fishing
- Shellfish
- Poultry/eggs
- Hogs
- Dairy cows/products
- Beef cattle
- Fruits
- Nursery stock
- Wheat
- Corn
- Rice
- Soybeans
- Cotton
- Timber/forest products
- Furniture
- Stone/gravel/cement
- Oil/gas
- Machinery
- Shipbuilding
- Rubber/plastics
- Chemistry
- Food processing
- Computers/electronics
- Tourism

FISH FARMS. Catfish, raised in large man-made ponds, account for almost half the value of all aquaculture in the U.S., and Mississippi is the leading producer.

BASICS

Statehood
November 21, 1789; 12th state

Total area (land and water)
53,819 sq mi (139,391 sq km)

Land area
48,618 sq mi (125,920 sq km)

Population
10,042,802

Capital
Raleigh
Population 451,066

Largest city
Charlotte
Population 827,097

Racial/ethnic groups
71.2% white; 22.1% African
American; 2.8% Asian; 1.6%
Native American; 9.1% Hispanic
(any race)

Foreign born
7.6%

Urban population
66.1% (2010)

Population density
2,174.7 per sq mi
(839.7 per sq km)

GEO WHIZ

The University of North Carolina
at Chapel Hill, which opened its
doors in 1795, is the oldest public
university in the United States.

The Biltmore estate in Asheville
is the largest private residence in
the United States. It was built by
Cornelius Vanderbilt to resemble a French chateau.

At 208 feet (63 m) high, Cape
Hatteras Light is the tallest
lighthouse in the U.S. Its
beacon can be seen some 20
miles (32 km) out to sea and
has warned sailors for more
than a century.

North Carolina

Before European contact, the land that became North Carolina was inhabited by numerous Native American groups. Early attempts to settle the area met with strong resistance, and one early colony established in 1587 on Roanoke Island disappeared without a trace. More attempts at settlement came in 1650, and in 1663 King Charles granted a charter for the Carolina colony, which included present-day North Carolina, South Carolina, and part of Georgia. In 1789 North Carolina became the 12th state, but in 1861 it joined the Confederacy, supplying more men and equipment to the Southern cause than any other state. In 1903 the Wright brothers piloted the first successful airplane near Kitty Hawk, foreshadowing the change and growth coming to the Tar Heel State. Traditional industries included agriculture, textiles, and furniture making. Today, these plus high-tech industries and education in the Raleigh-Durham Research Triangle area as well as banking and finance in Charlotte are important to the economy.

CARDINAL
FLOWERING
DOGWOOD

FAVORITE PASTIME.
With four of the state's major schools represented in the powerful Atlantic Coast Conference, it is not surprising that basketball is a popular sport among all ages, whether on the court or in the backyard.

TAKING FLIGHT.
The Wright Brothers Memorial on Kill Devil Hill, near Kitty Hawk on North Carolina's Outer Banks, marks the site of the first successful airplane flight in 1903.

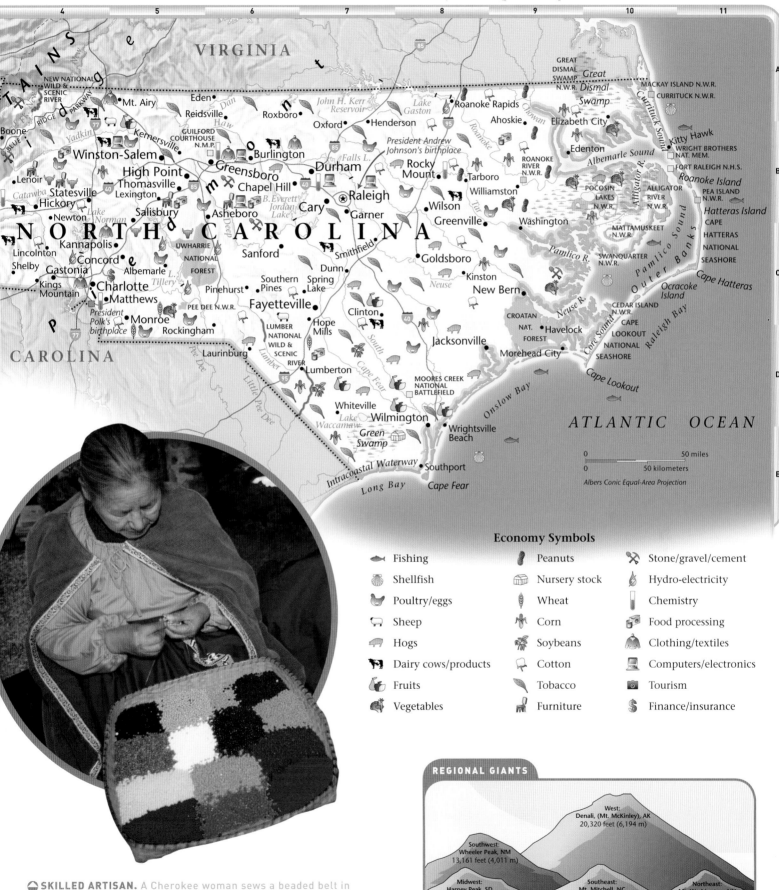

VIRGINIA

NORTH CAROLINA

CAROLINA

ATLANTIC OCEAN

0   50 miles
0   50 kilometers
Albers Conic Equal-Area Projection

Selected map labels:
Mt. Airy, Eden, Reidsville, Roxboro, Oxford, Henderson, Roanoke Rapids, Ahoskie, Elizabeth City, Great Dismal Swamp, Mackay Island N.W.R., Currituck N.W.R., Kitty Hawk, Wright Brothers Nat. Mem., Boone, Kernersville, Winston-Salem, Greensboro, Burlington, Durham, Rocky Mount, Tarboro, Williamston, Edenton, Fort Raleigh N.H.S., Roanoke Island, Pea Island N.W.R., Lenoir, High Point, Thomasville, Chapel Hill, Raleigh, Cary, Wilson, Greenville, Washington, Hatteras Island, Statesville, Lexington, Asheboro, Garner, Pocosin Lakes N.W.R., Alligator River N.W.R., Hickory, Salisbury, Smithfield, Goldsboro, Kinston, Mattamuskeet N.W.R., Swanquarter N.W.R., Cape Hatteras, Newton, Kannapolis, Sanford, Dunn, New Bern, Ocracoke Island, Lincolnton, Concord, Uwharrie National Forest, Spring Lake, Southern Pines, Pinehurst, Fayetteville, Clinton, Jacksonville, Havelock, Morehead City, Cape Lookout, Shelby, Gastonia, Albemarle, Kings Mountain, Charlotte, Matthews, President Polk's birthplace, Monroe, Rockingham, Lumber National Wild & Scenic River, Hope Mills, Moores Creek National Battlefield, Onslow Bay, Laurinburg, Lumberton, Whiteville, Wilmington, Wrightsville Beach, Southport, Cape Fear, Long Bay, President Andrew Johnson's birthplace, Guilford Courthouse N.M.P., New National Wild & Scenic River, Blue Ridge Parkway, Pee Dee N.W.R.

Economy Symbols

Fishing	Peanuts	Stone/gravel/cement
Shellfish	Nursery stock	Hydro-electricity
Poultry/eggs	Wheat	Chemistry
Sheep	Corn	Food processing
Hogs	Soybeans	Clothing/textiles
Dairy cows/products	Cotton	Computers/electronics
Fruits	Tobacco	Tourism
Vegetables	Furniture	Finance/insurance

SKILLED ARTISAN. A Cherokee woman sews a beaded belt in Oconaluftee Indian Village in western North Carolina. Cherokee in this mountainous region are descendants of Indians who hid in the hills to avoid the forced migration known as the Trail of Tears. The village preserves traditional 18th-century crafts, customs, and lifestyles.

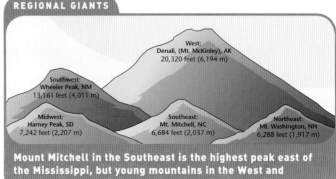

REGIONAL GIANTS

West:
Denali, (Mt. McKinley), AK
20,320 feet (6,194 m)

Southwest:
Wheeler Peak, NM
13,161 feet (4,011 m)

Midwest:
Harney Peak, SD
7,242 feet (2,207 m)

Southeast:
Mt. Mitchell, NC
6,684 feet (2,037 m)

Northeast:
Mt. Washington, NH
6,288 feet (1,917 m)

Mount Mitchell in the Southeast is the highest peak east of the Mississippi, but young mountains in the West and Southwest tower above older eastern peaks.

THE PALMETTO STATE:
SOUTH CAROLINA

BASICS

Statehood
May 23, 1788; 8th state

Total area (land and water)
32,020 sq mi (82,933 sq km)

Land area
30,061 sq mi
(77,857 sq km)

Population
4,896,146

Capital
Columbia
Population 133,803

Largest city
Columbia
Population 133,803

Racial/ethnic groups
68.4% white; 27.6% African American; 1.6% Asian; 0.5% Native American; 5.5% Hispanic (any race)

Foreign born
4.8%

Urban population
66.3% (2010)

Population density
162.9 per sq mi (62.8 per sq km)

GEO WHIZ

The loggerhead sea turtle, South Carolina's state reptile, is threatened throughout its range.

Congaree National Park, on the Congaree River, protects North America's largest remaining area of primary lowland hardwood forest.

Sweetgrass basketmaking, a traditional art form of African origin, has been a part of the Mount Pleasant community for more than 300 years. The baskets were originally used by slaves in the planting and processing of rice in coastal lowlands.

Bobcats are thriving on Kiawah Island, a resort community near Charleston. These elusive, nocturnal cats, which are about twice the size of an average house cat, help control the island's deer population.

South Carolina

Attempts in the 16th century by the Spanish and the French to colonize the area that would become South Carolina met fierce resistance from local Native American groups, but in 1670 the English were the first to establish a permanent European settlement at present-day Charleston. The colony prospered by relying on slave labor to produce first cotton, then rice and indigo. South Carolina became the eighth state in 1788 and the first to leave the Union just months before the first shots of the Civil War were fired on Fort Sumter in 1861. After the war South Carolina struggled to rebuild its economy. Early in the 20th century, textile mills introduced new jobs. Today, agriculture remains important, manufacturing and high-tech industries are expanding along interstate highway corridors, and tourists and retirees are drawn to the state's Atlantic coastline. But these coastal areas are not without risk. In 1989 Hurricane Hugo's 135-mile-an-hour (217-km/h) winds left a trail of destruction.

◷ **GLOW OF DAWN.** The rising sun reflects off the water along the Atlantic coast. Beaches attract visitors year-round, contributing to tourism, the state's largest industry.

YELLOW JESSAMINE
CAROLINA WREN

◷ **SOUTHERN CHARM.** Established in 1670, Charleston is famous for its stately antebellum homes. The city is an important port, located where the Ashley and Cooper Rivers merge before flowing to the Atlantic Ocean.

Map labels:
1 | 2
Highest point in South Carolina
Blue Ridge
CHATTOOGA NATIONAL WILD & SCENIC RIVER
SUMTER
Sassafras Mt. 3,560 ft 1,085 m
NATIONAL FOREST
Lake Keowee
Greenville
Easley • Gantt
Seneca • Clemson
Belton
Hartwell Lake
Anderson
Richard B. Russell Lake
Abbeville
Savannah
P

TRADE PARTNERS

Top shares of state export trade, 2014 data
(Other countries account for 28.7 percent.)

South Korea 2.1%
Netherlands 2.1%
Brazil 2.0%
Belgium 2.4%
Australia 3.0%
Japan 3.1%
Algeria 3.6%
United Kingdom 6.3%
Mexico 7.1%
Canada 12.2%
Germany 13.1%
China 14.3%

With more than $29 billion in export goods in 2014, export industries supported almost 25 percent of South Carolina's manufacturing jobs. Transportation equipment is the leading manufactured export.

0
50 miles

0
50 kilometers

Albers Conic Equal-Area Projection

SHOWING OFF. Feathers extended, a male wild turkey struts through Francis Beidler Forest, a wildlife sanctuary and the world's largest virgin cypress–tupelo swamp forest.

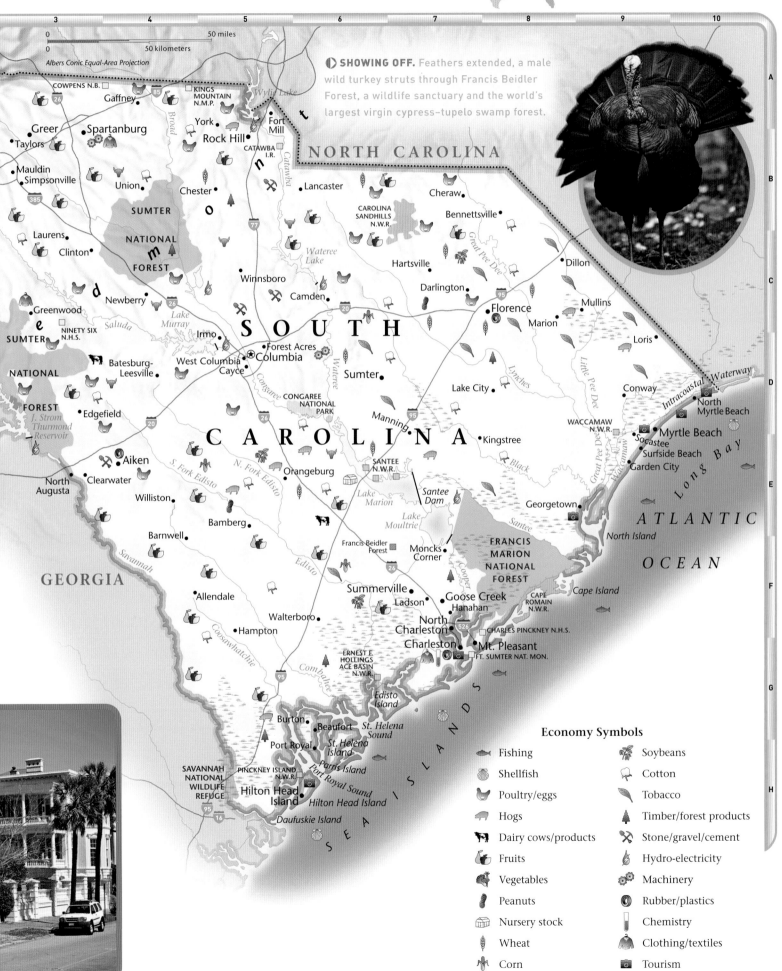

COWPENS N.B.

Gaffney

KINGS MOUNTAIN N.M.P.

Wylie Lake

NORTH CAROLINA

Greer

York

Fort Mill

Spartanburg

Rock Hill

Taylors

CATAWBA I.R.

Lancaster

Cheraw

Mauldin
Simpsonville

Union

Chester

Bennettsville

SUMTER

CAROLINA SANDHILLS N.W.R.

NATIONAL

Wateree Lake

Hartsville

Dillon

Laurens

FOREST

Winnsboro

Darlington

Mullins

Clinton

Camden

Florence

Greenwood

Newberry

Lake Murray

Marion

Loris

NINETY SIX N.H.S.

Saluda

SOUTH

SUMTER

Irmo

Forest Acres

Lake City

Conway

NATIONAL

West Columbia
Cayce

Columbia

Sumter

North Myrtle Beach

WACCAMAW N.W.R.

FOREST

Edgefield

CONGAREE NATIONAL PARK

Manning

Kingstree

Myrtle Beach
Socastee
Surfside Beach
Garden City

J. Strom Thurmond Reservoir

CAROLINA

Aiken

Orangeburg

SANTEE N.W.R.

North Augusta

Clearwater

Williston

Bamberg

Lake Marion

Santee Dam

Lake Moultrie

Georgetown

North Island

ATLANTIC

Barnwell

Francis Beidler Forest

Moncks Corner

FRANCIS MARION NATIONAL FOREST

Cape Island

OCEAN

GEORGIA

Allendale

Summerville

Goose Creek
Hanahan

CAPE ROMAIN N.W.R.

Walterboro

Ladson

Hampton

North Charleston

CHARLES PINCKNEY N.H.S.

Charleston

Mt. Pleasant

ERNEST F. HOLLINGS ACE BASIN N.W.R.

FT. SUMTER NAT. MON.

Edisto Island

Burton

Beaufort

St. Helena Sound

Port Royal

St. Helena Island

SAVANNAH NATIONAL WILDLIFE REFUGE

PINCKNEY ISLAND N.W.R.

Parris Island

Port Royal Sound

Hilton Head Island

Hilton Head Island

Daufuskie Island

SEA ISLANDS

Long Bay

Economy Symbols

Fishing		Soybeans
Shellfish		Cotton
Poultry/eggs		Tobacco
Hogs		Timber/forest products
Dairy cows/products		Stone/gravel/cement
Fruits		Hydro-electricity
Vegetables		Machinery
Peanuts		Rubber/plastics
Nursery stock		Chemistry
Wheat		Clothing/textiles
Corn		Tourism

BASICS

Statehood
June 1, 1796; 16th state

Total area (land and water)
42,144 sq mi (109,153 sq km)

Land area
41,235 sq mi (106,798 sq km)

Population
6,600,299

Capital
Nashville-Davidson County
Population 654,610

Largest city
Memphis
Population 655,770

Racial/ethnic groups
78.8% white; 17.1% African
American; 1.8% Asian; 0.4%
Native American; 5.2% Hispanic
(any race)

Foreign born
4.6%

Urban population
66.4% (2010)

Population density
160.1 per sq mi (61.8 per sq km)

GEO WHIZ

Great Smoky Mountains National
Park is known as the Salamander
Capital of the world for the 27
species of salamanders that live
there, including the five-foot
(1.5-m)-long hellbender.

The New Madrid Earthquakes
of 1811–1812, some of the
largest earthquakes in U.S.
history, created Reelfoot Lake
in northwestern Tennessee.
It is the state's only large,
natural lake; others were
created by damming waterways.

The Tennessee-Tombigbee
Waterway is a 234-mile
(376-km) artificial waterway
that connects the Tennessee
and Tombigbee Rivers. This
water transportation route
provides inland ports with an
outlet to the Gulf of Mexico.

Tennessee

Following the last ice age, Native Americans moved onto the fertile lands of Tennessee. The earliest Europeans in Tennessee were Spanish explorers who passed through in 1541. In 1673 both the English and French made claims on the land, hoping to develop trade with the powerful Cherokee, whose town, called *Tanasi,* gave the state its name. Originally part of North Carolina, Tennessee was ceded to the federal government and became the 16th state in 1796.

Tennessee was the last state to join the Confederacy and endured years of hardship after the war. Beginning in the 1930s, the federally funded Tennessee Valley Authority (TVA) set a high standard in water management in the state, and the hydropower it generated supported major industrial development. Tennessee played a key role in the civil rights movement of the 1960s. Today, visitors to Tennessee are drawn to national parks, Nashville's country music, and the mournful sound of the blues in Memphis.

MOCKINGBIRD
IRIS

◀ **OUT FOR A STROLL.**
Black bear cubs are usually born in January and remain with their mother for about 18 months. The Great Smoky Mountains National Park is one of the few remaining natural habitats for black bears in the eastern United States.

NATURE'S PLAYGROUND

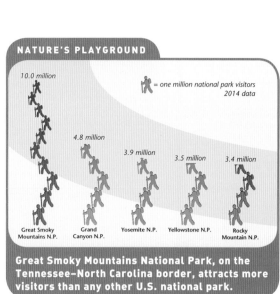

= one million national park visitors
2014 data

10.0 million — Great Smoky Mountains N.P.
4.8 million — Grand Canyon N.P.
3.9 million — Yosemite N.P.
3.5 million — Yellowstone N.P.
3.4 million — Rocky Mountain N.P.

Great Smoky Mountains National Park, on the Tennessee–North Carolina border, attracts more visitors than any other U.S. national park.

THE VOLUNTEER STATE:
TENNESSEE

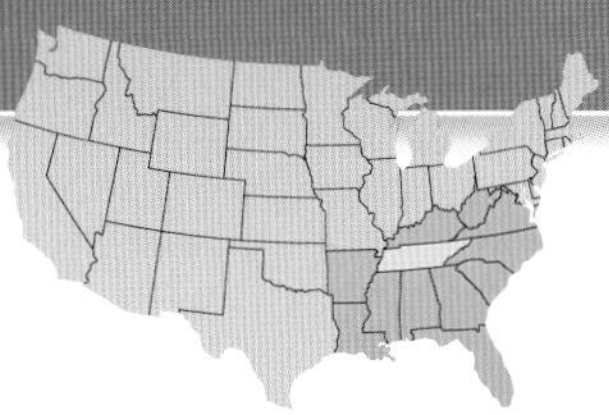

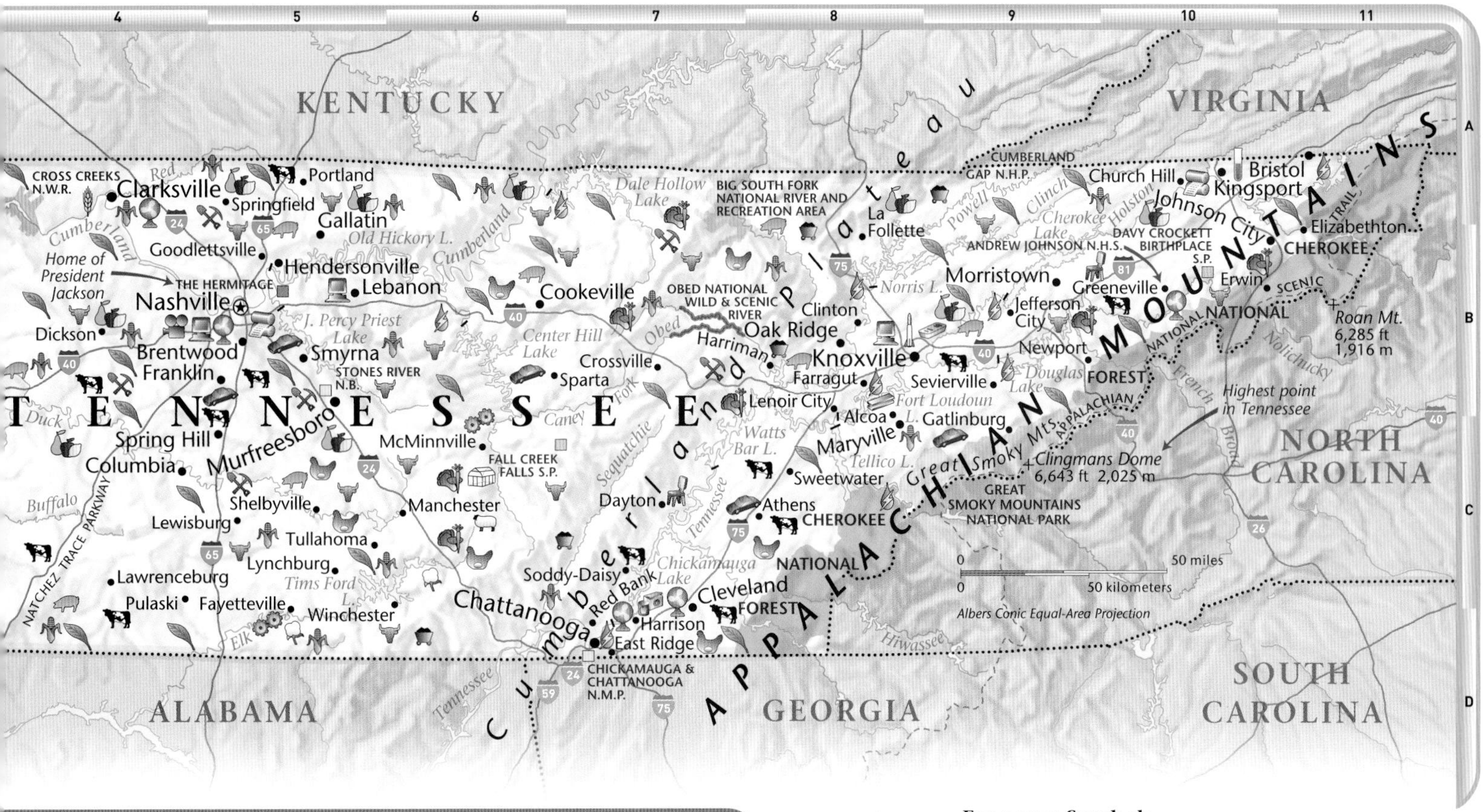
KENTUCKY
VIRGINIA
TENNESSEE
NORTH CAROLINA
SOUTH CAROLINA
GEORGIA
ALABAMA
Cumberland Plateau
APPALACHIAN MOUNTAINS
CROSS CREEKS N.W.R.
Clarksville
Portland
Springfield
Gallatin
Goodlettsville
Hendersonville
Lebanon
Home of President Jackson
THE HERMITAGE
Nashville
Dickson
Brentwood
Franklin
Smyrna
STONES RIVER N.B.
J. Percy Priest Lake
Old Hickory L.
Murfreesboro
Spring Hill
Columbia
Shelbyville
Lewisburg
Tullahoma
Lynchburg
Tims Ford L.
Lawrenceburg
Pulaski
Fayetteville
Winchester
Manchester
McMinnville
FALL CREEK FALLS S.P.
Cookeville
Center Hill Lake
Crossville
Sparta
Dale Hollow Lake
BIG SOUTH FORK NATIONAL RIVER AND RECREATION AREA
OBED NATIONAL WILD & SCENIC RIVER
La Follette
Clinton
Oak Ridge
Harriman
Knoxville
Farragut
Lenoir City
Alcoa
Maryville
Sweetwater
Watts Bar L.
Tellico L.
Athens
CHEROKEE
Dayton
Soddy-Daisy
Red Bank
Chattanooga
East Ridge
Harrison
Cleveland
Chickamauga Lake
NATIONAL FOREST
CHICKAMAUGA & CHATTANOOGA N.M.P.
CUMBERLAND GAP N.H.P.
Church Hill
Bristol
Kingsport
Johnson City
Elizabethton
CHEROKEE
ANDREW JOHNSON N.H.S.
DAVY CROCKETT BIRTHPLACE S.P.
Morristown
Greeneville
Jefferson City
Newport
Erwin
Norris L.
Douglas Lake
Fort Loudoun L.
Sevierville
Gatlinburg
Great Smoky Mts.
Clingmans Dome 6,643 ft 2,025 m
GREAT SMOKY MOUNTAINS NATIONAL PARK
CHEROKEE NATIONAL FOREST
Roan Mt. 6,285 ft 1,916 m
Highest point in Tennessee
APPALACHIAN SCENIC TRAIL
NATCHEZ TRACE PARKWAY
Cumberland
Tennessee
Duck
Buffalo
Elk
Caney Fork
Sequatchie
Clinch
Powell
Holston
French Broad
Nolichucky
Hiwassee
Obed
0 50 miles
0 50 kilometers
Albers Conic Equal-Area Projection

Economy Symbols

- Poultry/eggs
- Sheep
- Hogs
- Dairy cows/products
- Beef cattle
- Fruits
- Vegetables
- Nursery stock
- Wheat
- Corn
- Soybeans
- Cotton
- Tobacco
- Furniture
- Printing/publishing
- Stone/gravel/cement
- Mining
- Coal
- Hydro-electricity
- Machinery
- Metal manufacturing
- Motor vehicles/parts
- Chemistry
- Food processing
- Electrical equipment
- Computers/electronics
- Aerospace
- Motion picture/music industry

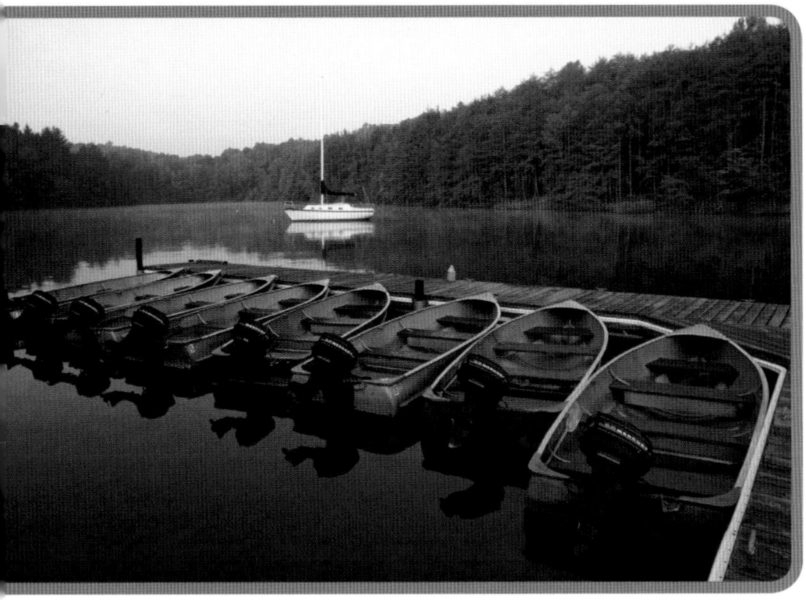

WATTS BAR DAM is one of nine TVA dams built on the Tennessee River to aid navigation and flood control and to supply power. The large reservoir behind the dam provides a recreation area that attracts millions of vacationers each year. Without the dam, cities such as Chattanooga would face devastating floods.

SOUTHERN TRADITION. Nashville's Grand Ole Opry is the home of country music. Originally a 1925 radio show called *WSM Barn Dance*, the Opry now occupies a theater with a seating capacity of 4,400 and the largest broadcasting studio in the world. Country music, using mainly stringed instruments, evolved from traditional folk tunes of the Appalachians.

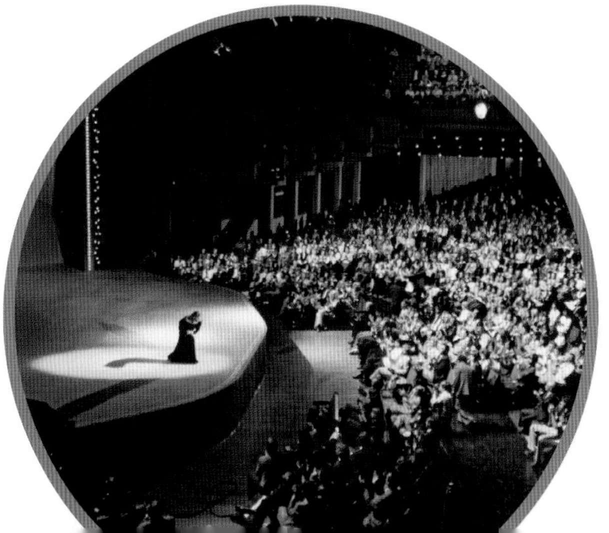

THE OLD DOMINION STATE:
VIRGINIA

BASICS

Statehood
June 25, 1788; 10th state

Total area (land and water)
42,775 sq mi (110,787 sq km)

Land area
39,490 sq mi (102,279 sq km)

Population
8,382,993

Capital
Richmond
Population 220,289

Largest city
Virginia Beach
Population 452,745

Racial/ethnic groups
70.2% white; 19.7% African American; 6.5% Asian; 0.5% Native American; 9.0% Hispanic (any race)

Foreign born
11.3%

Urban population
75.5% (2010)

Population density
212.3 per sq mi (82.0 per sq km)

GEO WHIZ

In the early 1700s, the bustling port of Hampton was a major target for pirates, including the notorious Blackbeard. Today, the city hosts the Blackbeard Festival each spring, complete with pirate re-enactors, live music, games, and fireworks.

During the Battle of Hampton Roads in 1862, the USS *Monitor* and the CSS *Virginia* (a rebuilt version of the USS *Merrimac*) met in one of the most famous naval engagements in U.S. history. The battle marked the dawn of a new era of naval warfare.

More than 200,000 telephone calls are made each day at the Pentagon, the headquarters for the U.S. Department of Defense, through phones connected by 100,000 miles (160,000 km) of telephone cable. The Pentagon is one of the world's largest office buildings.

FLOWERING
DOGWOOD

CARDINAL

Virginia

Long before Europeans arrived in present-day Virginia, Native Americans populated the area. Early Spanish attempts to establish a colony failed, but in 1607 merchants established the first permanent English settlement in North America at Jamestown. Virginia became a prosperous colony, growing tobacco using slave labor. Virginia played a key role in the drive for independence, and the final battle of the Revolutionary War was at Yorktown, near Jamestown. In 1861 Virginia joined the Confederacy and became a major battleground of the Civil War, which left the state in financial ruin.

EARLY ENTERTAINMENT. Dice made of bone, ivory, and lead, dating to 1607, were excavated at Jamestown, providing evidence of a popular form of entertainment during colonial times.

Today, Virginia has a diversified economy. Farmers still grow tobacco, along with other crops. The Hampton Roads area, near the mouth of Chesapeake Bay, is a center for shipbuilding and home to major U.S. naval bases. Northern Virginia, across the Potomac River from Washington, D.C., boasts federal government offices and high-tech businesses. And the state's natural beauty and many historic sites attract tourists from around the world.

NATURAL WONDER. Winding under the Appalachian Mountains, Luray Caverns formed as water dissolved limestone rocks and precipitated calcium deposits to form stalactites and stalagmites.

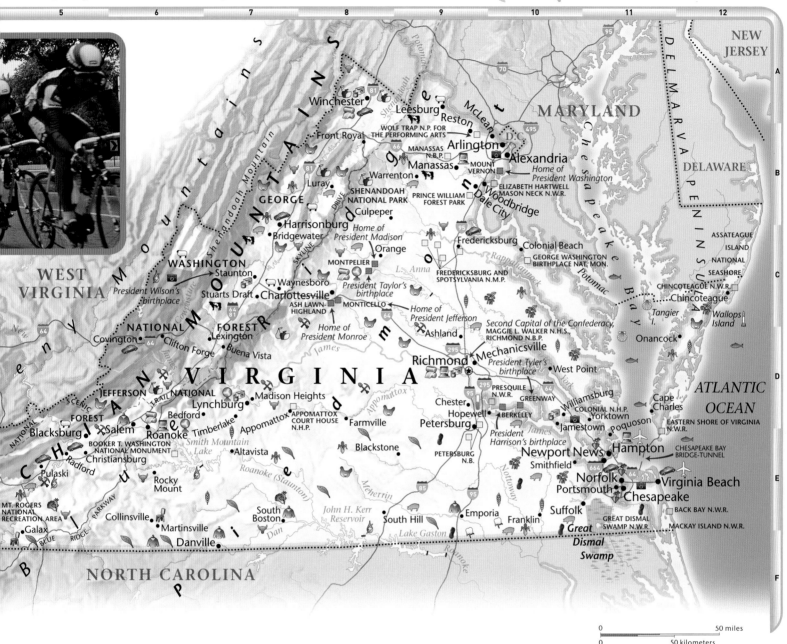

PAST AND PRESENT. Cyclists speed past a statue of Confederate General Robert E. Lee on Richmond's Monument Avenue. The street has drawn criticism for recognizing leaders of the Confederacy.

Economy Symbols

- Fishing
- Shellfish
- Poultry/eggs
- Sheep
- Hogs
- Dairy cows/products
- Beef cattle
- Fruits
- Vegetables
- Peanuts
- Wheat

- Corn
- Soybeans
- Cotton
- Tobacco
- Furniture
- Printing/publishing
- Stone/gravel/cement
- Coal
- Hydro-electricity
- Machinery
- Ship Building

- Motor vehicles/parts
- Chemistry
- Food processing
- Clothing/textiles
- Electrical equipment
- Computers/electronics
- Aircraft/parts
- Aerospace
- Tourism

MODERN CONNECTORS

17.6 mi (28.3 km)
Chesapeake Bay Bridge-Tunnel (Virginia Beach to Kiptopeke, VA)

15.8 miles (25.5 km)
Shanghai Yangtze Tunnel and Bridge (Pudong District to Chongming Island, China)

9.9 mi (15.0 km)
Oresund Connection (Sweden to Denmark)

8.7 mi (14.0 km)
Tokyo Bay Aqua Line (Kawasaki to Kisarazu, Japan)

5.1 miles (8.2 km)
Busan-Geoje Fixed Link (Busan to Geoje Island, South Korea)

Advanced engineering has made it possible to span wide expanses of water. The longest bridge-tunnel in the world is in Virginia.

BASICS

Statehood
June 20, 1863; 35th state

Total area (land and water)
24,230 sq mi (62,756 sq km)

Land area
24,038 sq mi (62,259 sq km)

Population
1,844,128

Capital
Charleston
Population 49,736

Largest city
Charleston
Population 49,736

Racial/ethnic groups
93.6% white; 3.6% African American; 0.8% Asian; 0.2% Native American; 1.5% Hispanic (any race)

Foreign born
1.4%

Urban population
48.7% (2010)

Population density
76.7 per sq mi (29.6 per sq km)

GEO WHIZ

The FBI Criminal Justice Information Center (CJIS) near Clarksburg has the largest collection of criminal finger-prints in the world. The center handles about 12 million inquiries each day.

The city of Weirton is nestled in the panhandle between Ohio and Pennsylvania. It is the only city in the U.S. that sits in one state and borders two others.

The first rural free mail delivery in the United States started in Charles Town on October 1, 1896.

West Virginia

Mountainous West Virginia was first settled by Native Americans who favored the wooded region for hunting. The first Europeans to settle in what originally was an extension of Virginia were Germans and Scotch-Irish, who came through mountain valleys of Pennsylvania in the early 1700s. Because farms in West Virginia did not depend on slaves, residents opposed secession during the Civil War and broke away from Virginia, becoming the 35th state in 1863. In the early 1800s West Virginia harvested forest products and mined salt, but it was the exploitation of vast coal deposits that brought industrialization to the state. Coal fueled steel mills, steamboats, and trains, and jobs in the mines attracted immigrants from far and near. However, poor work conditions resulted in a legacy of poverty, illness, and environmental degradation—problems the state continues to face. Today, the state is working to build a tourist industry based on its natural beauty and mountain crafts and culture.

HARD LABOR. Coal miners work under difficult conditions—some in underground mines; others in surface mines. In 2013 West Virginia's mines employed more than 20,000 people.

CARDINAL
RHODODENDRON

OHIO

Point Pleasant

Hurricane
Huntington
Kenova

Ohio
Big Sandy

Logan

Williamson

Tug Fork

Guyandotte

Kanawha

KENTUCKY

STRATEGIC LOCATION. Founded in 1751 by Robert Harper, who built a ferry to cross the Shenandoah River, Harpers Ferry was the focus of John Brown's historic 1859 raid on the town's U.S. arsenal as a first step in a planned slave uprising.

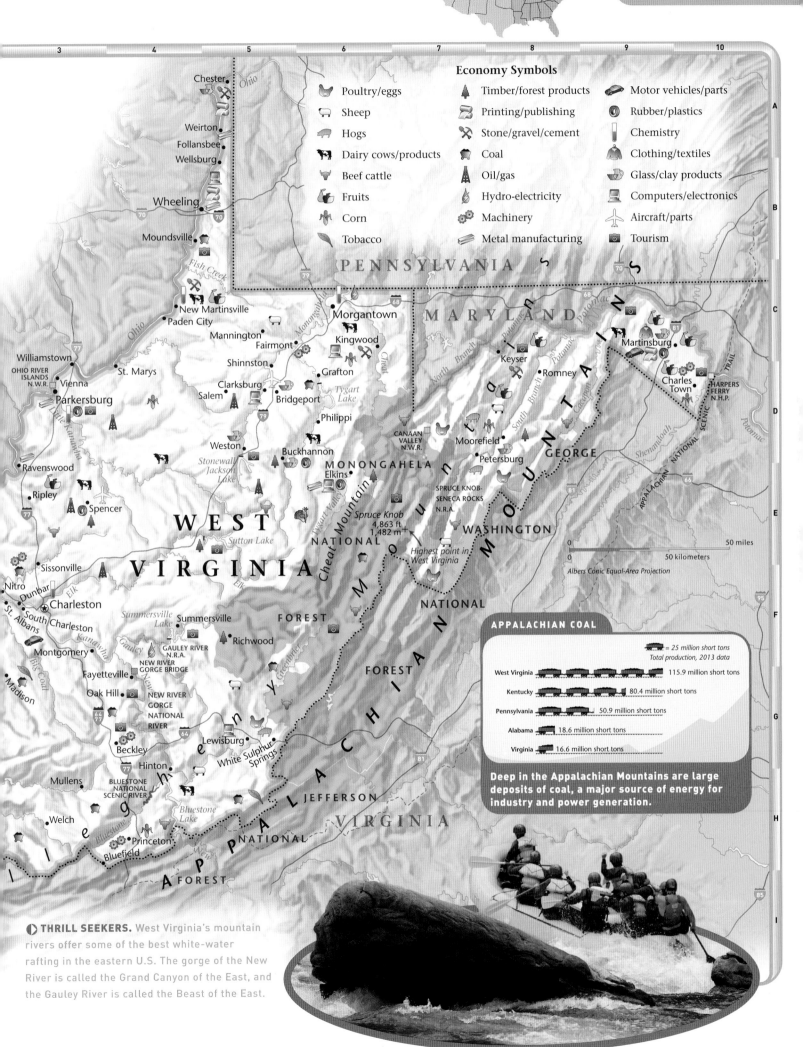

Economy Symbols

- Poultry/eggs
- Sheep
- Hogs
- Dairy cows/products
- Beef cattle
- Fruits
- Corn
- Tobacco
- Timber/forest products
- Printing/publishing
- Stone/gravel/cement
- Coal
- Oil/gas
- Hydro-electricity
- Machinery
- Metal manufacturing
- Motor vehicles/parts
- Rubber/plastics
- Chemistry
- Clothing/textiles
- Glass/clay products
- Computers/electronics
- Aircraft/parts
- Tourism

APPALACHIAN COAL

= 25 million short tons
Total production, 2013 data

West Virginia	115.9 million short tons
Kentucky	80.4 million short tons
Pennsylvania	50.9 million short tons
Alabama	18.6 million short tons
Virginia	16.6 million short tons

Deep in the Appalachian Mountains are large deposits of coal, a major source of energy for industry and power generation.

Spruce Knob
4,863 ft
1,482 m
Highest point in West Virginia

50 miles
50 kilometers
Albers Conic Equal-Area Projection

THRILL SEEKERS. West Virginia's mountain rivers offer some of the best white-water rafting in the eastern U.S. The gorge of the New River is called the Grand Canyon of the East, and the Gauley River is called the Beast of the East.

THE REGION

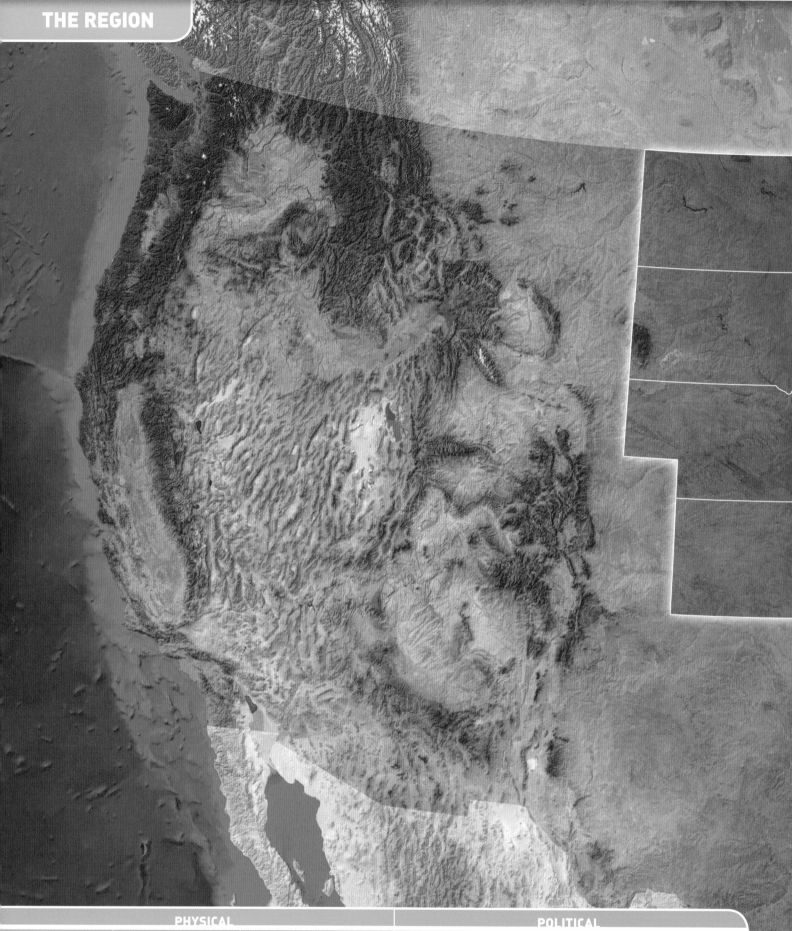

PHYSICAL			POLITICAL	
Total area (land and water) 821,726 sq mi (2,128,257 sq km)	**Lowest point** St. Francis River, MO 230 ft (70 m)	**Vegetation** Grassland; broadleaf, needleleaf, and mixed forest	**Total population** 67,907,403	**Smallest state** Indiana: 36,420 sq mi (94,326 sq km)
	Longest rivers Mississippi, Missouri, Arkansas, Ohio	**Climate** Continental to mild, ranging from cold winters and cool summers in the north to mild winters and humid summers in the south	**States (12):** Illinois, Indiana, Iowa, Kansas, Michigan, Minnesota, Missouri, Nebraska, North Dakota, Ohio, South Dakota, Wisconsin	**Most populous state** Illinois: 12,859,995
Highest point Harney Peak, SD 7,242 ft (2,207 m)				**Least populous state** North Dakota: 756,927
	Largest lakes Superior, Michigan, Huron, Erie		**Largest state** Michigan: 96,714 sq mi (250,487 sq km)	**Largest city proper** Chicago, IL: 2,720,546

The Midwest

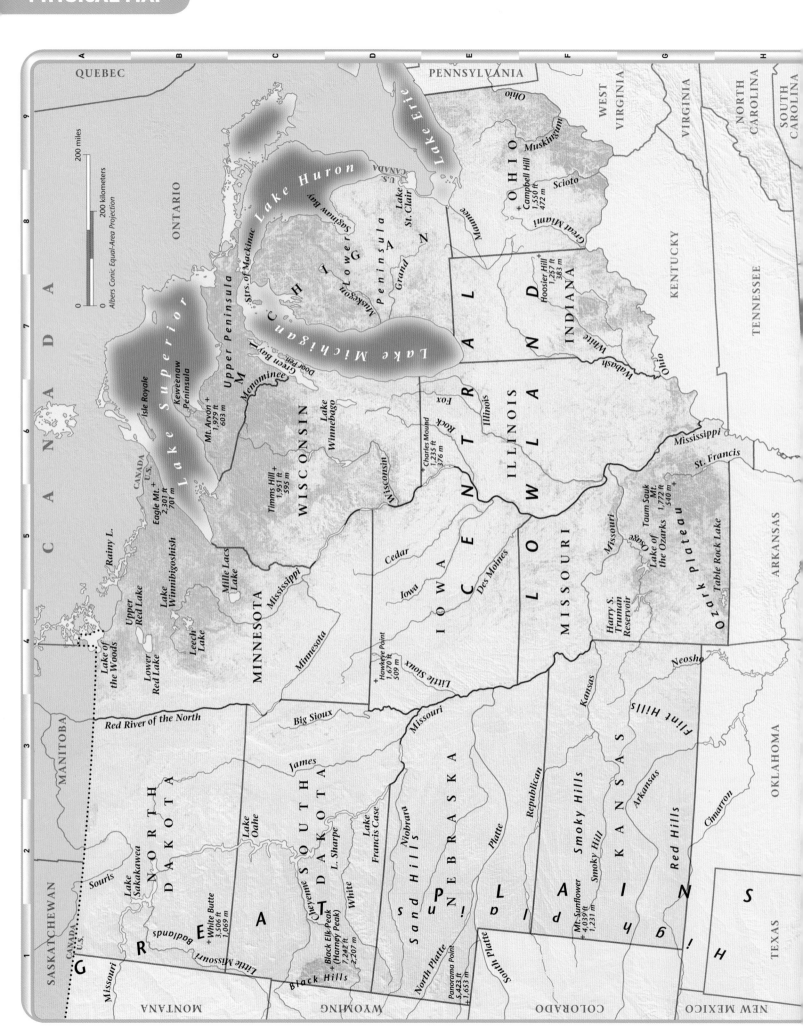

200 miles

200 kilometers
Albers Conic Equal-Area Projection

QUEBEC

PENNSYLVANIA

WEST VIRGINIA

VIRGINIA

NORTH CAROLINA

SOUTH CAROLINA

ONTARIO

Lake Erie

Lake Huron

Lake St. Clair

Ohio

O H I O

Muskingum

Campbell Hill
1,550 ft
472 m

Scioto

KENTUCKY

TENNESSEE

Lake Superior

Isle Royale

Keweenaw Peninsula

Upper Peninsula

Strs. of Mackinac

Saginaw Bay

Lower Peninsula

M I C H I G A N

Grand

Maumee

Great Miami

Hoosier Hill
1,257 ft
383 m

I N D I A N A

White

Wabash

Ohio

Eagle Mt.
2,301 ft
701 m

CANADA
U.S.

Mt. Arvon
1,979 ft
603 m

Menominee

Green Bay

Door Pen.

WISCONSIN

Lake Winnebago

Timms Hill
1,951 ft
595 m

Charles Mound
1,235 ft
376 m

Rock

Fox

Illinois

I L L I N O I S

C E N T R A L   L O W L A N D

Mississippi

St. Francis

Rainy L.

Lake Winnibigoshish

Mille Lacs Lake

Upper Red Lake

Leech Lake

Lake of the Woods

Lower Red Lake

Mississippi

M I N N E S O T A

Minnesota

Cedar

Iowa

Des Moines

I O W A

Hawkeye Point
1,670 ft
509 m

Little Sioux

Missouri

M I S S O U R I

Harry S. Truman Reservoir

Osage

Lake of the Ozarks

Taum Sauk Mt.
1,772 ft
540 m

Ozark Plateau

Table Rock Lake

ARKANSAS

CANADA
U.S.

MANITOBA

SASKATCHEWAN

C A N A D A

Red River of the North

Big Sioux

Missouri

James

Souris

Lake Sakakawea

N O R T H   D A K O T A

Little Missouri

White Butte
3,506 ft
1,069 m

Badlands

Missouri

G R E A T

Lake Oahe

Cheyenne

L. Sharpe

S O U T H   D A K O T A

Lake Francis Case

White

Black Elk Peak
(Harney Peak)
7,242 ft
2,207 m

Black Hills

Niobrara

Sand Hills

N E B R A S K A

North Platte

Panorama Point
5,423 ft
1,653 m

South Platte

Platte

P L A I N S

Republican

Kansas

K A N S A S

Smoky Hills

Smoky Hill

Mt. Sunflower
4,039 ft
1,231 m

Arkansas

Flint Hills

Red Hills

Cimarron

Neosho

OKLAHOMA

TEXAS

NEW MEXICO

COLORADO

WYOMING

MONTANA

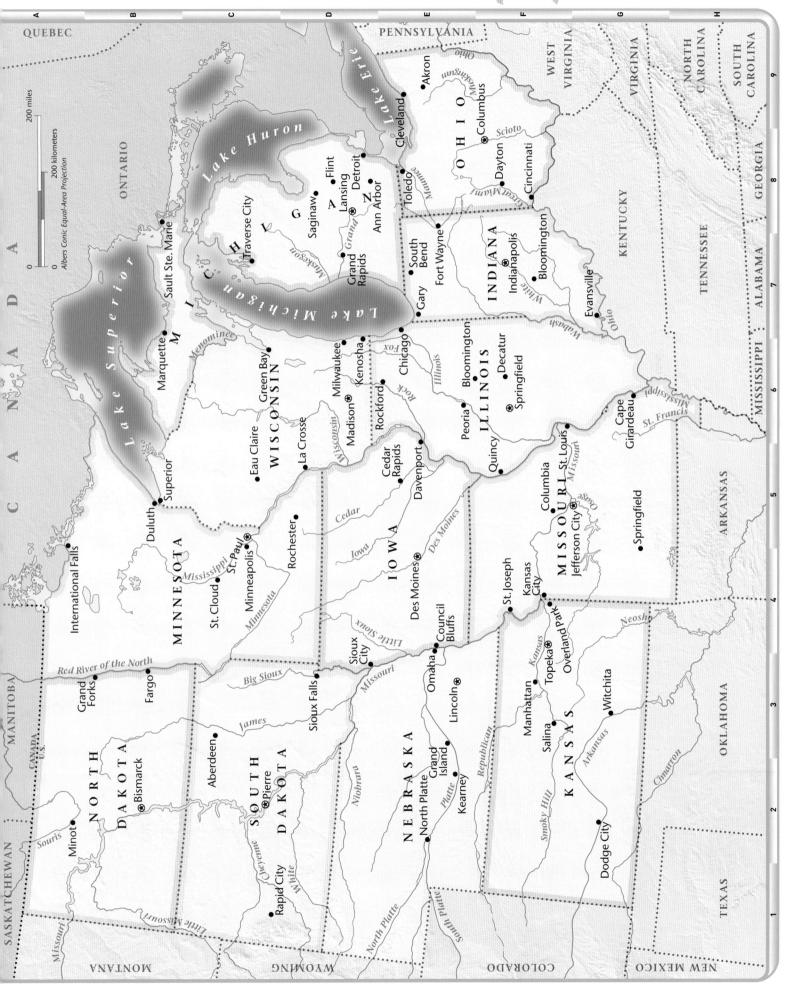

QUEBEC
PENNSYLVANIA

A   B   C   D   E   F   G   H

200 miles

0   200 kilometers   0

Albers Conic Equal-Area Projection

CANADA

ONTARIO

Lake Superior

Lake Huron

Lake Erie

Lake Michigan

WEST VIRGINIA

VIRGINIA

NORTH CAROLINA

SOUTH CAROLINA

GEORGIA

Akron
Cleveland
Columbus
Scioto

OHIO

Dayton
Cincinnati

Great Miami

Toledo
Maumee

Flint
Saginaw
Lansing
Detroit
Ann Arbor

M I C H I G A N

Traverse City
Grand Rapids
Muskegon
Grand

South Bend
Fort Wayne
Gary

INDIANA

Bloomington
Indianapolis
White
Evansville
Ohio

KENTUCKY

TENNESSEE

ALABAMA

MISSISSIPPI

Sault Ste. Marie
Marquette
Menominee

Green Bay
Milwaukee
Kenosha
Chicago
Fox

WISCONSIN

Eau Claire
La Crosse
Wisconsin
Madison
Rockford
Rock
Illinois

Bloomington
Decatur
Springfield

ILLINOIS

Peoria
Quincy

St. Louis
Missouri
Columbia
MISSOURI
Jefferson City
Osage

Cape Girardeau
St. Francis
Mississippi

ARKANSAS

Duluth
Superior

MINNESOTA

International Falls

St. Paul
Minneapolis
St. Cloud
Mississippi
Rochester
Cedar
Minnesota

Iowa

I O W A

Cedar Rapids
Davenport

Des Moines
Des Moines

Council Bluffs

Sioux City
Little Sioux

St. Joseph
Kansas City

Springfield

MANITOBA

SASKATCHEWAN

Red River of the North

Grand Forks
Fargo
James

NORTH DAKOTA

Bismarck

Minot
Souris

CANADA
U.S.

Aberdeen

SOUTH DAKOTA

Pierre

Rapid City
Cheyenne
White

Big Sioux

Sioux Falls

Missouri

NEBRASKA

Niobrara

Omaha
Lincoln
Council Bluffs

Grand Island
North Platte
Kearney
Platte

Republican

Little Missouri

Little Missouri

MONTANA

WYOMING

COLORADO

NEW MEXICO

TEXAS

OKLAHOMA

KANSAS

Manhattan
Topeka
Overland Park
Kansas
Salina
Witchita

Dodge City
Arkansas
Cimarron

Smoky Hill

Neosho

North Platte
South Platte

▶ FIERCE GIANT. Students in Chicago's Field Museum eye the skeleton of *Tyrannosaurus rex*, a dinosaur that roamed North America's plains 65 million years ago.

The Midwest

GREAT LAKES, GREAT RIVERS

The Midwest's early white settlers emigrated from eastern states or Europe, but recent immigrants come from all parts of the world. Hispanics, for example, are settling in communities large and small throughout the region, and many Arabs reside in Detroit and Dearborn, Michigan. Drained by three mighty rivers—the Mississippi, Missouri, and Ohio—the Midwestern lowlands and plains are one of the world's most bountiful farmlands. Though the number of farmers has declined, new technologies and equipment have made farms larger and more productive. Meanwhile, industrial cities of the Rust Belt are adjusting to an economy focused more on information and services than on manufacturing.

⬤ CROP CIRCLES. Much of the western part of the region receives less than 20 inches (50 cm) of rain yearly—not enough to support agriculture. Large, circular, center-pivot irrigation systems draw water from underground reserves called aquifers to provide life-giving water to crops.

⬤ DAIRY HEARTLAND. Dairy cows, such as these in Wisconsin, are sometimes treated with growth hormones to increase milk production. These animals play an important role in the economy of the Midwest, which supplies much of the country's milk, butter, and cheese.

MIDWEST URBAN HUB. Chicago, the third largest metropolitan area in the U.S., with almost 10 million people, is the economic and cultural core of the Midwest and a major transportation hub.

PRESERVING THE PAST.
A young Cherokee man, dressed in beaded costume and feathered headband, dances at a powwow in Milwaukee. Such gatherings provide Indians from across the country with a chance to share their traditions.

NATURE'S MOST VIOLENT STORMS.
Parts of the midwestern U.S. have earned the nickname Tornado Alley because these destructive, swirling storms, which develop in association with thunderstorms along eastward-moving cold fronts, occur here more than any other place on Earth.

WHERE THE PICTURES ARE

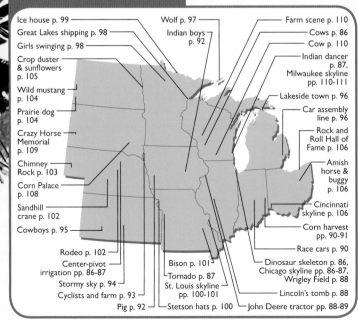

- Ice house p. 99
- Great Lakes shipping p. 98
- Girls swinging p. 98
- Crop duster & sunflowers p. 105
- Wild mustang p. 104
- Prairie dog p. 104
- Crazy Horse Memorial p. 109
- Chimney Rock p. 103
- Corn Palace p. 108
- Sandhill crane p. 102
- Cowboys p. 95
- Rodeo p. 102
- Center-pivot irrigation pp. 86-87
- Stormy sky p. 94
- Cyclists and farm p. 93
- Pig p. 92
- Stetson hats p. 100
- St. Louis skyline pp. 100-101
- Tornado p. 87
- Bison p. 101
- Wolf p. 97
- Indian boys p. 92
- Farm scene p. 110
- Cows p. 86
- Cow p. 110
- Indian dancer p. 87, Milwaukee skyline pp. 110-111
- Lakeside town p. 96
- Car assembly line p. 96
- Rock and Roll Hall of Fame p. 106
- Amish horse & buggy p. 106
- Cincinnati skyline p. 106
- Corn harvest pp. 90-91
- Race cars p. 90
- Dinosaur skeleton p. 86, Chicago skyline pp. 86-87, Wrigley Field p. 88
- Lincoln's tomb p. 88
- John Deere tractor pp. 88-89

THE LAND OF LINCOLN:
ILLINOIS

ILLINOIS

THE BASICS

Statehood
December 3, 1818; 21st state

Total area (land and water)
57,914 sq mi (149,995 sq km)

Land area
55,519 sq mi (143,793 sq km)

Population
12,859,995

Capital
Springfield
Population 116,565

Largest city
Chicago
Population 2,720,546

Racial/ethnic groups
77.3% white; 14.7% African American; 5.5% Asian; 0.6% Native American; 16.9% Hispanic (any race)

Foreign born
13.8%

Urban population
88.5% (2010)

Population density
231.6 per sq mi
(89.4 per sq km)

GEO WHIZ

A giant fossilized rain forest has been unearthed in an eastern Illinois coal mine near the town of Danville. Scientists believe an earthquake buried the entire forest 300 million years ago.

The Great Chicago fire of 1871 destroyed the city's waterworks, so firemen had to drag water in buckets from Lake Michigan and the Chicago River. The fire burned out of control for two days until rain finally put it out.

Illinois

Two rivers that now form the borders of Illinois aided the state's early white settlement. Frenchmen first explored the area in 1673 by traveling down the Mississippi, and the Ohio brought many 19th-century settlers to southern Illinois. Most Indians were forced out by the 1830s, more than a decade after Illinois became the 21st state. Ethnically diverse Chicago, the most populous city in the Midwest, is an economic giant and one of the country's busiest rail, highway, and air transit hubs. Barges from its port reach the Gulf of Mexico via rivers and canals, and ships reach the Atlantic Ocean via the Great Lakes and St. Lawrence Seaway. Flat terrain and fertile prairie soils in the northern and central regions help make the state a top producer of corn and soybeans. The more rugged, forested south has deposits of bituminous coal. Springfield, capital of the Land of Lincoln, welcomes tourists visiting the home and tomb of the country's 16th president.

VIOLET

CARDINAL

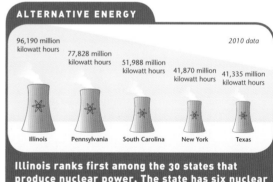

⚛ **REMEMBERING A PRESIDENT.**
Dedicated in 1874, the National Lincoln Monument in Springfield honors Abraham Lincoln, who was assassinated in 1865. A special vault holds the remains of the slain president, who led the country during the Civil War.

ALTERNATIVE ENERGY

2010 data

96,190 million kilowatt hours — Illinois
77,828 million kilowatt hours — Pennsylvania
51,988 million kilowatt hours — South Carolina
41,870 million kilowatt hours — New York
41,335 million kilowatt hours — Texas

Illinois ranks first among the 30 states that produce nuclear power. The state has six nuclear power plants with 11 reactors.

🔵 **PLAY BALL!** Wrigley Field, home to the Chicago Cubs baseball team, is affected by wind conditions more than any other Major League park due to its location near Lake Michigan.

🔵 **FIELDS OF GRAIN.** Illinois has long been a major grain producer, but farming today is highly mechanized. Above, a tractor with a front loader moves bales of rolled hay.

Economy Symbols

- Poultry/eggs
- Sheep
- Hogs
- Dairy cows/products
- Beef cattle
- Vegetables
- Nursery stock
- Wheat
- Corn
- Soybeans
- Printing/publishing
- Stone/gravel/cement
- Mining
- Coal
- Oil/gas
- Machinery
- Metal products
- Motor vehicles/parts
- Rubber/plastics
- Chemistry
- Food processing
- Computers/electronics
- Motion picture/music industry
- Tourism
- Finance/insurance

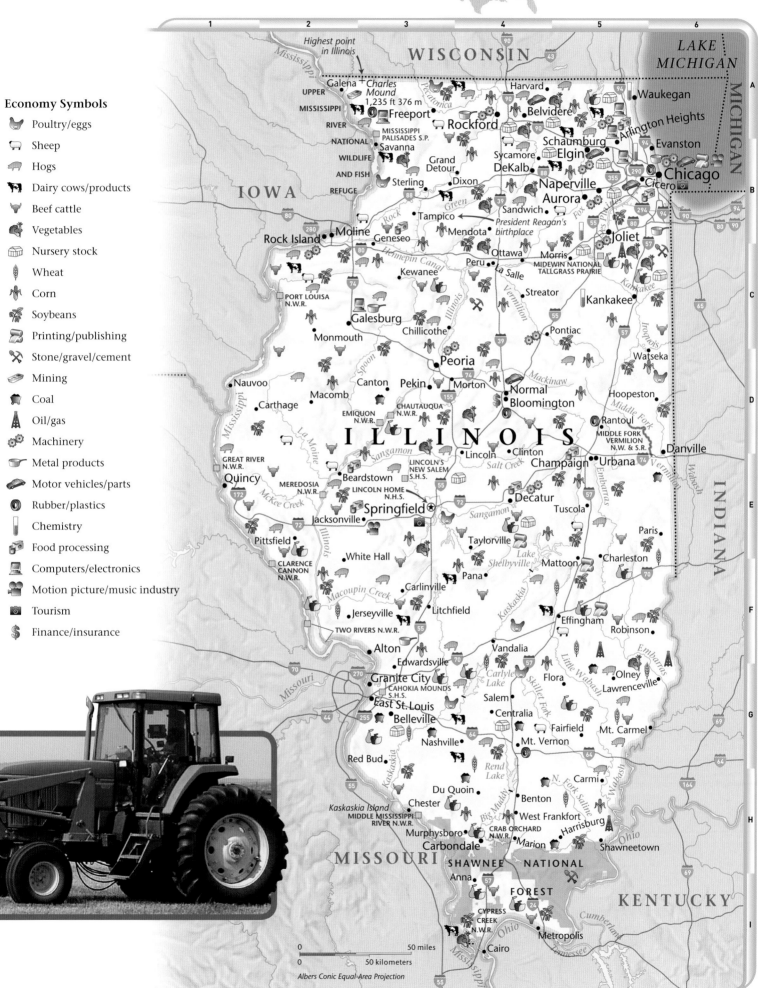

WISCONSIN

LAKE MICHIGAN

MICHIGAN

IOWA

INDIANA

MISSOURI

KENTUCKY

ILLINOIS

Highest point in Illinois
Galena Charles Mound 1,235 ft 376 m
UPPER MISSISSIPPI RIVER NATIONAL WILDLIFE AND FISH REFUGE
Freeport
Rockford
Harvard
Belvidere
Waukegan
Arlington Heights
Evanston
Schaumburg
Elgin
Chicago
Cicero
MISSISSIPPI PALISADES S.P.
Savanna
Grand Detour
Sycamore
DeKalb
Naperville
Aurora
Sterling
Dixon
Sandwich
Tampico
President Reagan's birthplace
Mendota
Joliet
Moline
Geneseo
Rock Island
Ottawa
Morris
MIDEWIN NATIONAL TALLGRASS PRAIRIE
Peru
La Salle
Streator
Kankakee
Kewanee
PORT LOUISA N.W.R.
Galesburg
Chillicothe
Pontiac
Watseka
Monmouth
Peoria
Canton
Pekin
Morton
Normal
Bloomington
Hoopeston
Nauvoo
Macomb
Rantoul
MIDDLE FORK VERMILION N.W. & S.R.
Carthage
EMIQUON N.W.R.
CHAUTAUQUA N.W.R.
Danville
GREAT RIVER N.W.R.
Lincoln
Clinton
Champaign
Urbana
Quincy
MEREDOSIA N.W.R.
Beardstown
LINCOLN'S NEW SALEM S.H.S.
LINCOLN HOME N.H.S.
Decatur
Tuscola
Paris
Jacksonville
Springfield
Taylorville
Charleston
Pittsfield
White Hall
Lake Shelbyville
Mattoon
CLARENCE CANNON N.W.R.
Pana
Carlinville
Effingham
Robinson
Jerseyville
Litchfield
TWO RIVERS N.W.R.
Alton
Vandalia
Edwardsville
Flora
Olney
Granite City
CAHOKIA MOUNDS S.H.S.
Salem
Lawrenceville
East St. Louis
Centralia
Fairfield
Mt. Carmel
Belleville
Nashville
Mt. Vernon
Red Bud
Du Quoin
Carmi
Chester
Benton
West Frankfort
Harrisburg
Kaskaskia Island
MIDDLE MISSISSIPPI RIVER N.W.R.
Murphysboro
CRAB ORCHARD N.W.R.
Marion
Shawneetown
Carbondale
SHAWNEE NATIONAL FOREST
Anna
CYPRESS CREEK N.W.R.
Metropolis
Cairo

0 50 miles
0 50 kilometers
Albers Conic Equal-Area Projection

THE BASICS

Statehood
December 11, 1816; 19th state

Total area (land and water)
36,420 sq mi (94,326 sq km)

Land area
35,826 sq mi (92,789 sq km)

Population
6,619,680

Capital
Indianapolis
Population 853,173

Largest city
Indianapolis
Population 853,173

Racial/ethnic groups
85.8% white; 9.6% African American; 2.1% Asian; 0.4% Native American; 6.7% Hispanic (any race)

Foreign born
4.7%

Urban population
72.4% (2010)

Population density
184.8 per sq mi (71.3 per sq km)

GEO WHIZ

Every July during Circus Festival in Peru, a couple hundred local kids and a couple thousand volunteers put on a three-ring circus complete with clowns, snow cones, and standing ovations from sellout crowds. The city is home to the International Circus Hall of Fame.

Every year Fort Wayne hosts the Johnny Appleseed Festival to honor John Chapman, the man who planted apple orchards from Pennsylvania to Illinois.

The Children's Museum of Indianapolis, the largest children's museum in the world, features life-size dinosaur replicas, a planetarium, hands-on science labs, and much more. About one million people visit the museum each year.

Indiana

Indiana's name, meaning "Land of the Indians," honors the tribes who lived in the region before the arrival of Europeans. The first permanent white settlement was Vincennes, established by the French in the early 1700s. Following statehood in 1816, most Indians were forced out to make way for white settlement. Lake Michigan, in the state's northwest corner, brings economic and recreational opportunities. The lakefront city of Gary anchors a major industrial region. Nearby, the natural beauty and shifting sands of the Indiana Dunes National Lakeshore attract many visitors. Corn, soybeans, and hogs are the most important products from Indiana's many farms. True to the state motto, "The Crossroads of America," highways from all directions converge at Indianapolis. Traveling at a much higher speed are cars on that city's famed Motor Speedway, home to the Indy 500 auto race since 1911. Cheering for a favorite high school or college team is a favorite pastime for many Hoosiers who catch basketball fever.

⬥ START YOUR ENGINES. The Indianapolis Motor Speedway seats up to 250,000 sports fans. Nicknamed the Brickyard, its track was once paved with 3.2 million bricks.

**CARDINAL
PEONY**

◗ FUEL FARMING.
Indiana farmers grow corn for many uses—livestock feed, additives used in human food products, and production of ethanol, a non–fossil fuel energy source.

HEAVY INDUSTRY

Indiana	27% (29.7 million tons)
Ohio	13% (14.3 million tons)
Michigan	6% (6.6 million tons)
Pennsylvania	5% (5.5 million tons)

*% = share of U.S. total production (110 million tons)
2015 data*

Steel production was the core of early industrialization in the United States. Indiana and Ohio lead in steel production, but the U.S. also imports much of the steel it uses.

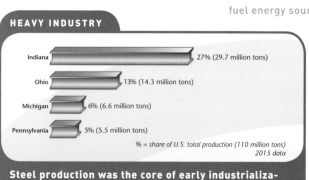

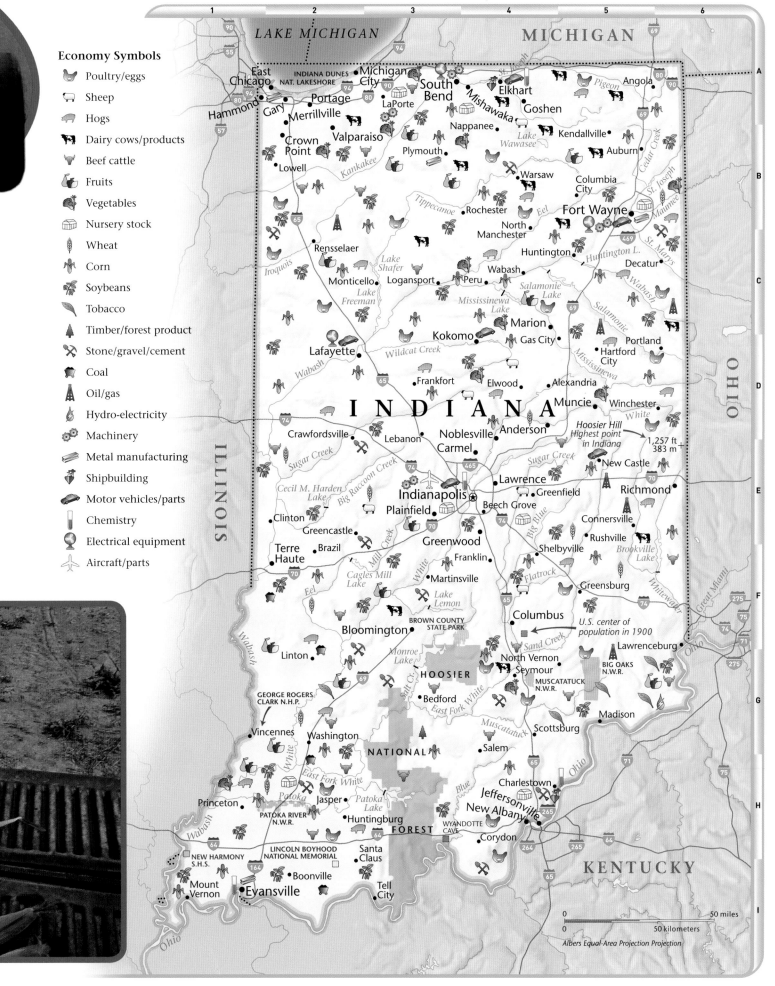

Economy Symbols

- Poultry/eggs
- Sheep
- Hogs
- Dairy cows/products
- Beef cattle
- Fruits
- Vegetables
- Nursery stock
- Wheat
- Corn
- Soybeans
- Tobacco
- Timber/forest product
- Stone/gravel/cement
- Coal
- Oil/gas
- Hydro-electricity
- Machinery
- Metal manufacturing
- Shipbuilding
- Motor vehicles/parts
- Chemistry
- Electrical equipment
- Aircraft/parts

LAKE MICHIGAN

MICHIGAN

ILLINOIS

OHIO

KENTUCKY

I N D I A N A

East Chicago
Hammond
Gary
Portage
Merrillville
Crown Point
Valparaiso
Lowell
Michigan City
LaPorte
South Bend
Mishawaka
Elkhart
Goshen
Nappanee
Angola
Kendallville
Auburn
Plymouth
Warsaw
Columbia City
Rochester
North Manchester
Fort Wayne
Huntington
Decatur
Rensselaer
Monticello
Logansport
Peru
Wabash
Lafayette
Frankfort
Kokomo
Marion
Gas City
Portland
Hartford City
Elwood
Alexandria
Muncie
Winchester
Crawfordsville
Lebanon
Noblesville
Carmel
Anderson
Hoosier Hill
Highest point in Indiana
1,257 ft
383 m
New Castle
Richmond
Indianapolis
Lawrence
Greenfield
Plainfield
Beech Grove
Clinton
Greencastle
Greenwood
Connersville
Brazil
Terre Haute
Franklin
Rushville
Shelbyville
Martinsville
Greensburg
Bloomington
BROWN COUNTY STATE PARK
Columbus
U.S. center of population in 1900
Lawrenceburg
Linton
North Vernon
Seymour
BIG OAKS N.W.R.
GEORGE ROGERS CLARK N.H.P.
MUSCATATUCK N.W.R.
Bedford
Madison
HOOSIER
Scottsburg
Vincennes
Washington
Salem
NATIONAL
Charlestown
Jeffersonville
New Albany
Princeton
Jasper
PATOKA RIVER N.W.R.
Huntingburg
WYANDOTTE CAVE
FOREST
Corydon
NEW HARMONY S.H.S.
LINCOLN BOYHOOD NATIONAL MEMORIAL
Santa Claus
Boonville
Tell City
Mount Vernon
Evansville

INDIANA DUNES NAT. LAKESHORE

Kankakee
Iroquois
Lake Shafer
Lake Freeman
Tippecanoe
Eel
Wildcat Creek
Wabash
Sugar Creek
Cecil M. Harden Lake
Big Raccoon Creek
Sugar Creek
Mill Creek
Cagles Mill Lake
Lake Lemon
White
Flatrock
Eel
Monroe Lake
Brookville Lake
Whitewater
Great Miami
Ohio
Wabash
Sand Creek
Salt Cr.
East Fork White
Muscatatuck
Blue
Patoka
Patoka Lake
White
East Fork White
Ohio
Lake Wawasee
Pigeon
St. Joseph
Cedar Creek
St. Joseph
Maumee
St. Marys
Huntington L.
Salamonie Lake
Salamonie
Mississinewa Lake
Mississinewa
White
Big Blue

0   50 miles
0   50 kilometers

Albers Equal-Area Projection Projection

THE HAWKEYE STATE:
IOWA

IOWA

THE BASICS

Statehood
December 28, 1846; 29th state

Total area (land and water)
56,273 sq mi (145,746 sq km)

Land area
55,857 sq mi (144,669 sq km)

Population
3,123,899

Capital
Des Moines
Population 210,330

Largest city
Des Moines
Population 210,330

Racial/ethnic groups
91.8% white; 3.5%
African American; 2.4%
Asian; 0.5% Native
American; 5.7% Hispanic
(any race)

Foreign born
4.5%

Urban population
64.0% (2010)

Population density
55.9 per sq mi (21.6 per sq km)

GEO WHIZ

One of the most famous houses in America is in Eldon. It was immortalized in Grant Wood's famous painting "American Gothic." The pitchfork-holding man and his wife shown in the art were not farmers at all. Wood's sister and his dentist posed for the painting.

Effigy Mounds National Monument, in northeast Iowa, is the only place in the country with such a large collection of mounds in the shapes of birds, mammals, and reptiles. Eastern Woodland Indians built these mounds from about 500 B.C. to A.D. 1300.

Iowa ranks second, after Texas, among wind energy producers. Just 12 states produce 80 percent of energy generated in the U.S. by wind.

Iowa

Iowa's prehistoric inhabitants built earthen mounds—some shaped like birds and bears—that are visible in the state's northeast. Nineteenth-century white settlers found rolling prairies covered by a sea of tall grasses that soon yielded to the plow. A decade after statehood in 1846, a group of religious German immigrants established the Amana Colonies, a communal society that still draws visitors. Blessed with ample precipitation and rich soils, Iowa is the heart of one of the world's most productive farming regions. The state is the country's top producer of corn, soybeans, hogs, and eggs. Food processing and manufacturing machinery are two of the biggest industries. Much of the grain crop feeds livestock destined to reach dinner plates in the United States and around the world.

An increasing amount of corn is used to make ethanol, which is mixed with gasoline to fuel cars and trucks. Des Moines, the capital and largest city, is a center of insurance and publishing.

PIG BUSINESS.
Hogs outnumber people almost seven to one in Iowa. The state raises nearly one third of the country's hogs, making it the leading producer.

WILD ROSE

AMERICAN GOLDFINCH

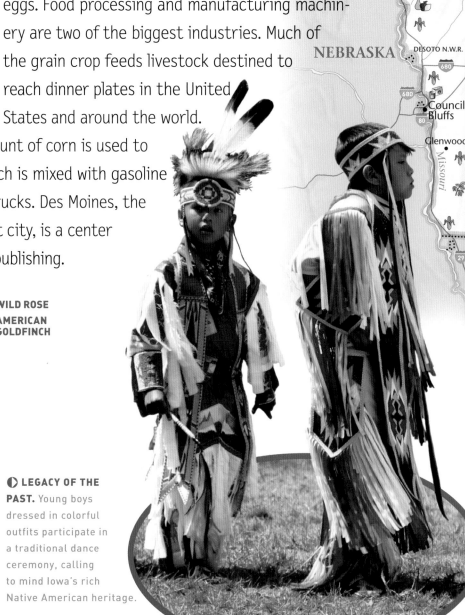

LEGACY OF THE PAST. Young boys dressed in colorful outfits participate in a traditional dance ceremony, calling to mind Iowa's rich Native American heritage.

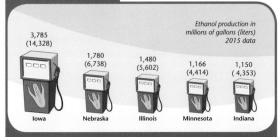

SOUTH DAKOTA

NEBRASKA

Hawkeye Point
1,670 ft
509 m

Highest point in Iowa

Sioux Center   Sheldon

Orange City

Le Mars

Sioux City

Onawa

DESOTO N.W.R.

Council Bluffs

Glenwood

Missouri

Big Sioux

Floyd

Little Sioux

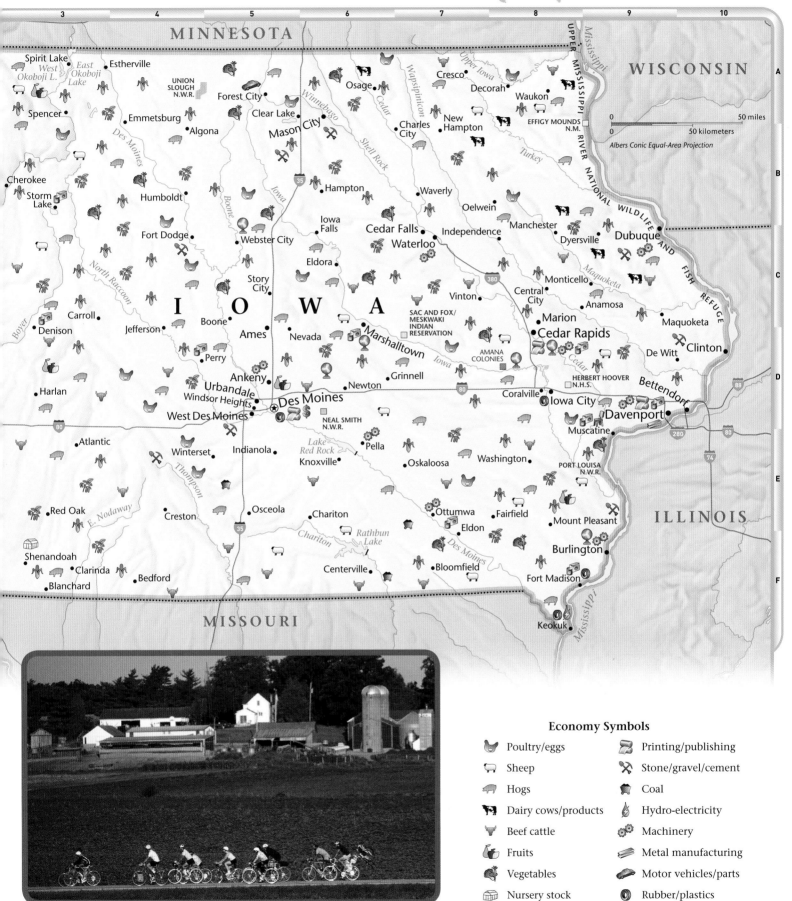

MINNESOTA

WISCONSIN

0 — 50 miles
0 — 50 kilometers
Albers Conic Equal-Area Projection

IOWA

ILLINOIS

MISSOURI

Spirit Lake, West Okoboji L., East Okoboji Lake, Estherville, Spencer, Cherokee, Storm Lake, Emmetsburg, Algona, Humboldt, Fort Dodge, Carroll, Denison, Jefferson, Harlan, Atlantic, Red Oak, Shenandoah, Clarinda, Blanchard, Bedford, Creston, Osceola, Winterset, Indianola, Knoxville, Chariton, Centerville, Forest City, Clear Lake, Mason City, Webster City, Story City, Boone, Ames, Nevada, Perry, Ankeny, Urbandale, Windsor Heights, West Des Moines, Des Moines, Pella, Oskaloosa, Bloomfield, Iowa Falls, Eldora, Marshalltown, Grinnell, Newton, Osage, Hampton, Charles City, Cedar Falls, Waterloo, Vinton, Cresco, Decorah, Waukon, New Hampton, Waverly, Oelwein, Independence, Manchester, Dyersville, Dubuque, Monticello, Central City, Marion, Cedar Rapids, Anamosa, Maquoketa, De Witt, Clinton, Coralville, Iowa City, Davenport, Bettendorf, Muscatine, Washington, Fairfield, Mount Pleasant, Ottumwa, Eldon, Burlington, Fort Madison, Keokuk, Effigy Mounds N.M., Amana Colonies, Herbert Hoover N.H.S., Neal Smith N.W.R., Lake Red Rock, Rathbun Lake, Port Louisa N.W.R., Union Slough N.W.R., Sac and Fox/Meskwaki Indian Reservation

⚙ **FITNESS RALLY.** Cyclists pass a cluster of farm buildings during the Annual Great Bicycle Ride across Iowa, sponsored by the *Des Moines Register*. Each year 10,000 riders participate in this event.

Economy Symbols

- Poultry/eggs
- Sheep
- Hogs
- Dairy cows/products
- Beef cattle
- Fruits
- Vegetables
- Nursery stock
- Corn
- Soybeans
- Furniture
- Printing/publishing
- Stone/gravel/cement
- Coal
- Hydro-electricity
- Machinery
- Metal manufacturing
- Motor vehicles/parts
- Rubber/plastics
- Food processing
- Electrical equipment
- Finance/insurance

KANSAS

THE BASICS

Statehood
January 29, 1861; 34th state

Total area (land and water)
82,278 sq mi (213,100 sq km)

Land area
81,759 sq mi (211,754 sq km)

Population
2,911,641

Capital
Topeka
Population 127,265

Largest city
Wichita
Population 389,965

Racial/ethnic groups
86.7% white; 6.3% African American; 2.9% Asian; 1.2% Native American; 11.6% Hispanic (any race)

Foreign born
6.7%

Urban population
74.2% (2010)

Population density
35.6 per sq mi (13.8 per sq km)

GEO WHIZ

Plesiosaur skeletons and many other marine reptile fossils have been unearthed in Kansas. The National Geographic IMAX film *Sea Monsters* explores the kinds of animals that lived in the prehistoric sea that covered Kansas and much of North America 82 million years ago.

The Tallgrass Prairie National Preserve, the nation's last great expanse of tallgrass prairie, is in the Flint Hills of Kansas.

Lindsborg is proud of its Swedish heritage and the fact that it is home to the Anatoly Karpov International School of Chess, named for the Russian who succeeded American Bobby Fischer as world champion in 1975.

Kansas

Considered by whites to be unsuitable for settlement, Kansas was made part of Indian Territory—a vast tract of land between Missouri and the Rockies—in the 1830s. By the 1850s whites were fighting Indians for more land and among themselves over the issue of slavery. In 1861 Kansas entered the Union as a free state. After the Civil War, cowboys drove Texas cattle to railheads in the Wild West towns of Abilene and Dodge City, where waiting trains hauled cattle to slaughterhouses in the East. Today, the state remains a major beef producer and the country's second largest wheat grower. Oil and natural gas wells dot the landscape, and factories in Wichita, the largest city, make aircraft equipment. A preserve in the Flint Hills boasts one of the few tallgrass prairies to escape farmers' plows. Heading west toward the Rockies, elevations climb slowly, and the climate gets drier. Threats of fierce thunderstorms accompanied by tornadoes have many Kansans keeping an eye on the sky.

SUNFLOWER

WESTERN MEADOWLARK

⬡ **OMINOUS SKY.** Lightning splits the sky as black clouds of a thunderstorm roll across a field of wheat. Such storms bring heavy rain and often spawn dangerous tornadoes.

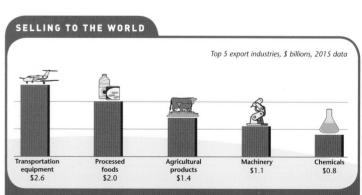

SELLING TO THE WORLD

Top 5 export industries, $ billions, 2015 data

| Transportation equipment $2.6 | Processed foods $2.0 | Agricultural products $1.4 | Machinery $1.1 | Chemicals $0.8 |

Participation in the global economy earns Kansas more than $10 billion each year. Top markets are Canada and Mexico. Aircraft and processed meat products make up much of export sales.

NEBRASKA

- Oberlin
- Norton
- Phillipsburg
- Lebanon
- Washington
- Belleville
- Marysville
- Seneca
- Hiawatha
- Atchison
- Concordia
- Clay Center
- Holton
- Leavenworth
- Lansing
- Kansas City
- Plainville
- Manhattan
- Wamego
- Bonne Springs
- WaKeeney
- Minneapolis
- Topeka
- Overland Park
- Hays
- Russell
- Abilene
- Junction City
- Lawrence
- Olathe
- Ellsworth
- Salina
- Council Grove
- Ottawa
- Paola
- Ness City
- Hoisington
- Lindsborg
- Emporia
- Osawatomie
- Great Bend
- McPherson
- Hillsboro
- Garnett
- Larned
- Lyons
- Burlington
- Hutchinson
- Hesston
- Newton
- Iola
- Fort Scott
- Kinsley
- El Dorado
- Eureka
- Chanute
- Dodge City
- Wichita
- Augusta
- Pratt
- Kingman
- Derby
- Fredonia
- Pittsburg
- Greensburg
- Mulvane
- Parsons
- Meade
- Medicine Lodge
- Wellington
- Winfield
- Independence
- Columbus
- Anthony
- Arkansas City
- Coffeyville
- Baxter Springs

Geographic center of the 48 contiguous states

KIRWIN N.W.R.
NICODEMUS N.H.S.
Smoky Hills
Cedar Bluff Reservoir
Wilson Lake
Kanopolis Lake
Cheyenne Bottoms
KANSAS
Red Hills
FORT LARNED N.H.S.
QUIVIRA N.W.R.
Cheney Reservoir
Marion Lake
TALLGRASS PRAIRIE NATIONAL PRESERVE
BROWN V. BOARD OF EDUCATION N.H.S.
Osage City
Hillsdale Lake
Perry Lake
Milford Lake
Tuttle Creek Lake
POTAWATOMI INDIAN RESERVATION
KICKAPOO INDIAN RESERVATION
SAC AND FOX I.R.
IOWA I.R.
El Dorado Lake
FLINT HILLS N.W.R.
John Redmond Reservoir
Flint Hills
Elk City Lake
FORT SCOTT N.H.S.
MARAIS DES CYGNES N.W.R.

MISSOURI

OKLAHOMA

50 miles
50 kilometers
Alber Conic Equal-Area Projection

Economy Symbols

- Poultry/eggs
- Sheep
- Hogs
- Dairy cows/products
- Beef cattle
- Vegetables
- Vegetable oil
- Wheat
- Corn
- Soybeans
- Printing/publishing
- Stone/gravel/cement
- Coal
- Oil/gas
- Railroad equipment
- Motor vehicles/parts
- Rubber/plastics
- Food processing
- Aircraft/parts
- Aerospace

MODERN-DAY COWBOYS. Dodge City traces its history to Fort Dodge, built on the Santa Fe Trail in 1865 to protect pioneer wagon trains and the mail service from Indian attacks. Frequented by cattle herders and bison hunters, the town was known for its lawlessness.

THE BASICS

Statehood
January 26, 1837; 26th state

Total area (land and water)
96,714 sq mi (250,487 sq km)

Land area
56,539 sq mi (146,435 sq km)

Population
9,922,576

Capital
Lansing
Population 115,056

Largest city
Detroit
Population 677,116

Racial/ethnic groups
79.7% white; 14.2% African American; 3.0% Asian; 0.7% Native American; 4.9% Hispanic (any race)

Foreign born
6.1%

Urban population
74.6% (2010)

Population density
175.5 per sq mi (67.8 per sq km)

GEO WHIZ

Researchers at the Seney National Wildlife Refuge on the Upper Peninsula have discovered why loons sound different on different lakes: The males change their calls when they move to new territories. Why they do this is still unknown.

The Keweenaw Peninsula offers adventurers a 100-mile (161-km) water trail for canoers, scores of wrecks for divers, 14 miles (23 km) of bike paths, and more than 150 miles (240 km) of hiking trails on nearby Isle Royale National Park.

The Great Lakes contain 20 percent of Earth's freshwater. Industrial dumping, agricultural runoff, and municipal use are some of the threats to the health of Lake Michigan and the other lakes, but the Alliance for the Great Lakes is working to restore their health.

APPLE BLOSSOM

ROBIN

Michigan

Indians had friendly relations with early French fur traders who came to what is now Michigan, but they waged battles with the British who later assumed control. Completion of New York's Erie Canal in 1825 made it easier for settlers to reach the area, and statehood came in 1837. Michigan consists of two large peninsulas that border four of the five Great Lakes—Erie, Huron, Michigan, and Superior. Most of the population is on the state's Lower Peninsula, while the Upper Peninsula, once a productive mining area, now is popular among vacationing nature lovers. The five-mile (8-km)-long Mackinac Bridge has linked the peninsulas since 1957. In the 20th century Michigan became the center of the American auto industry, and the state's fortunes have risen and fallen with those of the Big Three car companies. Though it remains a big producer of cars and trucks, the state is working to diversify its economy. Michigan's farms grow crops ranging from grains to fruits and vegetables.

⬤ **ASSEMBLY LINE.** More than 1,000 robots speed production at Chrysler's Sterling Heights assembly plant near Detroit by making it possible to build different car models on the same assembly line. Motor vehicle production is a major part of the state economy.

DRIVING FORCE

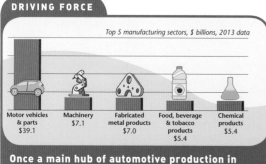

Top 5 manufacturing sectors, $ billions, 2013 data

Motor vehicles & parts	Machinery	Fabricated metal products	Food, beverage & tobacco products	Chemical products
$39.1	$7.1	$7.0	$5.4	$5.4

Once a main hub of automotive production in the U.S., Michigan is still among the top auto manufacturing states.

⬤ **REFLECTION OF THE PAST.** Victorian-style summer homes, built on Mackinac Island in the late 19th century by wealthy railroad families, now welcome vacationers to the island. To protect the environment, cars are not allowed.

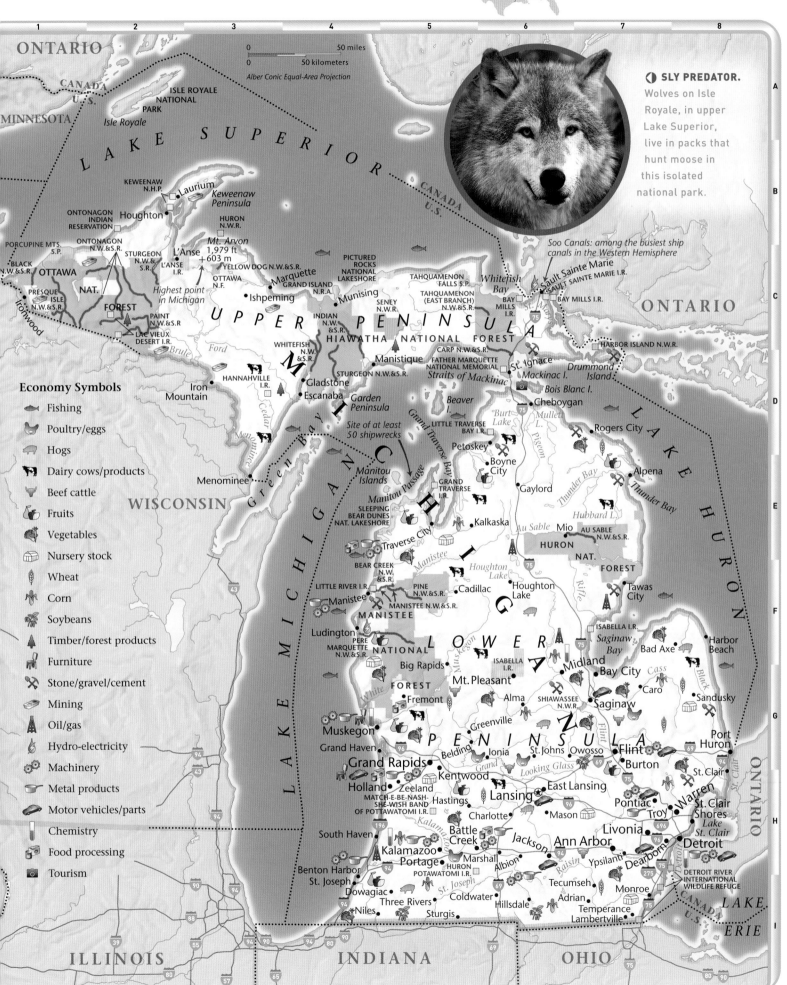

SLY PREDATOR. Wolves on Isle Royale, in upper Lake Superior, live in packs that hunt moose in this isolated national park.

Soo Canals: among the busiest ship canals in the Western Hemisphere

Economy Symbols

- Fishing
- Poultry/eggs
- Hogs
- Dairy cows/products
- Beef cattle
- Fruits
- Vegetables
- Nursery stock
- Wheat
- Corn
- Soybeans
- Timber/forest products
- Furniture
- Stone/gravel/cement
- Mining
- Oil/gas
- Hydro-electricity
- Machinery
- Metal products
- Motor vehicles/parts
- Chemistry
- Food processing
- Tourism

Map labels

ONTARIO
CANADA
U.S.
MINNESOTA

LAKE SUPERIOR

ISLE ROYALE NATIONAL PARK
Isle Royale

KEWEENAW N.H.P.
Laurium
Keweenaw Peninsula
ONTONAGON INDIAN RESERVATION
Houghton
HURON N.W.R.
PORCUPINE MTS. S.P.
ONTONAGON N.W.& S.R.
L'Anse
L'Anse I.R.
STURGEON N.W.& S.R.
BLACK N.W.& S.R.
OTTAWA
PRESQUE ISLE N.W.& S.R.
Ironwood
NAT.
PAINT N.W.& S.R.
FOREST
LAC VIEUX DESERT I.R.
Brule
Mt. Arvon 1,979 ft +603 m
Highest point in Michigan
Ford
YELLOW DOG N.W.& S.R.
OTTAWA N.F.
Marquette
GRAND ISLAND N.R.A.
PICTURED ROCKS NATIONAL LAKESHORE
Munising
Ishpeming
UPPER PENINSULA
INDIAN N.W.& S.R.
SENEY N.W.R.
HIAWATHA NATIONAL FOREST
TAHQUAMENON FALLS S.P.
TAHQUAMENON (EAST BRANCH) N.W.R.
Whitefish Bay
Sault Sainte Marie
SAULT SAINTE MARIE I.R.
ONTARIO
CANADA
U.S.
WHITEFISH N.W.& S.R.
Manistique
CARP N.W.& S.R.
FATHER MARQUETTE NATIONAL MEMORIAL
St. Ignace
Straits of Mackinac
Mackinac I.
HARBOR ISLAND N.W.R.
BAY MILLS I.R.
BAY MILLS I.R.
Drummond Island
HANNAHVILLE I.R.
Iron Mountain
Gladstone
STURGEON N.W.& S.R.
Escanaba
Garden Peninsula
Bois Blanc I.
Cheboygan
LAKE HURON
WISCONSIN
Menominee
Green Bay
Site of at least 50 shipwrecks
Manitou Islands
Manitou Passage
LITTLE TRAVERSE BAY I.R.
Burt Lake
Mullett L.
Rogers City
Piggon
Beaver I.
GRAND TRAVERSE BAY
Petoskey
Boyne City
Gaylord
Alpena
Thunder Bay
Thunder Bay
SLEEPING BEAR DUNES NAT. LAKESHORE
GRAND TRAVERSE I.R.
Hubbard L.
Traverse City
Kalkaska
Au Sable
Mio
AU SABLE N.W.& S.R.
HURON NAT. FOREST
BEAR CREEK N.W.& S.R.
LITTLE RIVER I.R.
Manistee
PINE N.W.& S.R.
MANISTEE N.W.& S.R.
Cadillac
Houghton Lake
Houghton Lake
Rifle
Tawas City
MANISTEE
Ludington
PERE MARQUETTE N.W.& S.R.
NATIONAL
Muskegon
ISABELLA I.R.
Saginaw Bay
Bad Axe
Harbor Beach
Big Rapids
ISABELLA I.R.
Midland
Bay City
Cass
FOREST
Mt. Pleasant
Alma
SHIAWASSEE N.W.R.
Saginaw
Caro
Sandusky
Fremont
Greenville
LOWER
PENINSULA
Belding
Ionia
St. Johns
Owosso
Flint
Black
Muskegon
Grand Haven
Grand Rapids
Kentwood
Holland
Zeeland
MATCH-E-BE-NASH-SHE-WISH BAND OF POTTAWATOMI I.R.
Hastings
Charlotte
Lansing
East Lansing
Mason
Pontiac
Troy
Port Huron
Burton
St. Clair
Warren
St. Clair Shores
Lake St. Clair
Livonia
Kalamazoo
South Haven
Battle Creek
Jackson
Ann Arbor
Detroit
Benton Harbor
St. Joseph
Portage
Marshall
Albion
Tecumseh
Ypsilanti
Dearborn
DETROIT RIVER INTERNATIONAL WILDLIFE REFUGE
Monroe
Dowagiac
Three Rivers
Coldwater
Hillsdale
Adrian
Temperance
Lambertville
Niles
Sturgis
HURON POTAWATOMI I.R.
St. Joseph
Kalamazoo
Raisin
ONTARIO
CANADA
U.S.
LAKE ERIE
LAKE MICHIGAN
ILLINOIS
INDIANA
OHIO

Scale

0   50 miles
0   50 kilometers
Alber Conic Equal-Area Projection

THE BASICS

Statehood
May 11, 1858; 32nd state

Total area (land and water)
86,936 sq mi (225,163 sq km)

Land area
79,627 sq mi (206,232 sq km)

Population
5,489,594

Capital
St. Paul
Population 300,851

Largest city
Minneapolis
Population 410,939

Racial/ethnic groups
85.4% white; 6.0% African American; 4.9% Asian; 1.3% Native American; 5.2% Hispanic (any race)

Foreign born
7.3%

Urban population
73.3% (2010)

Population density
68.9 per sq mi
(26.6 per sq km)

GEO WHIZ

Wild rice is the state grain of Minnesota. Nett Lake, in the Bois Forte Chippewa reservation, has the state's largest continuous beds of wild rice. Native Americans have been harvesting this grain, which they call *manoomin*, for thousands of years.

The Mayo Clinic, a world-famous medical research center founded in 1889 by Dr. William W. Mayo, is in Rochester.

The Boundary Waters Canoe Area Wilderness, along the Minnesota-Ontario border, was the first wilderness area in the U.S. to be set aside for canoeing.

Minnesota

French fur traders began arriving in present-day Minnesota in the mid-17th century. Statehood was established in 1858, and most remaining Indians were forced from the state after a decisive battle in 1862. During the late 1800s large numbers of Germans, Scandinavians, and other immigrants settled a land rich in wildlife, timber, minerals, and fertile soils. Today, farming is concentrated in the south and west. In the northeast, the Mesabi Range's open-pit mines make the state the country's leading source of iron ore. Most of the ore is shipped from Duluth. Both Duluth and nearby Superior in Wisconsin (see page 111) are leading Great Lakes ports. From these ports, ships can reach the Atlantic Ocean via the St. Lawrence Seaway. Scattered across the state's landscape are thousands of lakes—ancient footprints of retreating glaciers—that draw anglers and canoeists. One of those lakes, Lake Itasca, is the source of the mighty Mississippi River, which flows through the Twin Cities of Minneapolis and St. Paul.

COMMON LOON
SHOWY LADY'S SLIPPER

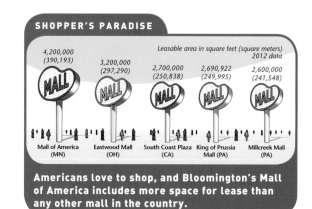

◯ **SUMMER FUN.** Young girls play on a rope swing near Leech Lake in northern Minnesota. The state's many lakes are remnants of the last ice age, when glaciers gouged depressions that filled with water as the ice sheets retreated.

SHOPPER'S PARADISE

Leasable area in square feet (square meters)
2012 data

4,200,000 (390,193) — Mall of America (MN)
3,200,000 (297,290) — Eastwood Mall (OH)
2,700,000 (250,838) — South Coast Plaza (CA)
2,690,922 (249,995) — King of Prussia Mall (PA)
2,600,000 (241,548) — Millcreek Mall (PA)

Americans love to shop, and Bloomington's Mall of America includes more space for lease than any other mall in the country.

◖ **INLAND PORT.** Duluth, on the northern shore of Lake Superior, is the westernmost deep-water port on the St. Lawrence Seaway. Barges and container ships move products such as iron ore and grain along the Great Lakes to the Atlantic Ocean and to markets around the world.

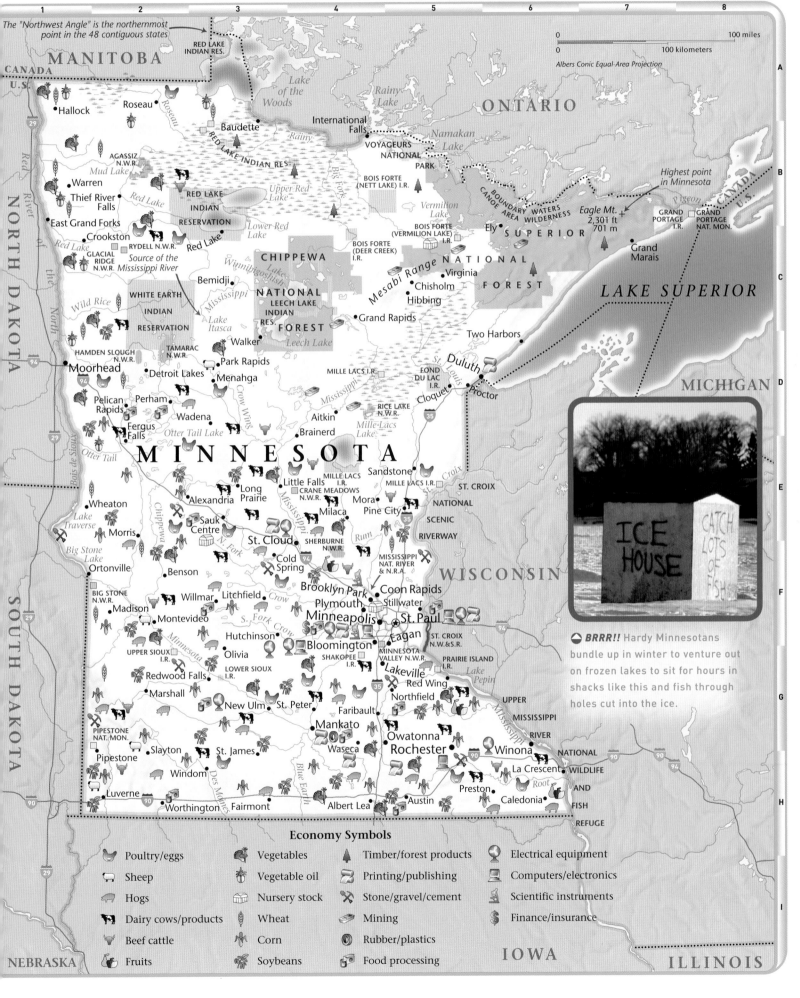

The "Northwest Angle" is the northernmost point in the 48 contiguous states

RED LAKE INDIAN RES.

MANITOBA

CANADA
U.S.

ONTARIO

0   100 miles
0   100 kilometers
Albers Conic Equal-Area Projection

Hallock •   Roseau •

Baudette

Lake of the Woods

Rainy Lake

International Falls

Namakan Lake

VOYAGEURS NATIONAL PARK

AGASSIZ N.W.R.

Mud Lake

Warren •
Thief River Falls •

RED LAKE INDIAN RES.

Red Lake

Upper Red Lake

Big Fork

BOIS FORTE (NETT LAKE) I.R.

Rainy

BOUNDARY WATERS CANOE AREA WILDERNESS

Highest point in Minnesota
Eagle Mt. 2,301 ft 701 m

CANADA
U.S.

East Grand Forks •
Crookston •

RED LAKE INDIAN RESERVATION

Lower Red Lake

Vermilion Lake

BOIS FORTE (VERMILION LAKE) I.R.

Ely •

SUPERIOR

GRAND PORTAGE I.R.

GRAND PORTAGE NAT. MON.

RYDELL N.W.R.
Source of the Mississippi River

Red Lake •

Winnibigoshish Lake

Mississippi

CHIPPEWA

BOIS FORTE (DEER CREEK) I.R.

NATIONAL

Grand Marais •

GLACIAL RIDGE N.W.R.

WHITE EARTH INDIAN RESERVATION

Bemidji •

Lake Itasca

LEECH LAKE INDIAN RES.

NATIONAL FOREST

Virginia •
Chisholm •
Hibbing •

FOREST

LAKE SUPERIOR

Mesabi Range

HAMDEN SLOUGH N.W.R.

TAMARAC N.W.R.

Walker •

Leech Lake

Grand Rapids •

St. Louis

Two Harbors •

Moorhead •
Detroit Lakes •

Park Rapids •
Menahga •

MILLE LACS I.R.

Duluth •
FOND DU LAC I.R.

Proctor •

MICHIGAN

Pelican Rapids •
Perham •
Wadena •

Aitkin •

Mississippi

RICE LAKE N.W.R.

Cloquet •

Fergus Falls •

Otter Tail Lake

Brainerd •

Mille Lacs Lake

MINNESOTA

Otter Tail

NORTH DAKOTA

Crow Wing

Sandstone •

St. Croix

Wheaton •

Lake Traverse

Little Falls •

MILLE LACS I.R.
CRANE MEADOWS N.W.R.

Mora •

Milaca •

MILLE LACS I.R.

ST. CROIX

Alexandria •
Long Prairie •

Mississippi

Pine City •

NATIONAL SCENIC RIVERWAY

Morris •

Sauk Centre •

N. Fork

Rum

St. Cloud •

SHERBURNE N.W.R.

MISSISSIPPI NAT. RIVER & N.R.A.

WISCONSIN

Big Stone Lake

Ortonville •

Benson •

Cold Spring •

Brooklyn Park •
Plymouth •

Coon Rapids •
Stillwater •

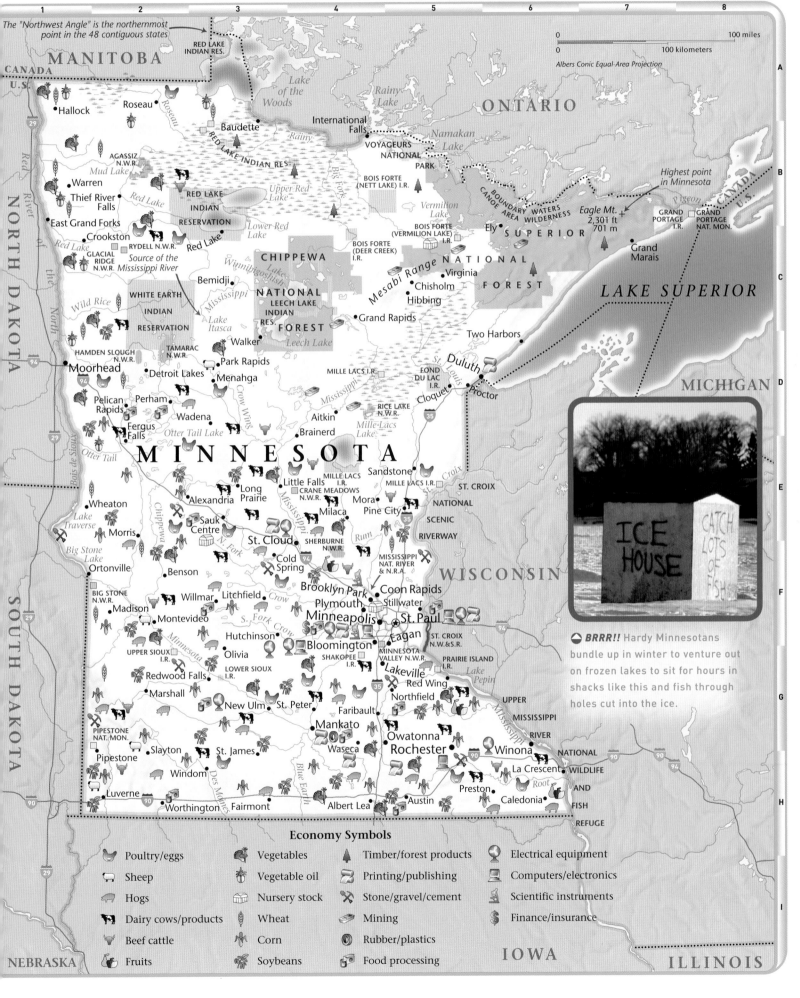

ICE HOUSE   CATCH LOTS OF FISH

🌀 ***BRRR!!*** Hardy Minnesotans bundle up in winter to venture out on frozen lakes to sit for hours in shacks like this and fish through holes cut into the ice.

BIG STONE N.W.R.

Willmar •
Litchfield •

Crow

Minneapolis

St. Paul •

Madison •
Montevideo •

S. Fork Crow

Eagan •

ST. CROIX N.W.&S.R.

UPPER SIOUX I.R.

Hutchinson •

Minnesota

Olivia •

Bloomington •
SHAKOPEE

MINNESOTA VALLEY N.W.R.

PRAIRIE ISLAND I.R.

LOWER SIOUX I.R.

Redwood Falls •

Lakeville •

Lake Pepin

SOUTH DAKOTA

Marshall •

New Ulm •
St. Peter •

Red Wing •
Northfield •

UPPER MISSISSIPPI RIVER

PIPESTONE NAT. MON.

Faribault •

Mankato •

Owatonna •

Rochester •

Winona •

NATIONAL WILDLIFE

Slayton •
Pipestone •

St. James •

Waseca •

La Crescent •

Des Moines

AND

Windom •

Blue Earth

Preston •

Caledonia •

FISH

Luverne •
Worthington •   Fairmont •

Albert Lea •
Austin •

Root

REFUGE

NEBRASKA

IOWA

ILLINOIS

Economy Symbols

🦃	Poultry/eggs	🥬	Vegetables	🌲	Timber/forest products	💡	Electrical equipment
🐑	Sheep	🌻	Vegetable oil	🖨	Printing/publishing	💻	Computers/electronics
🐖	Hogs	🏠	Nursery stock	✂	Stone/gravel/cement	🔬	Scientific instruments
🐄	Dairy cows/products	🌾	Wheat		Mining	$	Finance/insurance
🐂	Beef cattle	🌽	Corn	⊚	Rubber/plastics		
🍎	Fruits	🌱	Soybeans		Food processing		

THE SHOW-ME STATE:
MISSOURI

THE BASICS

Statehood
August 10, 1821; 24th state

Total area (land and water)
69,707 sq mi (180,540 sq km)

Land area
68,742 sq mi (178,040 sq km)

Population
6,083,672

Capital
Jefferson City
Population 43,132 (2014)

Largest city
Kansas City
Population 151,306

Racial/ethnic groups
83.3% white; 11.8% African
American; 2.0% Asian; 0.6%
Native American; 4.1% Hispanic
(any race)

Foreign born
3.9%

Urban population
70.4% (2010)

Population density
88.5 per sq mi (34.2 per sq km)

GEO WHIZ

Camp Wood, near St. Louis,
was the starting point for
Lewis and Clark's Corps of
Discovery, commissioned by
President Thomas Jefferson to
seek a water route to the Pacific.
Along the way their encounters
included hundreds of new
species of plants and animals,
nearly 50 Indian tribes, and the
Rocky Mountains.

In Ash Grove, near Springfield,
Father Moses Berry has turned
his family history into a museum
for slavery education. His was
one of the few families that
didn't flee the area after three
falsely accused black men were
lynched in 1906. The museum
is the only one of its kind in
the Ozark region.

Missouri

The Osage people were among the largest tribes in present-day Missouri when the French began establishing permanent settlements in the 1700s. The United States obtained the territory as part of the 1803 Louisiana Purchase, and Lewis and Clark began exploring the vast wilderness by paddling up the Missouri River from the St. Louis area. Missouri entered the Union as a slave state in 1821. Though it remained in the Union during the Civil War, sympathies were split between the North and South. For much of the 1800s the state was the staging ground for pioneers traveling to western frontiers on the Santa Fe and Oregon Trails. Today, Missouri leads the country in lead mining. Farmers raise cattle, hogs, poultry, corn, and soybeans. Cotton and rice are grown in the southeastern Bootheel region. Cross-state river-port rivals St. Louis and Kansas City are centers of transportation, manufacturing, and finance. Lakes, caves, scenic views, and Branson's country music shows bring many tourists to the Ozarks.

EASTERN BLUEBIRD
HAWTHORN

⬭ **TALL HATS.** Since its founding in 1865 in St. Joseph, the Stetson Company has been associated with Western hats worn by men and women around the world.

HISTORICAL MONUMENTS

630 feet (192 m)
570 feet (174 m)
555 feet (169 m)
352 feet (107 m)
351 feet (107 m)

Gateway Arch (MO)
San Jacinto Monument (TX)
Washington Monument (DC)
Perry's Victory and International Peace Memorial (OH)
Jefferson Davis Monument (KY)

The tallest of all monuments in the United States is Gateway Arch in St. Louis, which was the departure point for westward-bound pioneers during the 19th century.

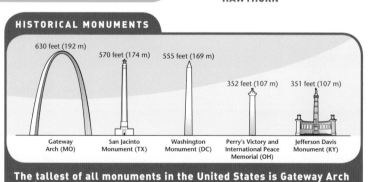

◗ **NATIONAL LANDMARK.** Named a National Historic Landmark in 1987, the steel and concrete Gateway Arch is the tallest arch in the world. Here it frames St. Louis and the Mississippi River.

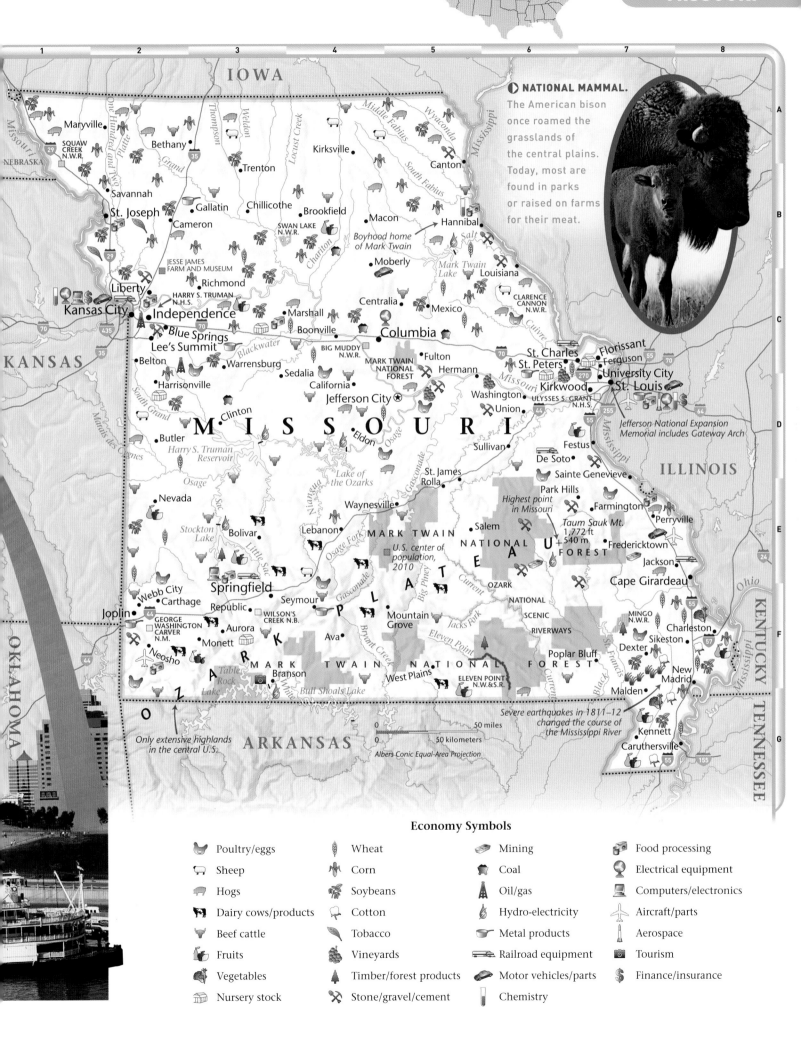

NATIONAL MAMMAL.
The American bison once roamed the grasslands of the central plains. Today, most are found in parks or raised on farms for their meat.

IOWA

NEBRASKA

KANSAS

OKLAHOMA

ARKANSAS

ILLINOIS

KENTUCKY

TENNESSEE

Maryville
SQUAW CREEK N.W.R.
Bethany
Trenton
Kirksville
Canton
Savannah
Gallatin
Chillicothe
Brookfield
Macon
Hannibal
St. Joseph
Cameron
SWAN LAKE N.W.R.
Boyhood home of Mark Twain
Salt
JESSE JAMES FARM AND MUSEUM
Richmond
Moberly
Mark Twain Lake
Louisiana
Liberty
HARRY S. TRUMAN N.H.S.
Centralia
CLARENCE CANNON N.W.R.
Kansas City
Independence
Marshall
Mexico
Columbia
Blue Springs
Lee's Summit
Boonville
BIG MUDDY N.W.R.
MARK TWAIN NATIONAL FOREST
St. Charles
Florissant
Ferguson
Belton
Warrensburg
Fulton
Hermann
St. Peters
University City
Harrisonville
Sedalia
California
Washington
Kirkwood
St. Louis
MISSOURI
Jefferson City
ULYSSES S. GRANT N.H.S.
Clinton
Union
Jefferson National Expansion Memorial includes Gateway Arch
Butler
Eldon
Sullivan
Festus
Harry S. Truman Reservoir
Osage
De Soto
Sainte Genevieve
Lake of the Ozarks
St. James
Rolla
Park Hills
Highest point in Missouri
Nevada
Waynesville
Farmington
Perryville
Stockton Lake
Bolivar
Lebanon
MARK TWAIN
Salem
Taum Sauk Mt. 1,772 ft +540 m
Fredericktown
NATIONAL
FOREST
Jackson
Webb City
Springfield
Seymour
U.S. center of population, 2010
OZARK
Cape Girardeau
Carthage
Republic
Mountain Grove
NATIONAL
MINGO N.W.R.
Joplin
GEORGE WASHINGTON CARVER N.M.
Aurora
Ava
SCENIC
Charleston
Monett
WILSON'S CREEK N.B.
RIVERWAYS
Sikeston
Neosho
Eleven Point
Dexter
Table Rock Lake
Branson
West Plains
ELEVEN POINT N.W.&S.R.
Poplar Bluff
New Madrid
Bull Shoals Lake
Malden
Severe earthquakes in 1811–12 changed the course of the Mississippi River
Kennett
Only extensive highlands in the central U.S.
Caruthersville

Mississippi
One Hundred and Two
Platte
Thompson
Grand
Weldon
Locust Creek
Middle Fabius
Wyaconda
South Fabius
Chariton
Cuivre
Blackwater
Missouri
Niangua
Gasconade
Marais des Cygnes
South Grand
Sac
Little Sac
Osage Fork
Big Piney
Current
Jacks Fork
Bryant Creek
Eleven Point
St. Francis
Black
Ohio
Mississippi
Table Rock Lake
White
Gasconade

0   50 miles
0   50 kilometers
Albers Conic Equal-Area Projection

Economy Symbols

Poultry/eggs
Sheep
Hogs
Dairy cows/products
Beef cattle
Fruits
Vegetables
Nursery stock

Wheat
Corn
Soybeans
Cotton
Tobacco
Vineyards
Timber/forest products

Mining
Coal
Oil/gas
Hydro-electricity
Metal products
Railroad equipment
Motor vehicles/parts
Chemistry

Food processing
Electrical equipment
Computers/electronics
Aircraft/parts
Aerospace
Tourism
Finance/insurance

THE BASICS

Statehood
March 1, 1867; 37th state

Total area (land and water)
77,348 sq mi (200,330 sq km)

Land area
76,824 sq mi
(198,974 sq km)

Population
1,896,190

Capital
Lincoln
Population 277,348

Largest city
Omaha
Population 443,885

Racial/ethnic groups
89.1% white; 5.0% African American; 2.3% Asian; 1.4% Native American; 10.4% Hispanic (any race)

Foreign born
6.3%

Urban population
73.1% (2010)

Population density
24.7 per sq mi (9.5 per sq km)

GEO WHIZ

Many of Nebraska's early settlers were called sodbusters because they cut chunks of the grassy prairie (sod) to build their houses. These building blocks became known as "Nebraska marble."

Nebraska's state fossil is the mammoth. The state estimates that as many as 10 of these prehistoric elephants are buried beneath an average square mile of territory.

Boys Town, a village-style community founded near Omaha in 1917 as a home for troubled boys, has provided a haven for girls, too, since 1979.

Nebraska

For thousands of westbound pioneers on the Oregon and California Trails, Scotts Bluff and Chimney Rock were unforgettable landmarks, towering above the North Platte River. Once reserved for Indians by the government, Nebraska was opened for white settlement in 1854. Following statehood in 1867, ranchers clashed with farmers in an unsuccessful bid to preserve open rangelands. Before white settlers arrived, Indians hunted bison and grew corn, pumpkins, beans, and squash. Today, farms and ranches cover nearly all of the state. Ranchers graze beef cattle on the grass-covered Sand Hills, and farmers grow corn, soybeans, and wheat elsewhere. The vast underground Ogallala Aquifer feeds center-pivot irrigation systems needed to water crops in areas that do not receive enough rain. Processing the state's farm products, especially meatpacking, is a big part of the economy. Omaha, which sits along the Missouri River, is a center of finance, insurance, and agribusiness. Lincoln, the state capital, has the only unicameral, or one-house, legislature in the country.

⬤ **TAKING FLIGHT.**
Migratory Sandhill cranes pass through in late winter, stopping in the Platte River Valley to feed and rest.

GOLDENROD
WESTERN MEADOWLARK

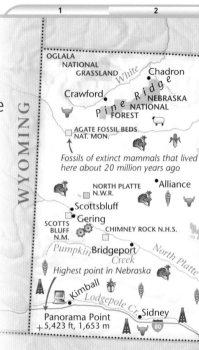

⬤ **RIDER DOWN.** The Big Rodeo is an annual event in tiny Burwell (population 1,213) in Nebraska's Sand Hills. The town, sometimes called "the place where the Wild West meets the 21st century," has hosted the rodeo for more than 80 years.

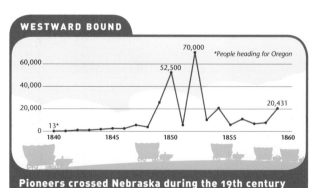

WESTWARD BOUND

*People heading for Oregon

70,000

60,000

52,500

40,000

20,000

20,431

13*

0

1840   1845   1850   1855   1860

Pioneers crossed Nebraska during the 19th century on their way to Oregon. Traffic fluctuated with the occurrence of cholera epidemics and Indian wars.

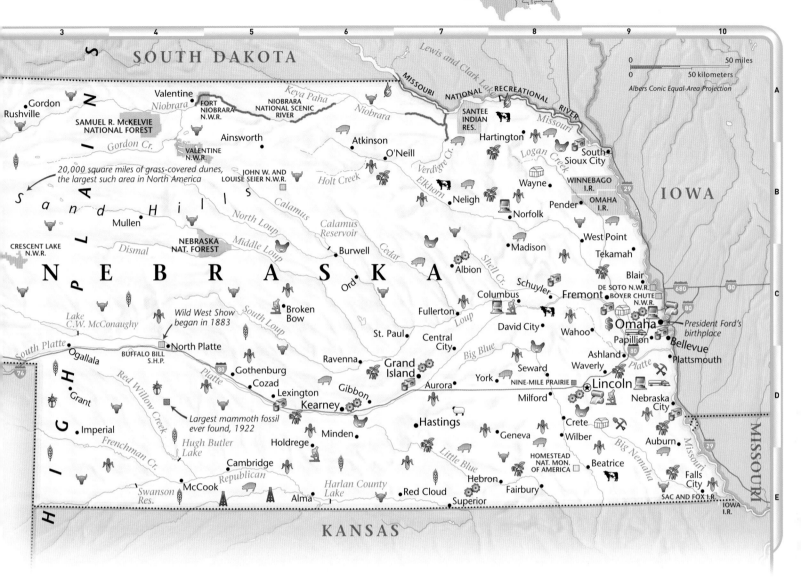

SOUTH DAKOTA

Gordon
Rushville
Valentine
FORT NIOBRARA N.W.R.
NIOBRARA NATIONAL SCENIC RIVER
Keya Paha
Niobrara
MISSOURI NATIONAL RECREATIONAL RIVER
Lewis and Clark Lake
SAMUEL R. McKELVIE NATIONAL FOREST
Gordon Cr.
Ainsworth
Atkinson
O'Neill
SANTEE INDIAN RES.
Hartington
Missouri
South Sioux City
IOWA
Mullen
VALENTINE N.W.R.
JOHN W. AND LOUISE SEIER N.W.R.
Holt Creek
Verdigre Cr.
Logan Creek
Wayne
WINNEBAGO I.R.
29
20,000 square miles of grass-covered dunes, the largest such area in North America
Calamus
North Loup
Calamus Reservoir
Elkhorn
Neligh
Pender
OMAHA I.R.
CRESCENT LAKE N.W.R.
Dismal
Middle Loup
NEBRASKA NAT. FOREST
Burwell
Cedar
Norfolk
West Point
Tekamah

N E B R A S K A

Ord
Albion
Madison
Blair
DE SOTO N.W.R.
Sand Hills
High Plains
Lake C.W. McConaughy
South Loup
Broken Bow
Fullerton
Loup
Schuyler
Columbus
Fremont
BOYER CHUTE N.W.R.
680
80
Wild West Show began in 1883
St. Paul
Central City
David City
Wahoo
Omaha
President Ford's birthplace
South Platte
Ogallala
BUFFALO BILL S.H.P.
North Platte
Gothenburg
Cozad
Lexington
Ravenna
Gibbon
Grand Island
Aurora
York
Seward
Ashland
Waverly
Papillion
80
Platte
Bellevue
Plattsmouth
76
Grant
Red Willow Creek
Platte
Kearney
Hastings
Milford
NINE-MILE PRAIRIE
Lincoln
Nebraska City
Largest mammoth fossil ever found, 1922
Imperial
Minden
Geneva
Crete
Wilber
Auburn
Frenchman Cr.
Hugh Butler Lake
Holdrege
Little Blue
HOMESTEAD NAT. MON. OF AMERICA
Beatrice
Big Nemaha
MISSOURI
Cambridge
Republican
Harlan County Lake
Red Cloud
Hebron
Fairbury
Falls City
29
Swanson Res.
McCook
Alma
Superior
SAC AND FOX I.R.
IOWA I.R.

KANSAS

0 — 50 miles
0 — 50 kilometers
Albers Conic Equal-Area Projection

Economy Symbols

Poultry/eggs	Printing/publishing
Sheep	Stone/gravel/cement
Hogs	Oil/gas
Dairy cows/products	Hydro-electricity
Beef cattle	Machinery
Vegetables	Railroad equipment
Vegetable oil	Food processing
Nursery stock	Computers/electronics
Wheat	Scientific instruments
Corn	Finance/insurance
Soybeans	

THE WAY WEST. Longhorn cattle and a bison stand knee-deep in grass below Chimney Rock, which rises more than 300 feet (91 m) above western Nebraska's rolling landscape. An important landmark on the Oregon Trail for 19th-century westbound pioneers and now a national historic site, the formation is being worn away by forces of erosion.

THE BASICS

Statehood
November 2, 1889; 39th state

Total area (land and water)
70,698 sq mi (183,108 sq km)

Land area
69,001 sq mi
(178,711 sq km)

Population
756,927

Capital
Bismarck
Population 71,167

Largest city
Fargo
Population 118,523

Racial/ethnic groups
88.6% white; 2.4% African American; 1.4% Asian; 5.5% Native American; 3.5% Hispanic (any race)

Foreign born
2.7%

Urban population
59.9% (2010)

Population density
11.0 per sq mi (4.2 per sq km)

GEO WHIZ

The state's largest reservoir is named in honor of Sacagawea (also known as Sakakawea), the teenage Indian guide who joined the Lewis and Clark expedition in the spring of 1805.

Devils Lake has earned the title Perch Capital of the World for the large number of walleye—a kind of perch—caught there.

North Dakota's landscape boasts some of the world's largest outdoor animal sculptures, including Salem Sue, the world's largest Holstein cow; a giant grasshopper; and a snowmobiling turtle.

North Dakota

During the winter of 1804–05 Lewis and Clark camped at a Mandan village where they met Sacagawea, the young Shoshone woman who helped guide them through the Rockies and on to the Pacific Ocean. White settlement of the vast grassy plains coincided with the growth of railroads, and statehood was gained in 1889. The geographic center of North America is southwest of Rugby. The state's interior location helps give it a huge annual temperature range. A record low temperature of -60°F (-51°C) and record high of 121°F (49°C) were recorded in 1936. Fargo, located on the northward flowing Red River of the North, is the state's largest city. Garrison Dam, on the Missouri River, generates electricity and provides water for irrigation. The state is a major producer of flaxseed, canola, sunflowers, and barley, but it is wheat, cattle, and soybeans that provide the greatest income. Oil and lignite coal are important in the western part of the state.

VIGILANT LOOKOUT.
A black-tailed prairie dog watches for signs of danger. This member of the squirrel family lives in burrows in the Great Plains.

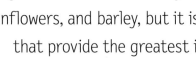

WILD PRAIRIE ROSE
WESTERN
MEADOWLARK

BREADBASKET

Wheat production in million bushels, 2015 data

North Dakota	Kansas	Montana	Washington	Texas
370.0	321.9	185.4	111.5	106.5

Favorable climate and soil along with technology advances have made North Dakota the leading producer of wheat in the U.S.

RUNNING FREE. A wild horse runs through a landscape dramatically eroded by the Little Missouri River in Theodore Roosevelt National Park in North Dakota's Badlands region.

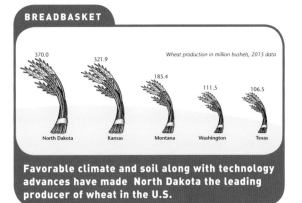

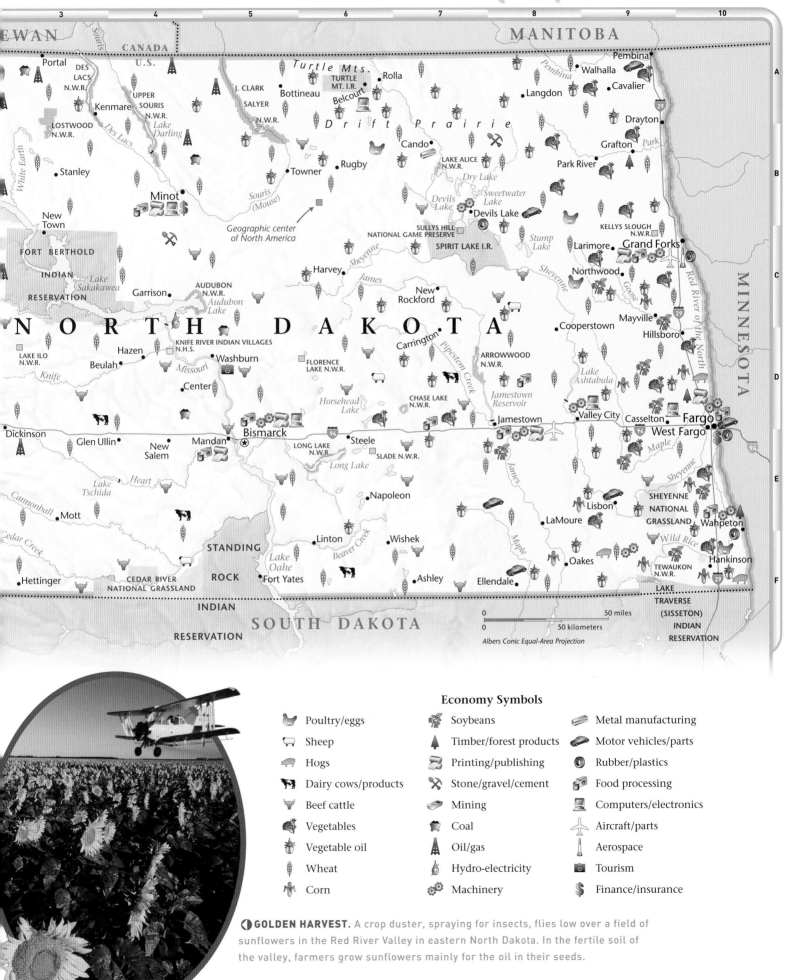

3   **4**   **5**   **6**   **7**   **8**   **9**   **10**

MANITOBA

CANADA
U.S.

EWAN

Souris

Portal
DES LACS N.W.R.
Kenmare
UPPER SOURIS N.W.R.
LOSTWOOD N.W.R.
Des Lacs
Stanley
White Earth
New Town
FORT BERTHOLD INDIAN RESERVATION
Lake Sakakawea
Garrison
Lake Darling
Minot
Souris (Mouse)

J. CLARK SALYER N.W.R.
Bottineau
Turtle Mts.
TURTLE MT. I.R.
Belcourt
Rolla
Drift Prairie
Towner
Rugby
Cando
Geographic center of North America

Pembina
Walhalla
Cavalier
Langdon
Drayton
Grafton
Park River
Pembina
Park

LAKE ALICE N.W.R.
Dry Lake
Devils Lake
Devils Lake
Sweetwater Lake
SULLYS HILL NATIONAL GAME PRESERVE
SPIRIT LAKE I.R.
Stump Lake
KELLYS SLOUGH N.W.R.
Larimore
Grand Forks
Northwood

AUDUBON N.W.R.
Audubon Lake
Harvey
Sheyenne
James
New Rockford
Carrington
Sheyenne
Cooperstown
Mayville
Hillsboro

N O R T H   **D A K O T A**

Goose
Red River of the North
MINNESOTA

LAKE ILO N.W.R.
Hazen
KNIFE RIVER INDIAN VILLAGES N.H.S.
Washburn
Beulah
Knife
Center
Missouri
FLORENCE LAKE N.W.R.
Horsehead Lake
CHASE LAKE N.W.R.
Pipestem Creek
ARROWWOOD N.W.R.
Jamestown Reservoir
Lake Ashtabula
Valley City
Casselton
Fargo

Dickinson
Glen Ullin
New Salem
Mandan
Bismarck
Steele
LONG LAKE N.W.R.
SLADE N.W.R.
Long Lake
Jamestown
West Fargo

Cannonball
Lake Tschida
Heart
Mott
Cedar Creek
Hettinger
Linton
Lake Oahe
Fort Yates
Wishek
Napoleon
Ashley
Ellendale
Oakes
LaMoure
Lisbon
Maple
James
Maple
SHEYENNE NATIONAL GRASSLAND
Sheyenne
Wahpeton
Wild Rice
Hankinson
TEWAUKON N.W.R.

STANDING ROCK INDIAN RESERVATION
CEDAR RIVER NATIONAL GRASSLAND

SOUTH DAKOTA

LAKE TRAVERSE (SISSETON) INDIAN RESERVATION

0   50 miles
0   50 kilometers
Albers Conic Equal-Area Projection

Economy Symbols

Poultry/eggs	Soybeans	Metal manufacturing
Sheep	Timber/forest products	Motor vehicles/parts
Hogs	Printing/publishing	Rubber/plastics
Dairy cows/products	Stone/gravel/cement	Food processing
Beef cattle	Mining	Computers/electronics
Vegetables	Coal	Aircraft/parts
Vegetable oil	Oil/gas	Aerospace
Wheat	Hydro-electricity	Tourism
Corn	Machinery	Finance/insurance

◗ **GOLDEN HARVEST.** A crop duster, spraying for insects, flies low over a field of sunflowers in the Red River Valley in eastern North Dakota. In the fertile soil of the valley, farmers grow sunflowers mainly for the oil in their seeds.

THE BUCKEYE STATE:
OHIO

THE BASICS

Statehood
March 1, 1803; 17th state

Total area (land and water)
44,826 sq mi (116,098 sq km)

Land area
40,861 sq mi (105,829 sq km)

Population
11,613,423

Capital
Columbus
Population 850,106

Largest city
Columbus
Population 850,106

Racial/ethnic groups
82.7% white; 12.7% African American; 2.1% Asian; 0.3% Native American; 3.6% Hispanic (any race)

Foreign born
4.0%

Urban population
77.9% (2010)

Population density
284.2 per sq mi (109.7 per sq km)

GEO WHIZ

Cedar Point Amusement Park, in Sandusky, is known as the Roller Coaster Capital of the World. Top Thrill Dragster, the tallest and fastest roller coaster on Earth when it was built in 2003, has a top speed of 120 miles an hour (193 km/h)!

Ohio's state tree is the buckeye, so-called because the nut it produces resembles the eye of a male deer, or buck.

The state insect is the ladybird beetle, more commonly known as the ladybug. Using these beetles to control plant-eating pests greatly reduces the need for chemical pesticides.

Ohio

Ohio and the rest of the Northwest Territory became part of the United States after the Revolutionary War. The movement of white settlers into the region led to conflicts with the native inhabitants until 1794, when Indian resistance was defeated at Fallen Timbers. Ohio entered the Union nine years later. Lake Erie in the north and the Ohio River in the south, along with canals and railroads, provided transportation links that spurred early immigration and commerce. The state became an industrial giant, producing steel, machinery, rubber, and glass. From 1869 to 1923, seven of twelve U.S. presidents were Ohioans. With 18 electoral votes, the seventh highest number in the country, Ohio is still a big player in presidential elections. Education, government, and finance employ many people in Columbus, the capital and largest city. Manufacturing in Cleveland, Toledo, Cincinnati, and other cities remains a vital segment of the state's economy. Farmers on Ohio's western plains, created by glaciers, grow soybeans and corn, the two largest cash crops.

🌐 **INLAND URBAN CENTER.** Cincinnati's skyline sparkles in the red glow of twilight. Founded in 1788, the modern city boasts education and medical centers as well as headquarters for companies such as Procter & Gamble.

**SCARLET CARNATION
CARDINAL**

🌐 **TRADITIONAL TRAVEL.** The horse and buggy is a familiar sight in central Ohio, location of the world's largest Amish population.

🌐 **SOUND OF MUSIC.** Colorful guitars mark the entrance to the Rock and Roll Hall of Fame in downtown Cleveland. The museum, through its Rockin' the Schools program, attracts thousands of students annually to experience the sounds of rock and roll music and learn about its history.

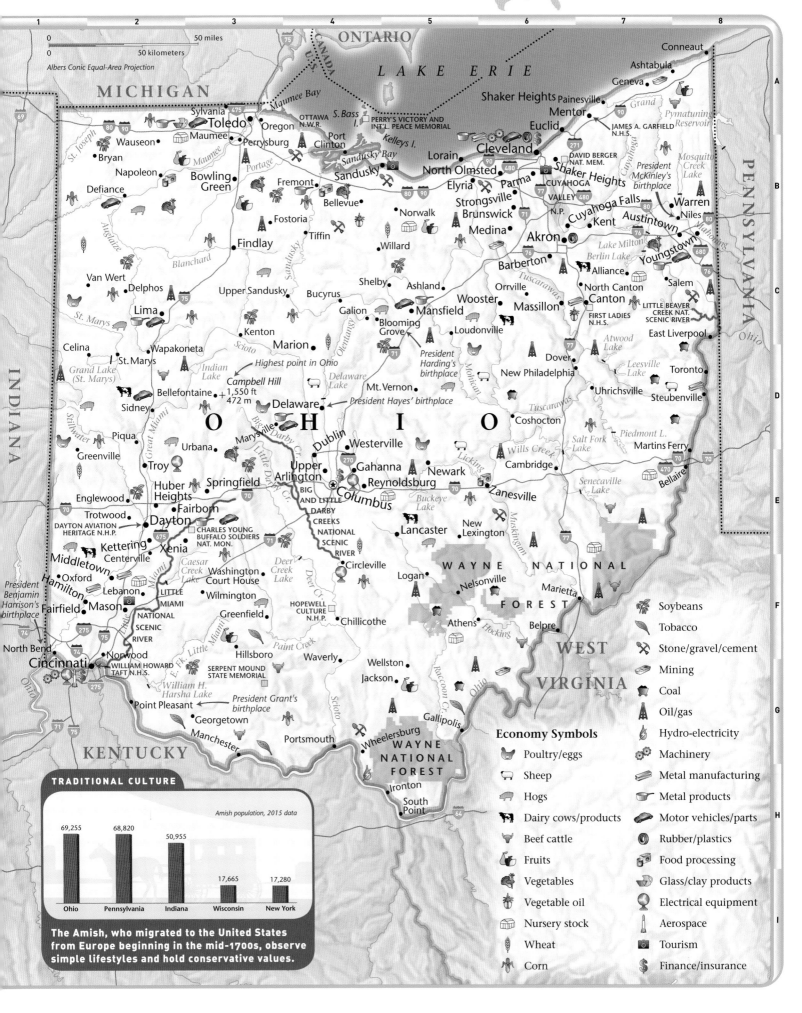

THE MIDWEST

Map of Ohio showing cities, rivers, highways, national forests, and economic activity symbols.

ONTARIO

LAKE ERIE

MICHIGAN

PENNSYLVANIA

INDIANA

WEST VIRGINIA

KENTUCKY

O H I O

Scale: 50 miles / 50 kilometers
Albers Conic Equal-Area Projection

Highest point in Ohio
Campbell Hill +1,550 ft / 472 m

Cities and features: Toledo, Sylvania, Oregon, Maumee, Perrysburg, Wauseon, Bryan, Napoleon, Bowling Green, Defiance, Fremont, Bellevue, Fostoria, Tiffin, Findlay, Norwalk, Willard, Van Wert, Delphos, Upper Sandusky, Bucyrus, Shelby, Ashland, Lima, Wapakoneta, Kenton, Galion, Mansfield, Blooming Grove, Loudonville, Celina, St. Marys, Marion, Sidney, Bellefontaine, Delaware, Mt. Vernon, Coshocton, Piqua, Urbana, Marysville, Dublin, Westerville, Greenville, Troy, Springfield, Upper Arlington, Gahanna, Reynoldsburg, Newark, Cambridge, Huber Heights, Columbus, Zanesville, Englewood, Trotwood, Dayton, Fairborn, Kettering, Xenia, Centerville, Middletown, Oxford, Lebanon, Washington Court House, Wilmington, Circleville, Lancaster, New Lexington, Logan, Nelsonville, Hamilton, Fairfield, Mason, Greenfield, Hillsboro, Waverly, Wellston, Jackson, Athens, Belpre, Marietta, Cincinnati, Norwood, North Bend, Point Pleasant, Georgetown, Manchester, Portsmouth, Wheelersburg, Ironton, South Point, Gallipolis, Chillicothe

Lake Erie cities: Port Clinton, Sandusky, Lorain, North Olmsted, Elyria, Strongsville, Brunswick, Medina, Cleveland, Parma, Shaker Heights, Euclid, Mentor, Painesville, Geneva, Ashtabula, Conneaut, Akron, Barberton, Wooster, Orrville, Massillon, Canton, North Canton, Alliance, Salem, East Liverpool, Toronto, Steubenville, Uhrichsville, New Philadelphia, Dover, Cuyahoga Falls, Kent, Austintown, Youngstown, Niles, Warren, Martins Ferry, Bellaire

National sites: Perry's Victory and Int'l. Peace Memorial, James A. Garfield N.H.S., David Berger Nat. Mem., Cuyahoga Valley N.P., President McKinley's birthplace, Little Beaver Creek Nat. Scenic River, First Ladies N.H.S., President Harding's birthplace, President Hayes' birthplace, Charles Young Buffalo Soldiers Nat. Mon., Big and Little Darby Creeks National Scenic River, Dayton Aviation Heritage N.H.P., President Benjamin Harrison's birthplace, William Howard Taft N.H.S., Little Miami National Scenic River, Hopewell Culture N.H.P., Serpent Mound State Memorial, President Grant's birthplace, William H. Harsha Lake, Wayne National Forest

Lakes/rivers: St. Joseph, Maumee, St. Marys, Auglaize, Blanchard, Portage, Sandusky Bay, Kelleys I., S. Bass I., Maumee Bay, Grand Lake (St. Marys), Indian Lake, Scioto, Olentangy, Delaware Lake, Great Miami, Little Miami, Caesar Creek Lake, Deer Creek Lake, Paint Creek, Stillwater, Mad, Wills Creek, Muskingum, Tuscarawas, Mohican, Licking, Hocking, Raccoon Cr., Ohio, Atwood Lake, Leesville Lake, Salt Fork Lake, Piedmont L., Senecaville Lake, Berlin Lake, Lake Milton, Mosquito Creek Lake, Pymatuning Reservoir, Mahoning, Buckeye Lake

Economy Symbols

- Poultry/eggs
- Sheep
- Hogs
- Dairy cows/products
- Beef cattle
- Fruits
- Vegetables
- Vegetable oil
- Nursery stock
- Wheat
- Corn
- Soybeans
- Tobacco
- Stone/gravel/cement
- Mining
- Coal
- Oil/gas
- Hydro-electricity
- Machinery
- Metal manufacturing
- Metal products
- Motor vehicles/parts
- Rubber/plastics
- Food processing
- Glass/clay products
- Electrical equipment
- Aerospace
- Tourism
- Finance/insurance

TRADITIONAL CULTURE

Amish population, 2015 data

Ohio	Pennsylvania	Indiana	Wisconsin	New York
69,255	68,820	50,955	17,665	17,280

The Amish, who migrated to the United States from Europe beginning in the mid-1700s, observe simple lifestyles and hold conservative values.

THE BASICS

Statehood
November 2, 1889; 40th state

Total area (land and water)
77,116 sq mi (199,729 sq km)

Land area
75,811 sq mi (196,350 sq km)

Population
858,469

Capital
Pierre
Population 14,054 (2014)

Largest city
Sioux Falls
Population 171,544

Racial/ethnic groups
85.5% white; 1.8% African
American; 1.4% Asian; 8.9%
Native American; 3.6%
Hispanic (any race)

Foreign born
2.8%

Urban population
56.7% (2010)

Population density
11.3 per sq mi (4.4 per sq km)

GEO WHIZ

Thanks to captive breeding
programs, the world's largest
population of wild black-footed
ferrets is thriving in a black-
tailed prairie dog colony in
south-central South Dakota.

Sometimes known as the Shrine
of Democracy, Mount Rushmore
National Monument features
the faces of four presidents:
Washington, Jefferson, Lincoln,
and Theodore Roosevelt.

Eight *Tyrannosaurus rex*
skeletons, including Sue, Stan,
Bucky, and WREX, were all dug
up in South Dakota.

South Dakota

After the discovery of Black Hills gold in 1874, prospectors poured in and established lawless mining towns such as Deadwood. Indians fought this invasion but were defeated, and statehood came in 1889. Today, South Dakota has several reservations, and nearly 9 percent of the state's people are Native Americans. The Missouri River flows through the center of the state, creating two distinct regions: To the east, farmers grow corn and soybeans on the fertile, rolling prairie; to the west, where it is too dry for most crops, farmers grow wheat and graze cattle and sheep on the vast plains. In the southwest the Black Hills, named for the dark coniferous trees blanketing their slopes, are still a rich source of gold. Millions of tourists visit the area to see Mount Rushmore and, nearby, a giant sculpture of Lakota leader Crazy Horse, which has been in the works since 1948. Nearby, the fossil-rich Badlands, a region of eroded buttes and pinnacles, dominate the landscape.

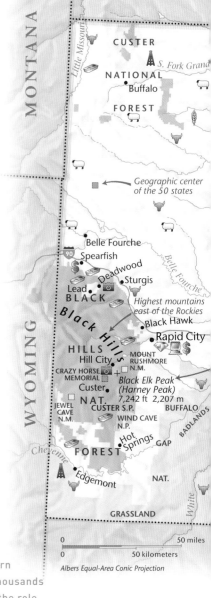

Albers Equal-Area Conic Projection

HONORING AGRICULTURE. The face of the Corn Palace in Mitchell is renewed each year using thousands of bushels of grain to create pictures depicting the role of agriculture in the state's history.

PASQUEFLOWER

RING-NECKED PHEASANT

OIL FROM SEEDS

*Total sunflower oil production in millions of pounds (kilograms)
2014 data*

877 (398) — South Dakota
849 (385) — North Dakota
137 (62) — Texas
92 (42) — Kansas
88 (40) — Minnesota

Sunflowers are an important source of seeds
and edible oil, which is obtained by crushing
the seeds of the flower.

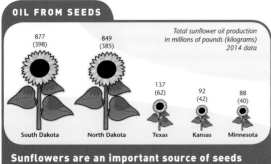

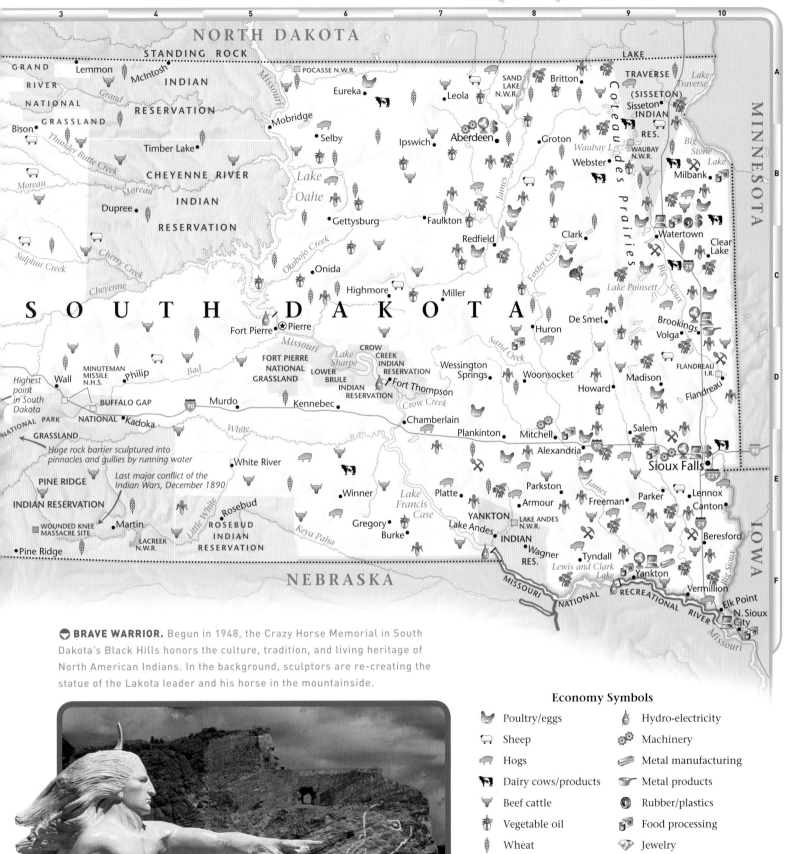

NORTH DAKOTA

STANDING ROCK

INDIAN

RESERVATION

GRAND RIVER NATIONAL GRASSLAND

Lemmon • McIntosh
□ POCASSE N.W.R.
Eureka
Leola
SAND LAKE N.W.R.
Britton
LAKE TRAVERSE (SISSETON) INDIAN RES.
Lake Traverse

Bison
Mobridge
Selby
Ipswich
Aberdeen
Groton
Webster
Milbank
Big Stone Lake

MINNESOTA

Timber Lake

CHEYENNE RIVER INDIAN RESERVATION

Dupree

Lake Oahe

Gettysburg
Faulkton
Redfield
Clark
Watertown
Clear Lake

Moreau

Sulphur Creek

Cherry Creek

Onida
Highmore
Miller
De Smet
Lake Poinsett
Brookings
Volga

S O U T H   D A K O T A

Cheyenne

Fort Pierre ⭐ Pierre
Huron
Wessington Springs
Woonsocket
Howard
Madison
FLANDREAU I.R.
Flandreau

Wall
Highest point in South Dakota
MINUTEMAN MISSILE N.H.S.
Philip
Bad
FORT PIERRE NATIONAL GRASSLAND
LOWER BRULE
Lake Sharpe
CROW CREEK INDIAN RESERVATION
Fort Thompson

Missouri

Murdo
BUFFALO GAP NATIONAL GRASSLAND
Kadoka
Kennebec
Chamberlain
Plankinton
Mitchell
Salem
Sioux Falls

White

Crow Creek

Huge rock barrier sculptured into pinnacles and gullies by running water

White River
Winner
Lake Francis Case
Platte
Parkston
Armour
Freeman
Parker
Lennox
Canton

PINE RIDGE INDIAN RESERVATION

Last major conflict of the Indian Wars, December 1890

□ WOUNDED KNEE MASSACRE SITE
Martin
LACREEK N.W.R.
Rosebud
ROSEBUD INDIAN RESERVATION
Keya Paha
Gregory
Burke
YANKTON
Lake Andes
LAKE ANDES N.W.R.
INDIAN RES.
Wagner
Tyndall
Yankton
Beresford

• Pine Ridge

Little White

Lewis and Clark Lake
Vermillion
Elk Point
N. Sioux City

NEBRASKA

MISSOURI NATIONAL RECREATIONAL RIVER

IOWA

🔷 **BRAVE WARRIOR.** Begun in 1948, the Crazy Horse Memorial in South Dakota's Black Hills honors the culture, tradition, and living heritage of North American Indians. In the background, sculptors are re-creating the statue of the Lakota leader and his horse in the mountainside.

Economy Symbols

🐔 Poultry/eggs	💧 Hydro-electricity
🐑 Sheep	⚙️ Machinery
🐖 Hogs	Metal manufacturing
🐄 Dairy cows/products	Metal products
🐂 Beef cattle	⚫ Rubber/plastics
🌿 Vegetable oil	Food processing
🌾 Wheat	💎 Jewelry
🌽 Corn	🌐 Electrical equipment
🌾 Soybeans	💻 Computers/electronics
⚒️ Stone/gravel/cement	📷 Tourism
Mining	💲 Finance/insurance
⛽ Oil/gas	

WISCONSIN

1848

THE BASICS

Statehood
May 29, 1848; 30th state

Total area (land and water)
65,496 sq mi (169,635 sq km)

Land area
54,158 sq mi (140,268 sq km)

Population
5,771,337

Capital
Madison
Population 248,951

Largest city
Milwaukee
Population 600,155

Racial/ethnic groups
87.6% white; 6.6% African American; 2.8% Asian; 1.1% Native American; 6.6% Hispanic (any race)

Foreign born
4.7%

Urban population
70.2% (2010)

Population density
106.6 per sq mi
(41.1 per sq km)

GEO WHIZ

The Indian Community School in Milwaukee has courses in native languages, history, and rituals, all stressing seven core values: bravery, love, truth, wisdom, humility, loyalty, and respect.

Bogs left by retreating ice-age glaciers provide excellent conditions for raising cranberries. Wisconsin leads the country in harvesting this fruit.

Wisconsin's nickname—Badger State—comes not from the animal but from miners who dug living spaces by burrowing like badgers into the hillsides during the 1820s.

Wisconsin

Frenchman Jean Nicolet was the first European to reach present-day Wisconsin when he stepped ashore from Green Bay in 1634. After decades of getting along, relations with the region's Indians soured as the number of settlers increased.

TASTY GRAZING. The largest concentration of Brown Swiss cows in the United States is in Wisconsin. The milk of this breed is prized by cheese manufacturers.

CITY BY THE LAKE. Milwaukee, on the shore of Lake Michigan, derives its name from the Algonquian word for "beautiful land." The city, known for brewing and manufacturing, also has a growing service sector.

The Black Hawk War in 1832 ended the last major Indian resistance, and statehood came in 1848. Many Milwaukee residents are descendants of German immigrants who labored in the city's breweries and meatpacking plants. Even as the economic importance of health care and other services has increased, food processing and the manufacture of machinery and metal products remains significant for the state. More than one million dairy cows graze in America's Dairyland, as the state is often called. Wisconsin leads the country in cheese production and is the second largest producer of milk and butter. Other farmers grow crops ranging from corn and soybeans to potatoes and cranberries. Northern Wisconsin is sparsely populated but heavily forested and is the source of paper and paper products produced by the state.

WOOD VIOLET
ROBIN

RURAL ECONOMY. The dairy industry is an important part of Wisconsin's rural economy, and dairy farmers control most of the state's farmland.

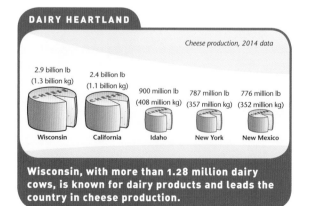

DAIRY HEARTLAND

Cheese production, 2014 data

Wisconsin	California	Idaho	New York	New Mexico
2.9 billion lb (1.3 billion kg)	2.4 billion lb (1.1 billion kg)	900 million lb (408 million kg)	787 million lb (357 million kg)	776 million lb (352 million kg)

Wisconsin, with more than 1.28 million dairy cows, is known for dairy products and leads the country in cheese production.

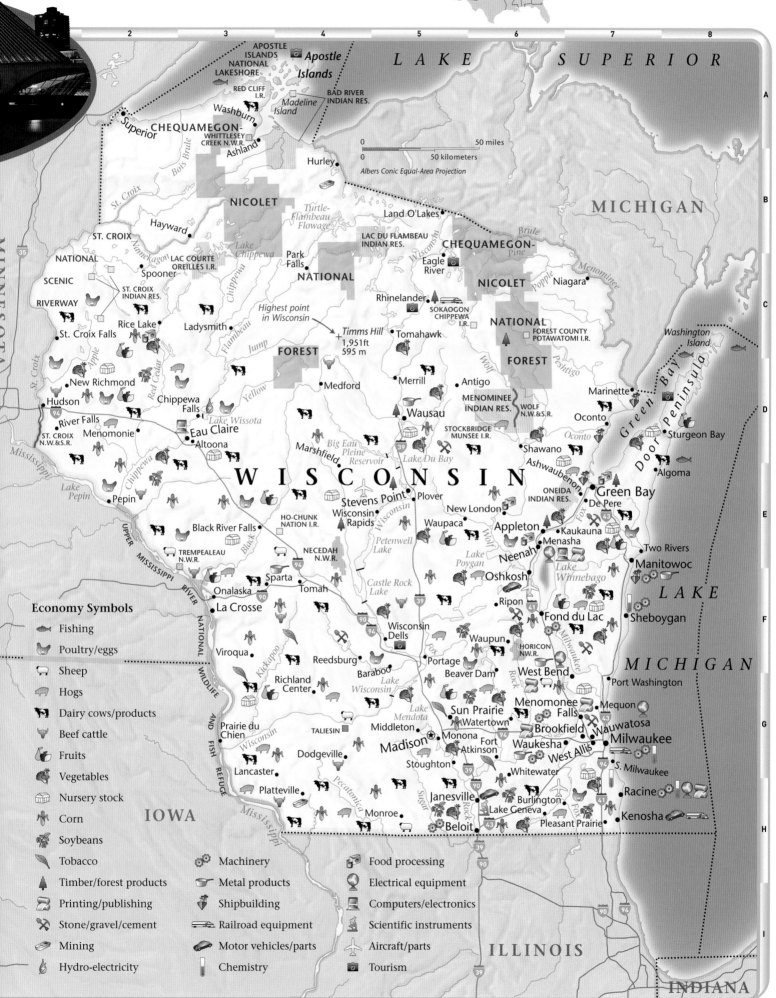

LAKE SUPERIOR

MICHIGAN

MINNESOTA

IOWA

ILLINOIS

INDIANA

LAKE MICHIGAN

WISCONSIN

APOSTLE ISLANDS NATIONAL LAKESHORE
Apostle Islands
RED CLIFF I.R.
Madeline Island
BAD RIVER INDIAN RES.
Washburn
Superior
CHEQUAMEGON-
WHITTLESEY CREEK N.W.R.
Ashland
Hurley
Bois Brule
St. Croix

50 miles
50 kilometers
Albers Conic Equal-Area Projection

NICOLET
Turtle-Flambeau Flowage
Land O'Lakes
Brule
LAC DU FLAMBEAU INDIAN RES.
CHEQUAMEGON-
Pine
Hayward
Lake Chippewa
Park Falls
Eagle River
Niagara
Menominee
Namekagon
ST. CROIX
NATIONAL
LAC COURTE OREILLES I.R.
NATIONAL
Wisconsin
NICOLET
SCENIC
Spooner
ST. CROIX INDIAN RES.
Chippewa
Rhinelander
SOKAOGON CHIPPEWA I.R.
NATIONAL
RIVERWAY
Rice Lake
Ladysmith
Flambeau
Highest point in Wisconsin
Timms Hill 1,951ft 595 m
Tomahawk
FOREST COUNTY POTAWATOMI I.R.
Washington Island
St. Croix Falls
Jump
FOREST
Merrill
Antigo
FOREST
Popple
Peshtigo
New Richmond
Chippewa Falls
Yellow
Medford
Wausau
MENOMINEE INDIAN RES.
Marinette
Green Bay
Door Peninsula
Hudson
Lake Wissota
Big Eau Pleine Reservoir
STOCKBRIDGE MUNSEE I.R.
WOLF N.W.&S.R.
Oconto
Sturgeon Bay
River Falls
Eau Claire
Altoona
Marshfield
Lake Du Bay
Wolf
Shawano
Ashwaubenon
Oconto
Algoma
Menomonie
ST. CROIX N.W.&S.R.
Chippewa
Stevens Point
Plover
New London
ONEIDA INDIAN RES.
Green Bay
De Pere
Lake Pepin
Wisconsin Rapids
Wisconsin
Waupaca
Appleton
Kaukauna
Two Rivers
Pepin
Black River Falls
HO-CHUNK NATION I.R.
Petenwell Lake
Lake Poygan
Menasha
Manitowoc
TREMPEALEAU N.W.R.
Black
NECEDAH N.W.R.
Castle Rock Lake
Neenah
Lake Winnebago
Sparta
Oshkosh
Onalaska
Tomah
Ripon
Sheboygan
La Crosse
Fond du Lac
Viroqua
Wisconsin
Wisconsin Dells
Kickapoo
Reedsburg
Portage
Waupun
HORICON NW.R.
Milwaukee
Richland Center
Baraboo
Lake Wisconsin
Beaver Dam
West Bend
Port Washington
Prairie du Chien
TALIESIN
Lake Mendota
Sun Prairie
Menomonee Falls
Mequon
Wisconsin
Middleton
Watertown
Brookfield
Wauwatosa
Dodgeville
Lake Monona
Madison
Monona
Fort Atkinson
Waukesha
Milwaukee
Lancaster
Stoughton
West Allis
S. Milwaukee
Platteville
Whitewater
Pecatonica
Janesville
Burlington
Racine
Monroe
Rock
Lake Geneva
Kenosha
Beloit
Pleasant Prairie
Sugar
Fox

Economy Symbols
- Fishing
- Poultry/eggs
- Sheep
- Hogs
- Dairy cows/products
- Beef cattle
- Fruits
- Vegetables
- Nursery stock
- Corn
- Soybeans
- Tobacco
- Timber/forest products
- Printing/publishing
- Stone/gravel/cement
- Mining
- Hydro-electricity
- Machinery
- Metal products
- Shipbuilding
- Railroad equipment
- Motor vehicles/parts
- Chemistry
- Food processing
- Electrical equipment
- Computers/electronics
- Scientific instruments
- Aircraft/parts
- Tourism

THE REGION

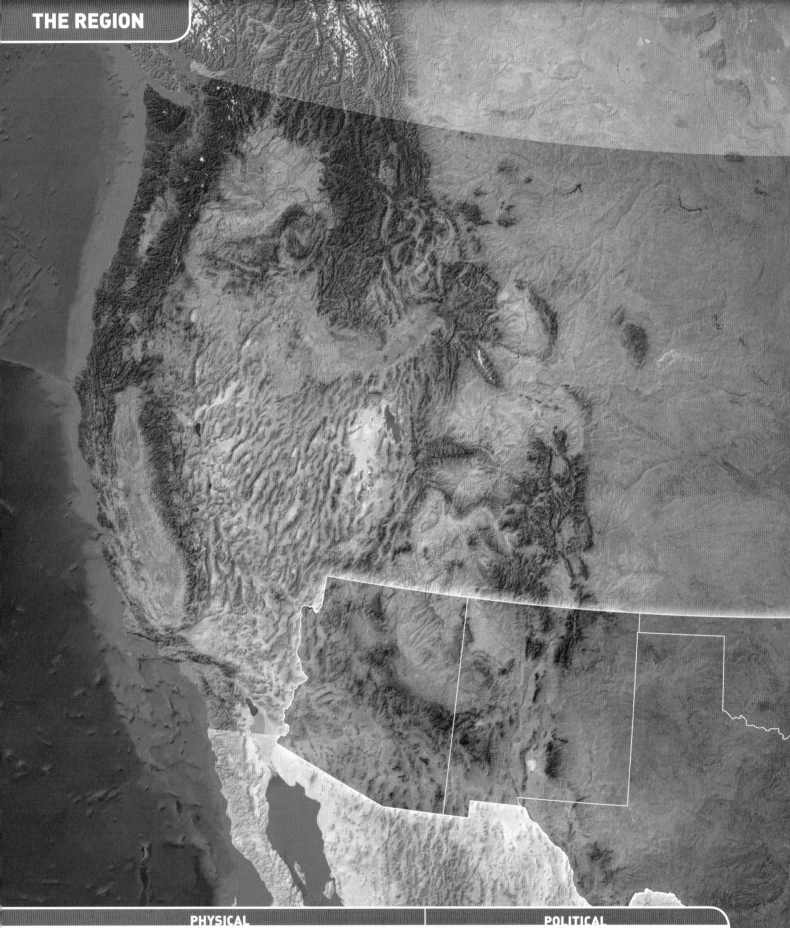

PHYSICAL

Total area (land and water) 574,075 sq mi (1,486,850 sq km)	**Lowest point** Sea level, shores of the Gulf of Mexico	**Vegetation** Mixed, broadleaf, and needleleaf forest; grassland; desert
Highest point Wheeler Peak, NM 13,161 ft (4,011 m)	**Longest rivers** Rio Grande, Arkansas, Colorado	**Climate** Humid subtropical, semiarid and arid, with warm to hot summers and cool winters
	Largest lakes Toledo Bend, Sam Rayburn, Eufaula (all reservoirs)	

POLITICAL

Total population 40,293,626	**Smallest state** Oklahoma: 69,899 sq mi (181,037 sq km)
States (4): Arizona, New Mexico, Oklahoma, Texas	**Most populous state** Texas: 27,469,114
	Least populous state New Mexico: 2,085,109
Largest state Texas: 268,596 sq mi (695,662 sq km)	**Largest city proper** Houston, 2,296,224

The Southwest

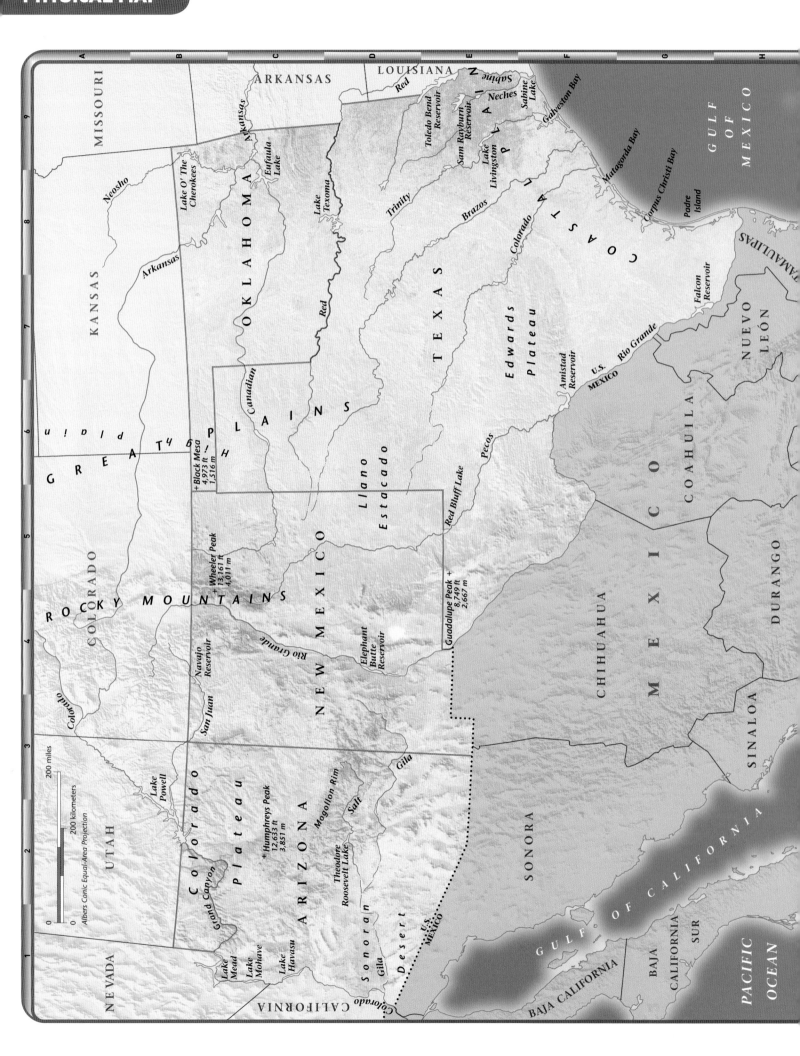

MISSOURI

ARKANSAS

LOUISIANA

Red

Neches

Sabine

Sabine Lake

Galveston Bay

GULF OF MEXICO

Arkansas

Neosho

KANSAS

Arkansas

Lake O' The Cherokees

Eufaula Lake

Lake Texoma

OKLAHOMA

Toledo Bend Reservoir

Sam Rayburn Reservoir

Lake Livingston

Trinity

Brazos

Colorado

Matagorda Bay

Corpus Christi Bay

Padre Island

TAMAULIPAS

GREAT PLAINS

Canadian

Red

TEXAS

COASTAL PLAIN

Edwards Plateau

Amistad Reservoir

U.S.
MEXICO

Rio Grande

Falcon Reservoir

NUEVO LEÓN

+ Black Mesa
4,973 ft
1,516 m

Llano Estacado

Pecos

Red Bluff Lake

COLORADO

GREAT PLAINS

COAHUILA

M E X I C O

200 miles

200 kilometers

Albers Conic Equal-Area Projection

ROCKY MOUNTAINS

+ Wheeler Peak
13,161 ft
4,011 m

NEW MEXICO

Guadalupe Peak +
8,749 ft
2,667 m

CHIHUAHUA

DURANGO

Colorado

UTAH

Lake Powell

Navajo Reservoir

San Juan

Rio Grande

Elephant Butte Reservoir

Colorado Plateau

+ Humphreys Peak
12,633 ft
3,851 m

Mogollon Rim

Gila

Salt

Theodore Roosevelt Lake

ARIZONA

SINALOA

SONORA

NEVADA

Grand Canyon

Lake Mead

Lake Mohave

Lake Havasu

Sonoran Desert

Gila

CALIFORNIA

Colorado

U.S.
MEXICO

BAJA CALIFORNIA

GULF OF CALIFORNIA

BAJA CALIFORNIA SUR

PACIFIC OCEAN

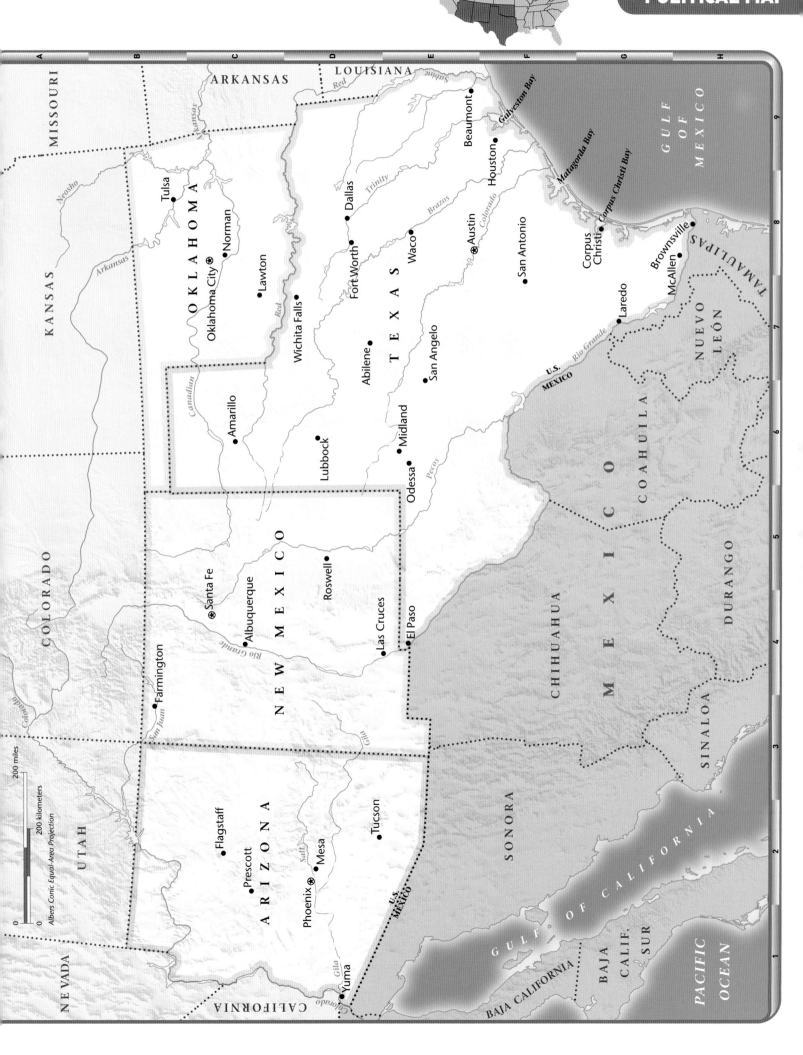

200 miles

200 kilometers

Albers Conic Equal-Area Projection

ABOUT THE
SOUTHWEST

◐ **SKY STONE.** According to Indian legend, turquoise stole its color from the sky. This Zuni woman is wearing turquoise jewelry for a festival in Phoenix. Zuni Indians, whose reservation is in western New Mexico, have made jewelry for more than one thousand years.

The Southwest
FROM CANYONS TO GRASSLANDS

Legendary cities of gold lured Spanish conquistadors to the Southwest in the 1500s. Today, the promise of economic opportunities brings people from other states as well as immigrants, both legal and illegal, from countries south of the border. This part of the Sunbelt region boasts future-oriented cities while preserving Wild West tales and Native American traditions. Its climate ranges from humid subtropical along the Gulf Coast to arid in Arizona's deserts, and the landscape ranges from sprawling plains in the east to plateaus cut by dramatic canyons in the west. Water is a major concern in the Southwest, one of the country's fastest-growing regions.

◕ **HIGH SOCIETY.** Dressed in an elegant ball gown, a young woman participates in the Society of Martha Washington Pageant in Laredo, Texas. This event presents daughters of wealthy and long-established Hispanic families to the local community.

MODERN METROPOLIS. Towering skyscrapers tell a story of success and wealth. Although incorporated as a town in 1856, it was not until 1930 that Dallas, Texas, experienced explosive growth and prosperity due to the discovery of oil. Today, the city is a center of the U.S. oil industry and a leader in technology-based industries.

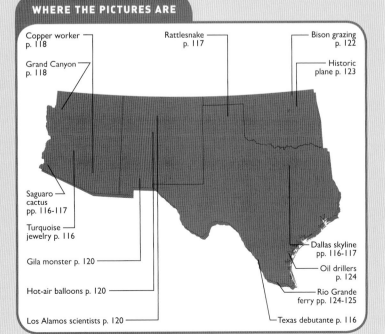

DEADLY VIPER. Shaking the rattles on the tip of its tail, this diamondback rattlesnake—coiled for attack—warns intruders to stay away. Common throughout the arid Southwest, the snake eats mainly small rodents.

STANDING TALL.
The saguaro cactus, which often rises more than 30 feet (9 m) above the shrubs of the Sonoran Desert, frequently has several branches and produces creamy-white flowers that bloom at night. The Sonoran, the hottest desert in North America, is located in the borderlands of southern Arizona and California and extends into northern Mexico.

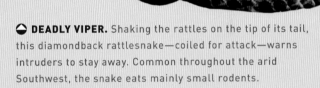

WHERE THE PICTURES ARE

Copper worker p. 118
Grand Canyon p. 118
Saguaro cactus pp. 116-117
Turquoise jewelry p. 116
Gila monster p. 120
Hot-air balloons p. 120
Los Alamos scientists p. 120

Rattlesnake p. 117

Bison grazing p. 122
Historic plane p. 123

Dallas skyline pp. 116-117
Oil drillers p. 124
Rio Grande ferry pp. 124-125
Texas debutante p. 116

THE BASICS

Statehood
February 14, 1912; 48th state

Total area (land and water)
113,990 sq mi (295,234 sq km)

Land area
113,594 sq mi (294,207 sq km)

Population
6,828,065

Capital
Phoenix
Population 1,563,025

Largest city
Phoenix
Population 1,563,025

Racial/ethnic groups
83.5% white; 4.8% African American; 3.4% Asian; 5.3% Native American; 30.7% Hispanic (any race)

Foreign born
13.4%

Urban population
89.8% (2010)

Population density
60.1 per sq mi (23.2 per sq km)

GEO WHIZ

The California condor, once common throughout the Southwest, nearly became extinct in 1987. Through captive breeding and other conservation measures, the species has been reintroduced to the wild in areas such as the Grand Canyon.

People have been carving pictures called petroglyphs into rock cliffs in Verde Valley near Flagstaff for thousands of years. The meanings of most are a mystery, but some reveal plants and animals of bygone eras.

Introduced as wild game for sportspeople, bullfrogs have made Arizona their new home on the range. With no natural predators and plenty to eat, bullfrogs are taking over.

Arizona

The first Europeans to visit what is now Arizona were the Spanish in the 1500s. The territory passed from Spain to Mexico and then to the United States over the next three centuries. In the 1800s settlers clashed with the Apache warriors Cochise and Geronimo—and with one another in lawless towns like Tombstone. Youngest of the 48 contiguous states, Arizona achieved statehood in 1912. Arizona's economy was long based on the Five C's: copper, cattle, cotton, citrus, and climate—but manufacturing and service industries have gained prominence. A fast-growing population, sprawling cities, and agricultural irrigation strain limited water supplies in this dry state, which depends on water from the Colorado River and underground aquifers. Tourists flock to the Colorado Plateau in the north to see stunning vistas of the Grand Canyon, Painted Desert, and Monument Valley. To the south, the Sonoran Desert's unique ecosystem includes the giant saguaro cactus. Indian reservations scattered around the state offer visitors the chance to learn about tribal history and culture.

CACTUS WREN

SAGUARO

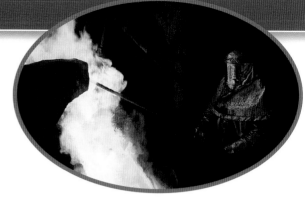

⊖ **HOT WORK.** A man in protective clothing works near a furnace that melts and refines copper ore at Magma Copper Company near Tucson. Arizona is one of the largest copper-producing regions in the world.

INDIAN RESERVATIONS

169,321

Number of people, 2010 data

Navajo AZ-NM-UT	Pine Ridge SD-NE	Fort Apache AZ	Gila River AZ	Osage OK
	16,906	13,041	11,251	9,920

More than 200,000 Indians live on reservations in the Southwest. The most populous is the Navajo Reservation in Arizona and adjoining states.

⊖ **NATURAL WONDER.** Carved by the rushing waters of the Colorado River, the Grand Canyon's geologic features and fossil record reveal almost two billion years of Earth's history. Archaeological evidence indicates human habitation dating back 12,000 years.

THE GRAND CANYON STATE:
ARIZONA

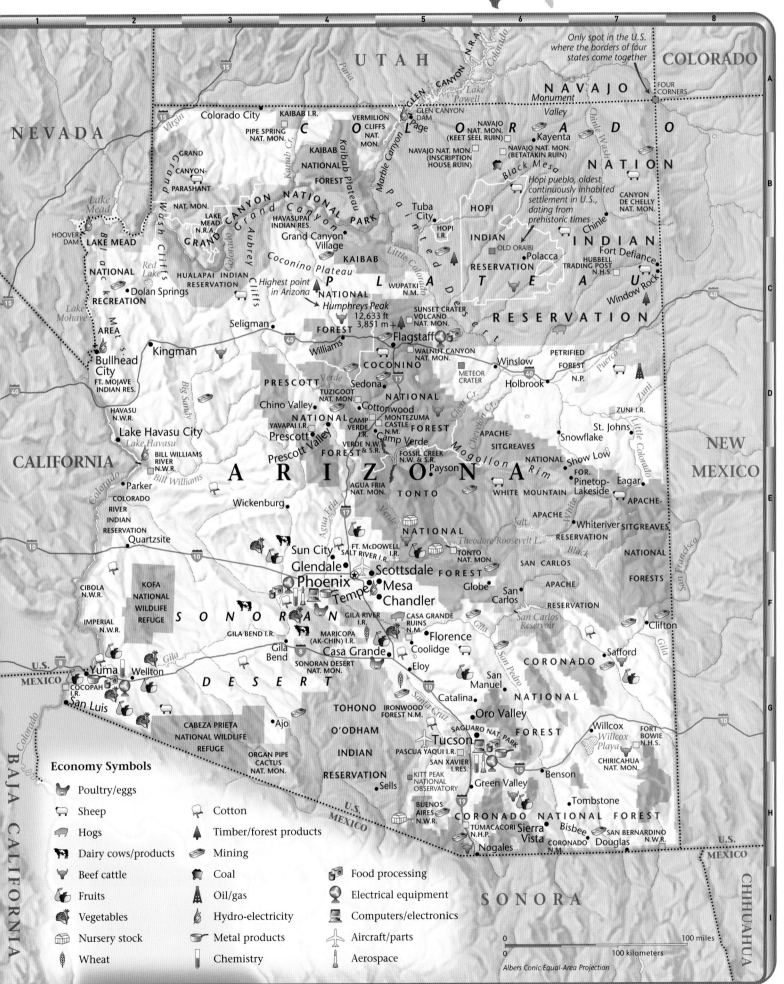

THE LAND OF ENCHANTMENT STATE:
NEW MEXICO

THE BASICS

Statehood
January 6, 1912; 47th state

Total area (land and water)
121,590 sq mi (314,917 sq km)

Land area
121,298 sq mi (314,161 sq km)

Population
2,085,109

Capital
Santa Fe
Population 84,099

Largest city
Albuquerque
Population 559,121

Racial/ethnic groups
82.5% white; 2.6% African American; 1.7% Asian; 10.5% Native American; 48.0% Hispanic (any race)

Foreign born
9.8%

Urban population
77.4% (2010)

Population density
17.2 per sq mi (6.6 per sq km)

GEO WHIZ

Carlsbad Caverns National Park has more than a hundred caves, including the deepest limestone cavern in the U.S. From May through October visitors can watch hundreds of thousands of Mexican free-tailed bats emerge from the caverns on their nightly search for food.

Taos Pueblo, in north-central New Mexico, has been continuously inhabited by Pueblo people for more than 1,000 years. When Spanish explorers reached it in 1540, they thought they had found one of the fabled golden cities of Cibola.

In 2011 Spaceport America officially opened in the high desert near Truth or Consequences. Private companies hope to offer sub-orbital space flights from this port in the near future.

New Mexico

New Mexico is among the youngest states—statehood was established in 1912—but its capital city is the country's oldest. The Spanish founded Santa Fe in 1610, a decade before the *Mayflower* reached America. Beginning in the 1820s, the Santa Fe Trail brought trade and settlers, and the United States acquired the territory from Mexico by 1853. Most large cities are in the center of the state, along the Rio Grande. The Rocky Mountains divide the plains in the east from eroded mesas and canyons in the west. Cattle and sheep ranching on the plains is the chief agricultural activity, but hay, onions, and chili peppers are also important. Copper, potash, and natural gas produce mineral wealth. Cultural richness created by the historic interaction of Indian, Hispanic, and Anglo peoples abounds. Visitors experience this unique culture in the state's spicy cuisine, the famous art galleries of Taos, and the crafts made by Indians on the state's many reservations.

○ PAINFUL BITE. The most poisonous lizard native to the United States is the strikingly patterned gila monster, which lives in desert areas of the Southwest.

ROADRUNNER
YUCCA

◒ FLYING HIGH. Brightly colored balloons rise into a brilliant blue October sky during Albuquerque's annual International Balloon Fiesta, the largest such event in the world. During the nine-day festival more than 500 hot-air balloons drift on variable air currents created by surrounding mountains.

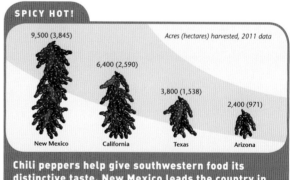

SPICY HOT!

9,500 (3,845)   6,400 (2,590)   3,800 (1,538)   2,400 (971)

Acres (hectares) harvested, 2011 data

New Mexico   California   Texas   Arizona

Chili peppers help give southwestern food its distinctive taste. New Mexico leads the country in acres planted in this fiery flavor enhancer.

◑ NUCLEAR MYSTERIES. Scientists at Los Alamos National Laboratory, a leading scientific and engineering research institution, use 3-D simulations to study nuclear explosions.

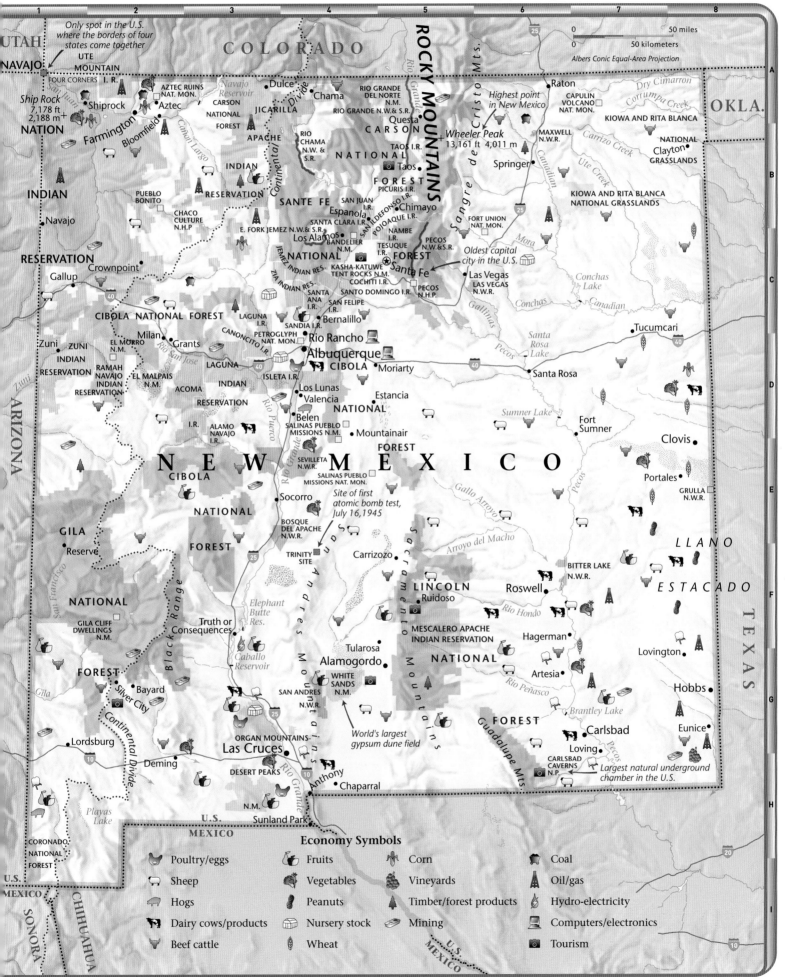

Only spot in the U.S. where the borders of four states come together

COLORADO

ROCKY MOUNTAINS

Highest point in New Mexico

Wheeler Peak 13,161 ft 4,011 m

OKLA.

Ship Rock 7,178 ft 2,188 m

FOUR CORNERS
UTE MOUNTAIN I.R.
NAVAJO

NATION

Shiprock • Aztec
AZTEC RUINS NAT. MON.
Farmington • Bloomfield
Dulce Chama
CARSON NATIONAL FOREST
JICARILLA
APACHE
INDIAN RESERVATION

Raton
CAPULIN VOLCANO NAT. MON.
Dry Cimarron
Corrumpa Creek

RIO GRANDE DEL NORTE N.M.
RIO GRANDE N.W.& S.R.
Questa
CARSON
NATIONAL FOREST
TAOS I.R.
Taos
PICURIS I.R.

MAXWELL N.W.R.
Springer
KIOWA AND RITA BLANCA
NATIONAL Clayton GRASSLANDS
Carrizo Creek

INDIAN
Navajo

RESERVATION
Gallup

PUEBLO BONITO
CHACO CULTURE N.H.P.
RIO CHAMA N.W.& S.R.
SANTE FE
San Juan I.R.
Espanola
SANTA CLARA I.R.
SAN ILDEFONSO I.R.
Chimayo
POJOAQUE I.R.
NAMBE I.R.
TESUQUE I.R.
PECOS N.W.&S.R.

FORT UNION NAT. MON.
Las Vegas
LAS VEGAS N.W.R.
Conchas Lake

Ute Creek
KIOWA AND RITA BLANCA
NATIONAL GRASSLANDS

Crownpoint
E. FORK JEMEZ N.W.& S.R.
Los Alamos
BANDELIER N.M.
JEMEZ INDIAN RES.
NATIONAL
KASHA-KATUWE TENT ROCKS N.M.
COCHITI I.R.
Santa Fe
Oldest capital city in the U.S.

Mora
Canadian
Conchas

Zuni
ZUNI INDIAN RESERVATION
Milan Grants
EL MORRO N.M.
RAMAH NAVAJO INDIAN RESERVATION
EL MALPAIS N.M.
CIBOLA NATIONAL FOREST
LAGUNA I.R.
CANONCITO I.R.
ZIA INDIAN RES.
SANTA ANA I.R.
SANDIA I.R.
SAN FELIPE I.R.
SANTO DOMINGO I.R.
Bernalillo
PETROGLYPH NAT. MON.
Rio Rancho
Albuquerque
CIBOLA
Moriarty

PECOS N.H.P.
Gallinas
Santa Rosa Lake
Tucumcari

Santa Rosa

ACOMA
LAGUNA INDIAN RESERVATION
ISLETA I.R.
Los Lunas
Valencia
NATIONAL
Estancia
Sumner Lake
Fort Sumner
Clovis

I.R.
ALAMO NAVAJO I.R.
Belen
SALINAS PUEBLO MISSIONS N.M.
Mountainair
FOREST
Portales
GRULLA N.W.R.

N E W   **M E X I C O**

CIBOLA
NATIONAL
FOREST
SEVILLETA N.W.R.
SALINAS PUEBLO MISSIONS NAT. MON.
Socorro
Site of first atomic bomb test, July 16, 1945
BOSQUE DEL APACHE N.W.R.
TRINITY SITE
Carrizozo
LINCOLN
Ruidoso
Roswell
BITTER LAKE N.W.R.

L L A N O
E S T A C A D O

Gallo Arroyo
Arroyo del Macho

GILA
Reserve

NATIONAL

FOREST

Elephant Butte Res.
Truth or Consequences
Caballo Reservoir

San Andres Mountains
MESCALERO APACHE INDIAN RESERVATION
Tularosa
Alamogordo
WHITE SANDS N.M.
World's largest gypsum dune field

Rio Hondo
Hagerman
NATIONAL
Artesia
Rio Peñasco

Lovington

Hobbs

T E X A S

GILA CLIFF DWELLINGS N.M.
FOREST
Bayard
Silver City
Continental Divide
Lordsburg
Gila
Deming

SAN ANDRES N.W.R.
ORGAN MOUNTAINS-DESERT PEAKS N.M.
Las Cruces
Anthony
Chaparral
Sunland Park

Guadalupe Mts.
FOREST
Brantley Lake
Carlsbad
Loving
CARLSBAD CAVERNS N.P.
Eunice
Largest natural underground chamber in the U.S.

Playas Lake
U.S.
MEXICO

CORONADO NATIONAL FOREST
U.S. MEXICO
SONORA
CHIHUAHUA

Economy Symbols

Poultry/eggs
Sheep
Hogs
Dairy cows/products
Beef cattle

Fruits
Vegetables
Peanuts
Nursery stock
Wheat

Corn
Vineyards
Timber/forest products
Mining

Coal
Oil/gas
Hydro-electricity
Computers/electronics
Tourism

Albers Conic Equal-Area Projection

0   50 miles
0   50 kilometers

ARIZONA

UTAH

OKLAHOMA

THE BASICS

Statehood
November 16, 1907; 46th state

Total area (land and water)
69,899 sq mi (181,037 sq km)

Land area
68,595 sq mi (177,660 sq km)

Population
3,911,338

Capital
Oklahoma City
Population 631,346

Largest city
Oklahoma City
Population 631,346

Racial/ethnic groups
74.8% white; 7.8% African American; 2.2% Asian; 9.1% Native American; 10.1% Hispanic (any race)

Foreign born
5.5%

Urban population
66.2% (2010)

Population density
57.0 per sq mi (22.0 per sq km)

GEO WHIZ

An area of Oklahoma City has earned the nickname Little Saigon. In the 1960s the city opened its doors to tens of thousands of refugees from Vietnam. Today, the area is a thriving business district that includes people of many Asian nationalities.

"Hillbilly Speed Bump" is one of several nicknames for the armadillo. Native to South America, large populations of this armor-plated mammal are found as far north as Oklahoma.

Before it became a state in 1907, Oklahoma was known as Indian Territory. Today 39 tribes, including Cherokee, Osage, Creek, and Choctaw, have their headquarters in the state.

Oklahoma

The U.S. government declared most of present-day Oklahoma as an Indian Territory in 1834. To reach this new homeland, south-eastern Indians were forced to travel the Trail of Tears, named for its brutal conditions. By 1889 areas were opened for white homesteaders who staked claims in frenzied land runs. White and Indian lands were combined to form the state of Oklahoma in 1907. During the 1930s many Oklahoma natives fled drought and dust storms that smothered everything in sight. Some traveled as far as California in search of work. Better farming methods and the return of rain helped agriculture recover, and today cattle and wheat are among the chief products. Oil and natural gas wells are found throughout the state. The Red River, colored by the region's iron-rich soils, marks the state's southern boundary. Along the eastern border, the Ozark Plateau and Ouachita Mountains form rugged bluffs and valleys. To the west, rolling plains rise toward the High Plains in the state's panhandle.

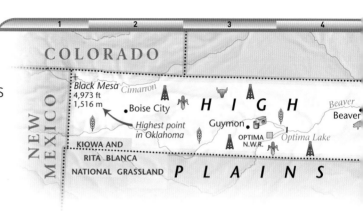

MISTLETOE
SCISSOR-TAILED
FLYCATCHER

FOOD SUPPLIER

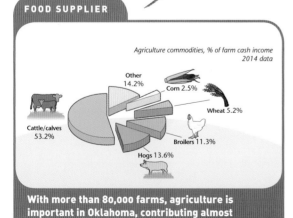

Agriculture commodities, % of farm cash income
2014 data

Other 14.2%
Corn 2.5%
Wheat 5.2%
Cattle/calves 53.2%
Broilers 11.3%
Hogs 13.6%

With more than 80,000 farms, agriculture is important in Oklahoma, contributing almost $8 billion to the state's economy.

◉ **NATURAL LANDSCAPE.** A bison herd grazes in the Tallgrass Prairie Preserve, near Pawhuska. In years when rain is abundant, the grasses can grow as tall as 8 feet (2.5 m). Tallgrass prairie once covered 140 million acres (57 million ha), extending from Minnesota to Texas, but today less than 10 percent remains because of urban sprawl and cropland expansion.

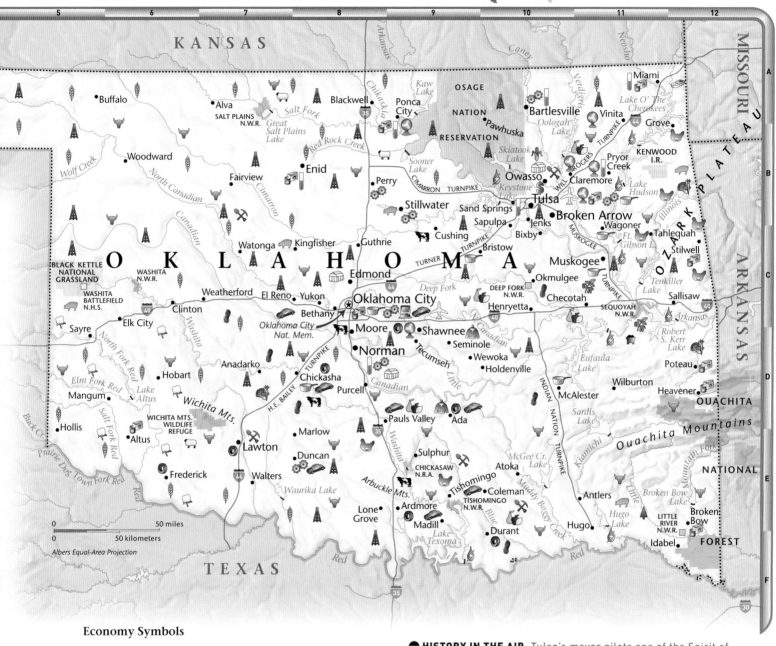

KANSAS

MISSOURI

TEXAS

OKLAHOMA

ARKANSAS

OZARK PLATEAU

OUACHITA

Ouachita Mountains

NATIONAL

FOREST

0   50 miles
0   50 kilometers
Albers Equal-Area Projection

Economy Symbols

Poultry/eggs		Coal	
Sheep		Oil/gas	
Hogs		Hydro-electricity	
Dairy cows/products		Machinery	
Beef cattle		Metal products	
Fruits		Motor vehicles/parts	
Vegetables		Rubber/plastics	
Peanuts		Chemistry	
Nursery stock		Food processing	
Wheat		Clothing/textiles	
Corn		Electrical equipment	
Soybeans		Computers/electronics	
Cotton		Aircraft/parts	
Stone/gravel/cement		Finance/insurance	
Mining			

HISTORY IN THE AIR. Tulsa's mayor pilots one of the Spirit of Tulsa Squadron's vintage PT-17 airplanes above the city. In 1990 the squadron became part of the Commemorative Air Force, a national organization committed to preserving aviation history by restoring and flying World War II aircraft.

THE BASICS

Statehood
December 29, 1845; 28th state

Total area (land and water)
268,596 sq mi (695,662 sq km)

Land area
261,232 sq mi (676,587 sq km)

Population
27,469,114

Capital
Austin
Population 931,830

Largest city
Houston
Population 2,296,224

Racial/ethnic groups
79.7% white; 12.5% African American; 4.7% Asian; 1.0% Native American; 38.8% Hispanic (any race)

Foreign born
16.3%

Urban population
84.7% (2010)

Population density
105.2 per sq mi (40.6 per sq km)

GEO WHIZ

The Fossil Rim Wildlife Research Center in the Texas Hill Country is breeding black rhinos and other endangered African animals. The center's goal is to reintroduce offspring into the wild in their native environment. Meanwhile, visitors get a chance to see a bit of Africa in Texas.

Six national flags have flown over Texas during the course of its history—Spanish, French, Mexican, Texan, Confederate, and American.

Texas has a long history of Bigfoot sightings. The ape-man creature was part of local Indian lore, and white settlers told stories about a wild woman along the Navidad River. Most sightings have been in the eastern part of the state near rivers or lakes.

Texas

Huge size, geographic diversity, and rich natural resources make Texas seem like its own country. In fact, it was an independent republic after throwing off Mexican rule in 1836. A famous battle in the fight for independence produced the Texan battle cry "Remember the Alamo!" In 1845 Texas was annexed by the U.S. Texas is the second largest state (behind Alaska) and the second most populous (behind California). It is a top producer of many agricultural products, including cattle, sheep, cotton, citrus fruits, vegetables, rice, and pecans. It also has huge oil and natural gas fields and is a manufacturing powerhouse. Pine forests cover East Texas, the wettest region. The Gulf Coast has swamps and extensive barrier islands. Grassy plains stretch across the northern panhandle, and the rolling Hill Country is famous for beautiful wildflowers. Mountains, valleys, and sandy plains sprawl across dry West Texas. The Rio Grande, sometimes barely a trickle, separates Texas and Mexico.

◐ **BLACK GOLD.** Workers plug an oil well. Discovery of oil early in the 20th century transformed life in Texas. Today, the state leads the U.S. in oil and natural gas production.

MOCKINGBIRD
BLUEBONNET

◐ **BORDERLAND RELIC.** Los Ebanos Ferry, which takes its name from a grove of ebony trees growing nearby, is the last remaining government-licensed, hand-pulled ferry on any U.S. border. The privately owned ferry near Mission, Texas, can carry three cars at a time across the Rio Grande.

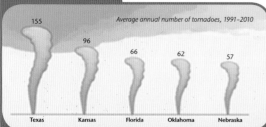

WHIRLING DANGER

Average annual number of tornadoes, 1991–2010

Texas	Kansas	Florida	Oklahoma	Nebraska
155	96	66	62	57

Every state in the U.S. has experienced a tornado, but Texas has more than any other. These violent storms occur when cold air collides with warm, moist air.

Economy Symbols

Fishing
Shellfish
Poultry/eggs
Sheep
Hogs
Dairy cows/products
Beef cattle
Fruits
Vegetables

Peanuts
Nursery stock
Wheat
Corn
Rice
Soybeans
Cotton
Timber/forest products
Stone/gravel/cement
Mining

Oil/gas
Hydro-electricity
Machinery
Metal manufacturing
Metal products
Motor vehicles/parts
Rubber/plastics
Chemistry
Food processing
Clothing/textiles
Leather products
Computers/electronic
Aircraft/parts
Tourism

OKLAHOMA
ARKANSAS
LOUISIANA
COAHUILA
NUEVO LEÓN
TAMAULIPAS
MEXICO

HIGH PLAINS

LLANO ESTACADO

TEXAS

Edwards Plateau

Hill Country

GULF OF MEXICO

KIOWA AND RITA BLANCA NATIONAL GRASSLAND
BLACK KETTLE N.G.
Perryton
Dumas
Borger
Pampa
LAKE MEREDITH N.R.A.
ALIBATES FLINT QUARRIES N.M.
McCLELLAN CREEK N.G.
Amarillo
Canyon
BUFFALO LAKE N.W.R.
PALO DURO CANYON S.P.
Hereford
Prairie Dog Town Fork Red
MULESHOE N.W.R.
Plainview
Childress
Levelland
Lubbock
Vernon
Burkburnett
Wichita Falls
Nocona
Denison
Sherman
Paris
CADDO NATIONAL GRASSLAND
Texarkana
President Eisenhower's birthplace
HAGERMAN N.W.R.
LYNDON B. JOHNSON N.G.
Brownfield
Lamesa
Snyder
Breckenridge
Mineral Wells
Denton
Plano
Sulphur Springs
Mt. Pleasant
Andrews
Big Spring
Sweetwater
Abilene
Stephenville
Glen Rose
Fort Worth
Irving
Arlington
Dallas
Garland
Marshall
Longview
Midland
Odessa
Coleman
Brownwood
Corsicana
Tyler
NECHES RIVER N.W.R.
Palestine
SABINE
Nacogdoches
NAT. FOR.
Toledo Bend Reservoir
Monahans
San Angelo
Gatesville
Waco
DAVY CROCKETT N.F.
Lufkin
ANGELINA N.F.
Sam Rayburn Res.
Fort Stockton
Brady
President Lyndon Johnson's birthplace
Copperas Cove
Killeen
Temple
Belton
Huntsville
ALABAMA & COUSHATTA I.R.
BIG THICKET NATIONAL PRESERVE
Ozona
BALCONES CANYONLANDS N.W.R.
Georgetown
Bryan
College Station
SAM HOUSTON N.F.
Conroe
TRINITY RIVER N.W.R.
Beaumont
Sonora
LYNDON B. JOHNSON N.H.P.
Round Rock
Austin
Brenham
Port Arthur
Kerrville
New Braunfels
San Marcos
ATTWATER PRAIRIE CHICKEN N.W.R.
Houston
Baytown
TEXAS POINT N.W.R.
McFADDIN N.W.R.
AMISTAD N.R.A.
San Antonio
Sugar Land
ANAHUAC N.W.R.
BIG BEND NATIONAL PARK
RIO GRANDE WILD AND SCENIC RIVER
Amistad Reservoir
Del Rio
Uvalde
SAN ANTONIO MISSIONS N.H.P.
Yoakum
El Campo
Galveston
BRAZORIA N.W.R.
Pearsall
Victoria
Bay City
Freeport
SAN BERNARD N.W.R.
Eagle Pass
Port Lavaca
BIG BOGGY N.W.R.
Carrizo Springs
Beeville
ARANSAS N.W.R.
Robstown
Rockport
Portland
Corpus Christi
Alice
Laredo
Kingsville
Falfurrias
PADRE ISLAND NATIONAL SEASHORE
Zapata
Falcon Reservoir
Rio Grande City
McAllen
SANTA ANA N.W.R.
LAGUNA ATASCOSA N.W.R.
Mission
Harlingen
LOWER RIO GRANDE VALLEY N.W.R.
PALO ALTO BATTLEFIELD N.H.S.
Brownsville

0   100 miles
0   100 kilometers
Albers Conic Equal-Area Projection

THE REGION

The West

PHYSICAL

Total area (land and water)
1,637,673 sq mi
(4,241,549 sq km)

Highest point
Denali (Mount McKinley), AK:
20,320 ft (6,194 m)

Lowest point
Death Valley, CA:
-282 ft (-86 m)

Longest rivers
Missouri, Yukon,
Rio Grande, Colorado

Largest lakes
Great Salt, Iliamna,
Becharof

Vegetation
Needleleaf, broadleaf, and mixed
forest; grassland; desert; tundra
(Alaska); tropical (Hawai'i)

Climate
Mild along the coast, with warm
summers and mild winters; semiarid
to arid inland; polar in parts of
Alaska; tropical in Hawai'i

POLITICAL

Total population
67,131,505

States (11):
Alaska, California, Colorado, Hawai'i,
Idaho, Montana, Nevada, Oregon, Utah,
Washington, Wyoming

Largest state
Alaska: 665,384 sq mi
(1,723,337 sq km)

Smallest state
Hawai'i: 10,932 sq mi (28,311 sq km)

Most populous state
California: 39,144,818

Least populous state
Wyoming: 586,107

Largest city proper
Los Angeles, CA: 3,971,883

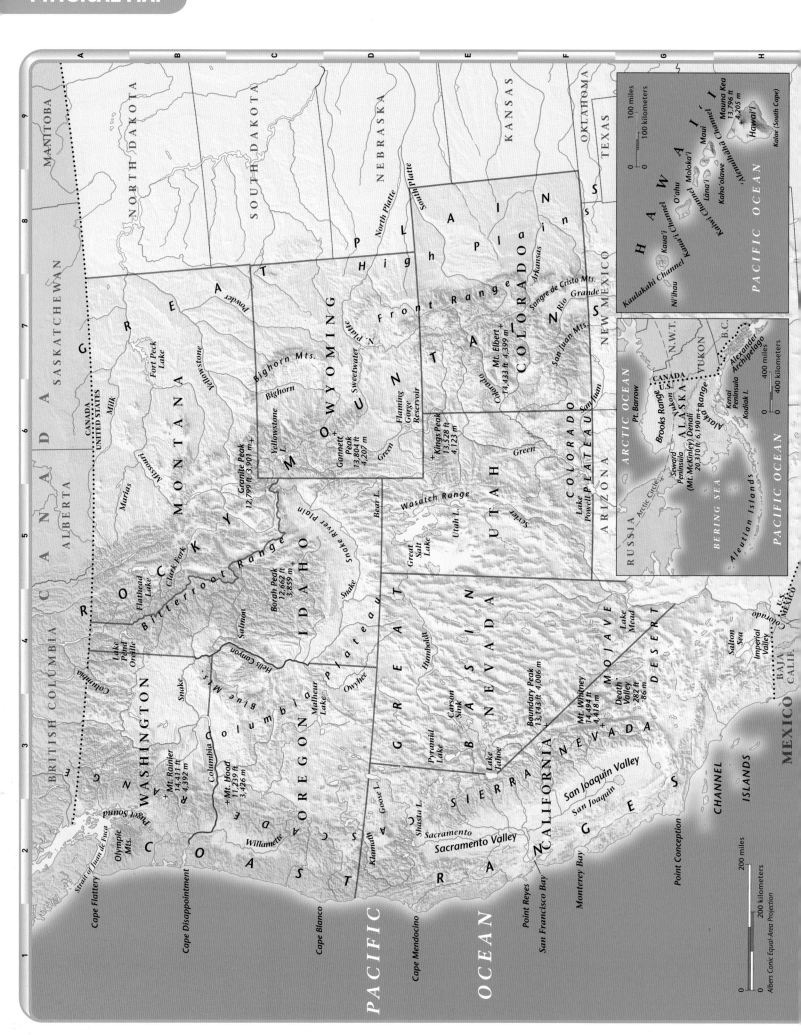

PACIFIC OCEAN

HAWAI'I

100 miles
100 kilometers

Ni'ihau Kaua'i O'ahu Honolulu Moloka'i Maui Lāna'i Kaho'olawe Hilo Hawai'i

ALASKA

ARCTIC OCEAN
Arctic Circle
Barrow
Prudhoe Bay
RUSSIA
BERING SEA
Nome
Yukon
Fairbanks
Koyukuk
Anchorage
Kodiak I.
Aleutian Islands
PACIFIC OCEAN
CANADA
U.S.
N.W.T.
YUKON
B.C.
Juneau

400 miles
400 kilometers

CANADA

MANITOBA
SASKATCHEWAN
ALBERTA
BRITISH COLUMBIA
CANADA
UNITED STATES

NORTH DAKOTA
SOUTH DAKOTA
NEBRASKA
KANSAS
OKLAHOMA
TEXAS
NEW MEXICO

MONTANA
Great Falls
Missoula
Helena
Butte
Bozeman
Billings
Cody

Milk
Missouri
Marias
Yellowstone
Powder
Bighorn

WYOMING
Gillette
Casper
Cheyenne
Laramie
Rock Springs

Sweetwater
Green
North Platte
South Platte

COLORADO
Fort Collins
Boulder
Denver
Colorado Springs
Pueblo
Grand Junction

Colorado
Arkansas
Rio Grande
San Juan
Green

IDAHO
Coeur d'Alene
Lewiston
Boise
Idaho Falls
Pocatello
Twin Falls

Snake
Salmon
Owyhee
Humboldt

UTAH
Logan
Ogden
Salt Lake City
Provo
St. George

Great Salt Lake
Sevier

WASHINGTON
Bellingham
Seattle
Tacoma
Olympia
Spokane
Yakima
Vancouver
Walla Walla

Columbia
Snake

OREGON
Portland
Salem
Eugene
Bend
Pendleton
Medford
Klamath Falls

Klamath
Columbia

NEVADA
Elko
Reno
Carson City
Las Vegas
Henderson

ARIZONA

CALIFORNIA
Eureka
Redding
Santa Rosa
Sacramento
Stockton
San Francisco
Oakland
San Jose
Salinas
Fresno
Bakersfield
San Bernardino
Riverside
Los Angeles
Long Beach
Oceanside
San Diego

Sacramento
San Joaquin

BAJA CALIF.
MEXICO
SONORA
U.S.
MEXICO
Colorado

PACIFIC OCEAN

200 miles
200 kilometers

Albers Conic Equal-Area Projection

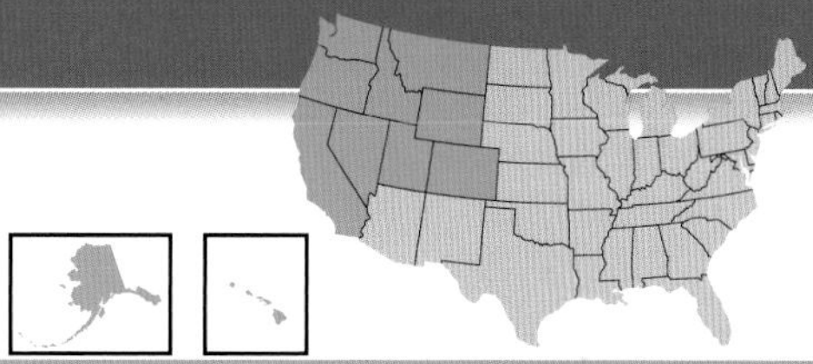

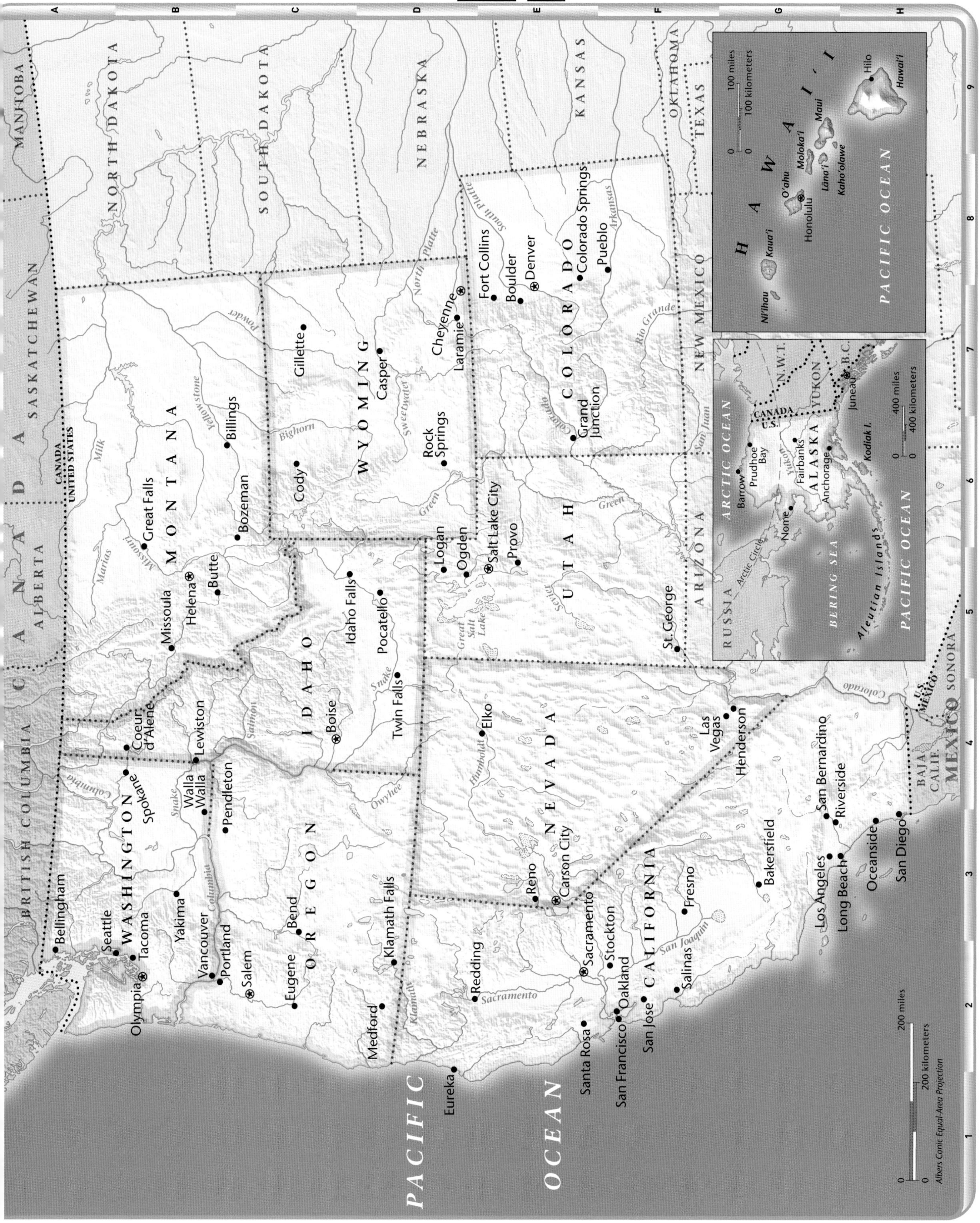

◗ **OLD AND NEW.** A cable car carries passengers in San Francisco. In the background, modern buildings, including the Transamerica Pyramid, rise above older neighborhoods in this earthquake-prone city.

The West

THE HIGH FRONTIER

T he western states, which make up almost half of the country's land area, have diverse landscapes and climates, ranging from the frozen heights of Denali, in Alaska, to the desolation of Death Valley, in California, and the lush, tropical islands of Hawai'i. More than half the region's population lives in California, and the Los Angeles metropolitan area is second in population only to that of New York City. Yet many parts of the region are sparsely populated, and much of the land is set aside as parkland and military bases. The region also faces many natural hazards—earthquakes, landslides, wildfires, and even volcanic eruptions.

◗ **NORTHERN GIANT.**
Denali, a name meaning "High One" in the Athabascan language, rises more than 20,000 feet (6,100 m) in the Alaska Range. Also known as Mount McKinley, it is North America's highest peak. The same tectonic forces that trigger earthquakes in Alaska are slowly pushing this huge block of granite ever higher.

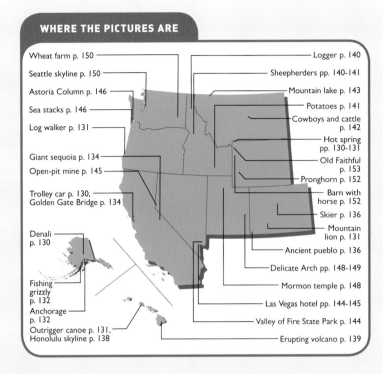

WHERE THE PICTURES ARE

Wheat farm p. 150
Seattle skyline p. 150
Astoria Column p. 146
Sea stacks p. 146
Log walker p. 131
Giant sequoia p. 134
Open-pit mine p. 145
Trolley car p. 130,
Golden Gate Bridge p. 134
Denali p. 130
Fishing grizzly p. 132
Anchorage p. 132
Outrigger canoe p. 131,
Honolulu skyline p. 138

Logger p. 140
Sheepherders pp. 140-141
Mountain lake p. 143
Potatoes p. 141
Cowboys and cattle p. 142
Hot spring pp. 130-131
Old Faithful p. 153
Pronghorn p. 152
Barn with horse p. 152
Skier p. 136
Mountain lion p. 131
Ancient pueblo p. 136
Delicate Arch pp. 148-149
Mormon temple p. 148
Las Vegas hotel pp. 144-145
Valley of Fire State Park p. 144
Erupting volcano p. 139

⬤ **ELUSIVE PREDATOR.** Known by many names, including cougar and mountain lion, these big cats are found mainly in remote mountainous areas of the West, where they hunt deer and smaller animals.

◐ **STEAMY BATH.** Colorful, mineral-rich hot springs are just one geothermal feature of Yellowstone National Park. Runoff from rain and snowmelt seeps into cracks in the ground, sinking to a depth of 10,000 feet (3,050 m), where it is heated by molten rock before rising back to the surface.

⬤ **BALANCING ACT.** For many years rivers have been used to move logs from forest to market, taking advantage of the buoyancy of logs and the power of moving water. A logger stands on a floating log raft in Coos Bay, Oregon.

⬤ **TRADITIONAL SAILING CRAFT.** A Hawaiian outrigger canoe on Waikiki Beach promises fun in the surf for visitors to the 50th state. An important part of Polynesian culture, the canoes were once used to travel from island to island.

THE LAST FRONTIER STATE:
ALASKA

THE BASICS

Statehood
January 3, 1959; 49th state

Total area (land and water)
665,384 sq mi
(1,723,337 sq km)

Land area
570,641 sq mi
(1,477,953 sq km)

Population
738,432

Capital
Juneau
Population 32,406 (2014)

Largest city
Anchorage
Population 110,229

Racial/ethnic groups
66.5% white; 3.9% African
American; 6.3% Asian; 14.8%
Native American; 7.0% Hispanic
(any race)

Foreign born
7.0%

Urban population
66.0% (2010)

Population density
1.3 per sq mi (0.5 per sq km)

GEO WHIZ

During the summer, migrating
humpback whales work together
in Alaskan waters to catch fish.
While swimming in circles, the
whales blow bubbles that form
a net around schools of herring.
Each whale can eat hundreds of
fish in one gulp.

Climate change and population
growth are changing the route
of the famous Iditarod sled-dog
race. Since 2002, lack of snow in
Wasilla has forced the starting
point for the competition first
to Willow and then as far north
as Fairbanks.

The Tongass National Forest is
the largest national forest in
the United States.

Alaska

Alaska—from Alyeska, an Aleut word meaning "great land"—was purchased by the U.S. from Russia in 1867 for just two cents an acre. Many people thought it was a bad investment, but it soon paid off when gold was discovered, and again when major petroleum deposits were discovered in 1968. Today, an 800-mile (1,287-km)-long pipeline links North Slope oil fields to the ice-free port at Valdez, but critics worry about the long-term environmental impact. Everything is big in Alaska. It is the largest state, with one-sixth of the country's land area; it has the highest peak in the United States, Denali (Mount McKinley); and the largest earthquake ever recorded in the United States—a 9.2 magnitude—occurred there in 1964. It is first in forestland, a leading source of seafood, and a major oil producer. Alaska's population has a higher percentage of native people than that of any other state.

🍴 **TIME FOR LUNCH.**
A grizzly bear wades into
the rushing waters of
Brooks Falls, in Katmai
National Park, to catch
a leaping salmon.

FORGET-ME-NOT
WILLOW PTARMIGAN

◖ **NORTHERN METROPOLIS.** Anchorage, established in
1915 as a construction port for the Alaska Railroad, sits
in the shadow of the snow-covered Chugach Mountains.

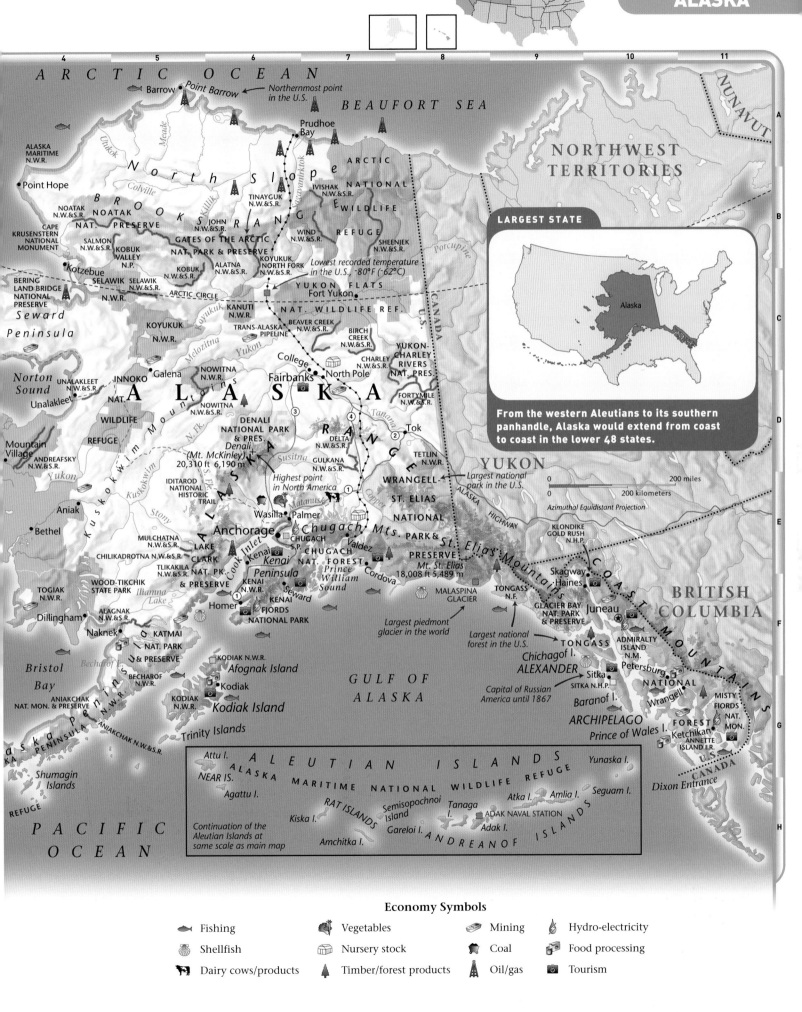

ARCTIC OCEAN

BEAUFORT SEA

Barrow • Point Barrow ← Northernmost point in the U.S.

Prudhoe Bay

NORTHWEST TERRITORIES

NUNAVUT

North Slope

ARCTIC NATIONAL WILDLIFE REFUGE

Point Hope

ALASKA MARITIME N.W.R.

Colville

Utukok

Meade

B R O O K S R A N G E

NOATAK NATIONAL PRESERVE

NOATAK N.W.&S.R.

TINAYGUK N.W.&S.R.

IVISHAK N.W.&S.R.

GATES OF THE ARCTIC NAT. PARK & PRESERVE

JOHN N.W.&S.R.

WIND N.W.&S.R.

SHEENJEK N.W.&S.R.

CAPE KRUSENSTERN NATIONAL MONUMENT

SALMON N.W.&S.R.

KOBUK VALLEY N.P.

ALATNA N.W.&S.R.

KOYUKUK, NORTH FORK N.W.&S.R.

Lowest recorded temperature in the U.S., -80°F (-62°C)

Porcupine

CANADA U.S.

Kotzebue

KOBUK N.W.&S.R.

SELAWIK SELAWIK N.W.&S.R.

ARCTIC CIRCLE

BERING LAND BRIDGE NATIONAL PRESERVE

Seward Peninsula

Norton Sound

UNALAKLEET N.W.&S.R.

Unalakleet

Mountain Village

Aniak

Bethel

KANUTI N.W.R.

KOYUKUK N.W.R.

INNOKO NAT. WILDLIFE REFUGE

Galena

NOWITNA N.W.R.

NOWITNA N.W.&S.R.

Melozitna

Yukon

ANDREAFSKY N.W.&S.R.

Yukon

A L A S K A

Fairbanks

College

North Pole

BEAVER CREEK N.W.&S.R.

BIRCH CREEK N.W.&S.R.

CHARLEY N.W.&S.R.

YUKON FLATS NAT. WILDLIFE REF.

Fort Yukon

YUKON-CHARLEY RIVERS NAT. PRES.

FORTYMILE N.W.&S.R.

TRANS-ALASKA PIPELINE

Kuskokwim Mountains

DENALI NATIONAL PARK & PRES.

Denali (Mt. McKinley) 20,310 ft 6,190 m

Highest point in North America

IDITAROD NATIONAL HISTORIC TRAIL

MULCHATNA N.W.&S.R.

CHILIKADROTNA N.W.&S.R.

TLIKAKILA N.W.&S.R.

LAKE CLARK NAT. PK. & PRESERVE

KENAI N.W.R.

③

④

② Tok

TETLIN N.W.R.

WRANGELL-ST. ELIAS NATIONAL PARK & PRESERVE

Mt. St. Elias 18,008 ft 5,489 m

Largest national park in the U.S.

YUKON

ALASKA HIGHWAY

A L A S K A R A N G E

DELTA N.W.&S.R.

GULKANA N.W.&S.R.

Tanana

Susitna

①

Wasilla • Palmer

Anchorage

CHUGACH S.P.

Cook Inlet

Kenai

Kenai Peninsula

KENAI FJORDS NATIONAL PARK

Homer

①

Seward

CHUGACH NAT. FOREST

Chugach Mts.

Valdez

Cordova

Prince William Sound

Copper

MALASPINA GLACIER

Largest piedmont glacier in the world

St. Elias Mountains

TONGASS N.F.

Largest national forest in the U.S.

KLONDIKE GOLD RUSH N.H.P.

Skagway

Haines

GLACIER BAY NAT. PARK & PRESERVE

Juneau ⍟

COAST MOUNTAINS

BRITISH COLUMBIA

TONGASS

Chichagof I.

ALEXANDER

ADMIRALTY ISLAND N.M.

Petersburg

NATIONAL

Sitka

SITKA N.H.P.

Capital of Russian America until 1867

Baranof I.

ARCHIPELAGO

Prince of Wales I.

Wrangell

FOREST

MISTY FIORDS NAT. MON.

Ketchikan

ANNETTE ISLAND I.R.

U.S. CANADA

Dixon Entrance

GULF OF ALASKA

TOGIAK N.W.R.

WOOD-TIKCHIK STATE PARK

ALAGNAK N.W.&S.R.

Dillingham

Iliamna Lake

Naknek

KATMAI NAT. PARK & PRESERVE

Becharof L.

BECHAROF N.W.R.

Bristol Bay

ANIAKCHAK NAT. MON. & PRESERVE

ANIAKCHAK N.W.&S.R.

KODIAK N.W.R.

Afognak Island

KODIAK N.W.R.

Kodiak

Kodiak Island

Trinity Islands

Alaska Peninsula

Shumagin Islands

REFUGE

PACIFIC OCEAN

Attu I.

NEAR IS.

Agattu I.

A L E U T I A N   I S L A N D S

ALASKA MARITIME NATIONAL WILDLIFE REFUGE

Yunaska I.

RAT ISLANDS

Kiska I.

Amchitka I.

Semisopochnoi Island

Garelol I.

Tanaga I.

Adak I.

ADAK NAVAL STATION

Atka I.

Amlia I.

Seguam I.

A N D R E A N O F   I S L A N D S

Continuation of the Aleutian Islands at same scale as main map

Economy Symbols

Fishing
Shellfish
Dairy cows/products

Vegetables
Nursery stock
Timber/forest products

Mining
Coal
Oil/gas

Hydro-electricity
Food processing
Tourism

CALIFORNIA REPUBLIC

THE BASICS

Statehood
September 9, 1850; 31st state

Total area (land and water)
163,695 sq mi (423,967 sq km)

Land area
155,779 sq mi (403,466 sq km)

Population
39,144,818

Capital
Sacramento
Population 490,712

Largest city
Los Angeles
Population 3,971,883

Racial/ethnic groups
72.9% white; 6.5% African American; 14.7% Asian; 1.7% Native American; 38.8% Hispanic (any race)

Foreign born
27.0%

Urban population
95.0% (2010)

Population density
251.3 per sq mi (97.0 per sq km)

GEO WHIZ

Every December, one of the largest gatherings of northern elephant seals in the world converges on the beaches of Año Nuevo State Reserve, south of San Francisco, to rest, mate, and give birth.

The Monterey Bay Aquarium has been working to save endangered sea otters for more than 20 years. Rescued animals that cannot be rehabilitated for re-release into the wild find a permanent home here.

Castroville, known as the Artichoke Capital of the World, crowned future movie legend Marilyn Monroe its first ever artichoke queen in 1947.

California

The coast of what is now California was visited by Spanish and English explorers in the mid-1500s, but colonization did not begin until 1769 when the first of 21 Spanish missions was established in San Diego. The missions, built to bring Christianity to the many native people living in the area, eventually extended up the coast as far as Sonoma along a road known as El Camino Real. The United States gained control of California in 1847, following a war with Mexico. The next year, gold was discovered near Sutter's Mill, triggering a gold rush and migration from the eastern United States and around the world. Today, California is the most populous state, and its economy ranks above that of most of the world's countries.

It is a major source of fruits, nuts, and vegetables, accounting for more than half of the U.S. output. The state is an industrial leader, producing jet aircraft, ships, and high-tech equipment. It is also a center for the entertainment industry.

ENGINEERING WONDER. Stretching more than a mile (1.6 km) across the entrance to San Francisco Bay, the Golden Gate Bridge opened to traffic in 1937. The bridge is painted vermilion orange, a color chosen in part because it is visible in fog.

**CALIFORNIA QUAIL
GOLDEN POPPY**

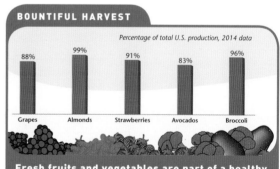

BOUNTIFUL HARVEST

Percentage of total U.S. production, 2014 data

Grapes	Almonds	Strawberries	Avocados	Broccoli
88%	99%	91%	83%	96%

Fresh fruits and vegetables are part of a healthy diet. California leads the country in the overall production of these beneficial crops.

FOREST GIANT. Sequoias in Yosemite National Park's Mariposa Grove exceed 200 feet (61 m), making them the world's tallest trees. The trees, some of which are 3,000 years old, grow in isolated groves on the western slopes of the Sierra Nevada.

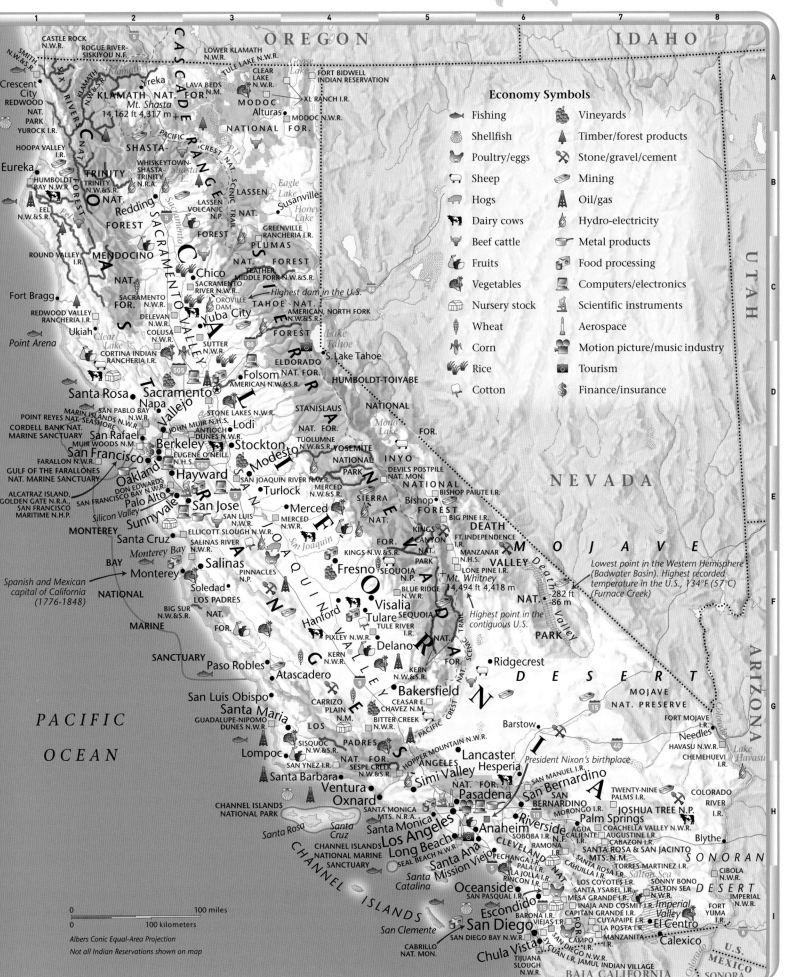

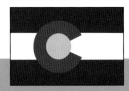

THE BASICS

Statehood
August 1, 1876; 38th state

Total area (land and water)
104,094 sq mi (269,601 sq km)

Land area
103,642 sq mi (268,431 sq km)

Population
5,456,574

Capital
Denver
Population 682,545

Largest city
Denver
Population 682,545

Racial/ethnic groups
87.5% white; 4.5% African American; 3.2% Asian; 1.6% Native American; 21.3% Hispanic (any race)

Foreign born
9.7%

Urban population
86.2% (2010)

Population density
52.7 per sq mi (20.3 per sq km)

GEO WHIZ

The Black Canyon of the Gunnison is one of the newest national parks in the Rockies. As it flows through the canyon, the Gunnison River drops an average of 95 feet (29 m) per mile—one of the steepest descents in North America. The craggy rock walls are a mecca for rock climbers.

Colorado's lynx population is making a comeback, thanks to a program that releases wild cats captured in Canada into Colorado's southern Rockies. Since 1999 when the program began, more than 200 cats have been released, and at least 141 lynx kittens have been born.

Colorado

Indians were the earliest inhabitants of present-day Colorado. Some were cliff dwellers; others were plains dwellers. Spanish explorers arrived in Colorado in 1541. In 1803 eastern Colorado became U.S. territory as part of the Louisiana Purchase. Gold was discovered in 1858, and thousands were attracted by the prospect of quick wealth. The sudden jump in population led to conflict with native Cheyenne and Arapaho over control of the land, but the settlers prevailed. Completion of the transcontinental railroad in 1869 helped link Colorado to the eastern states and opened its

**COLUMBINE
LARK BUNTING**

doors for growth. Cattle ranching and farming developed on the High Plains of eastern Colorado, while mining was the focus in the mountainous western part of the state. Mining is still important in Colorado, but the focus has shifted to energy resources—oil, natural gas, and coal. Agriculture is also a major source of income, with cattle accounting for half of farm income. And Colorado's majestic mountains attract thousands of tourists each year.

🜨 **THRILLING SPORT.**
Colorado's snow-covered mountains attract winter sports enthusiasts from near and far. In the past, skis were used by gold prospectors. Today, skiing and snowboarding are big moneymakers in the state's recreation and tourism industry.

◖ **ANCIENT CULTURE.** Ancestral Puebloans lived from about A.D. 600 to A.D. 1300 in the canyons that today are a part of Mesa Verde National Park. More than 600 stone structures were built on protected cliffs of the canyon walls; others were located on mesas. These dwellings hold many clues to a past way of life.

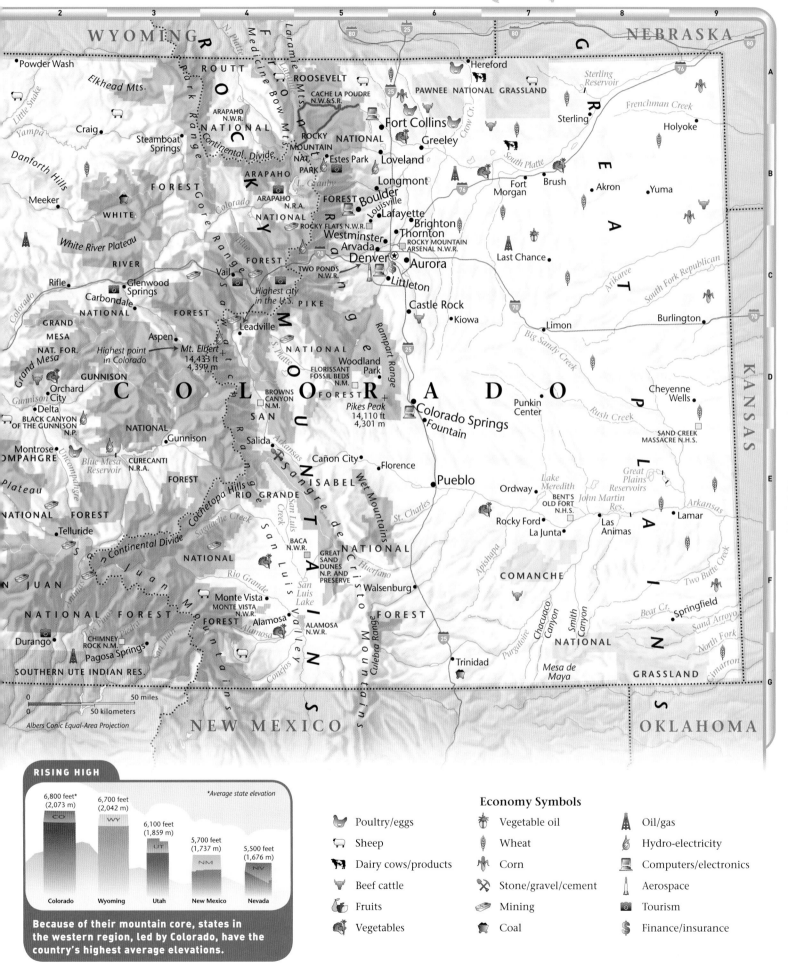

WYOMING

NEBRASKA

Powder Wash
Elkhead Mts.
Little Snake
Yampa
Craig
Danforth Hills
Meeker
ROUTT
NATIONAL
ROOSEVELT
CACHE LA POUDRE N.W.&S.R.
ROCKY MOUNTAIN NAT. PARK
Estes Park
L. Granby
ARAPAHO N.W.R.
ARAPAHO NATIONAL FOREST
Fort Collins
Greeley
Loveland
Longmont
Boulder
Louisville
Lafayette
Brighton
Thornton
Westminster
Arvada
Denver
Aurora
Littleton
Hereford
PAWNEE NATIONAL GRASSLAND
Sterling Reservoir
Sterling
Holyoke
Frenchman Creek
Fort Morgan
Brush
Akron
Yuma
South Platte
Crow Cr.
Last Chance
ROCKY MOUNTAIN ARSENAL N.W.R.
Steamboat Springs
Continental Divide
ARAPAHO N.R.A.
ROCKY FLATS N.W.R.
TWO PONDS N.W.R.
Highest city in the U.S.
WHITE
White River Plateau
RIVER
Rifle
Glenwood Springs
Carbondale
NATIONAL FOREST
Vail
Aspen
Leadville
PIKE
Mt. Elbert 14,433 ft 4,399 m
Highest point in Colorado
GRAND MESA
NAT. FOR.
Orchard City
Delta
BLACK CANYON OF THE GUNNISON N.P.
Montrose
UNCOMPAHGRE
Plateau
NATIONAL FOREST
Telluride
Durango
CHIMNEY ROCK N.M.
Pagosa Springs
SOUTHERN UTE INDIAN RES.
GUNNISON
Gunnison
Blue Mesa Reservoir
CURECANTI N.R.A.
NATIONAL FOREST
SAN
Salida
Cañon City
Florence
NATIONAL FOREST
BROWNS CANYON N.M.
FLORISSANT FOSSIL BEDS N.M.
Woodland Park
Pikes Peak 14,110 ft 4,301 m
Colorado Springs
Fountain
Castle Rock
Kiowa
Limon
Big Sandy Creek
Cheyenne Wells
Burlington
Punkin Center
Rush Creek
COLORADO
Gunnison
RIO GRANDE
Cochetopa Hills
Saguache Creek
Continental Divide
ISABEL
Wet Mountains
St. Charles
Pueblo
Ordway
Lake Meredith
BENT'S OLD FORT N.H.S.
Great Plains Reservoirs
John Martin Res.
Arkansas
Lamar
Rocky Ford
La Junta
Las Animas
SAND CREEK MASSACRE N.H.S.
SAN JUAN NATIONAL FOREST
SAN LUIS VALLEY
Monte Vista
MONTE VISTA N.W.R.
Alamosa
ALAMOSA N.W.R.
San Luis Lake
BACA N.W.R.
GREAT SAND DUNES N.P. AND PRESERVE
San Luis
NATIONAL
Sangre de Cristo Mountains
Huerfano
Walsenburg
FOREST
COMANCHE
Apishapa
Springfield
Bear Cr.
Sand Arroyo
NATIONAL GRASSLAND
Rio Grande
Conejos
Culebra Range
Trinidad
Mesa de Maya
Purgatoire
Chacuaco Canyon
Smith Canyon
Two Butte Creek
North Fork
Cimarron

0   50 miles
0   50 kilometers
Albers Conic Equal-Area Projection

NEW MEXICO   **OKLAHOMA**

KANSAS

GREAT PLAINS

RISING HIGH

6,800 feet* (2,073 m)	6,700 feet (2,042 m)	6,100 feet (1,859 m)	5,700 feet (1,737 m)	5,500 feet (1,676 m)
CO	WY	UT	NM	NV
Colorado	Wyoming	Utah	New Mexico	Nevada

*Average state elevation

Because of their mountain core, states in the western region, led by Colorado, have the country's highest average elevations.

Economy Symbols

Poultry/eggs
Sheep
Dairy cows/products
Beef cattle
Fruits
Vegetables

Vegetable oil
Wheat
Corn
Stone/gravel/cement
Mining
Coal

Oil/gas
Hydro-electricity
Computers/electronics
Aerospace
Tourism
Finance/insurance

THE BASICS

Statehood
August 21, 1959; 50th state

Total area (land and water)
10,932 sq mi (28,313 sq km)

Land area
6,423 sq mi (16,635 sq km)

Population
1,431,603

Capital
Honolulu
Population 352,769

Largest city
Honolulu
Population 352,769

Racial/ethnic groups
26.7% white; 2.6% African American; 37.3% Asian; 9.9% Pacific Islander; 10.4% Hispanic (any race)

Foreign born
17.9%

Urban population
91.9% (2010)

Population density
222.9 per sq mi (86.1 per sq km)

GEO WHIZ

Hawai'i is more than 2,300 miles (3,700 km) from California, 3,850 miles (6,196 km) from Japan, and 4,900 miles (7,886 km) from China, making it Earth's most isolated population center.

Everywhere else in the world caterpillars feed on plants. In Hawai'i there are 20 species that eat meat. Scientists have recorded the world's only known carnivorous caterpillars munching on ants.

You can ski two different ways on the same day in Hawai'i: on water at the beach and on snow on the slopes of Mauna Kea, a 13,796-foot (4,205-m)-high volcano on the Big Island.

HIBISCUS
HAWAIIAN GOOSE (NENE)

Hawai'i

Some 1,500 years ago Polynesians traveling in large canoes arrived from the south to settle the volcanic islands that make up Hawai'i. In 1778 Captain James Cook claimed the islands for Britain, and soon Hawai'i became a center of the whaling industry and a major producer of sugarcane. The spread of sugarcane plantations led to the importation of workers from Asia. Hawai'i became a U.S. territory in 1900. Naval installations, established as fueling depots and to protect U.S. interests in the Pacific, were attacked by the Japanese in 1941, an act that officially brought the United States into World War II. In 1959 Hawai'i became the 50th state. Tourism, agriculture, and the military, with bases centered on O'ahu's Pearl Harbor, are the cornerstone of Hawai'i's economy today. Jet airline service makes the state accessible to tourists from both the mainland United States and Asia as well as from Australia and New Zealand. Hawai'i is still a major producer of sugarcane, along with nursery products and pineapples.

ISLAND PARADISE. Hotels line Waikiki Beach, the center of Honolulu's tourist industry. Thousands of visitors flock to the islands each year to enjoy the warm climate, sandy beaches, and rich, multicultural heritage of Hawai'i.

One of the world's rainiest spots

KAUA'I

Princeville — KILAUEA POINT N.W.R.
HANALEI N.W.R.
Wai'ale'ale 5,148 ft 1,569 m
Kapa'a
Lehua I.
Hanamā'ulu
Kekaha — Līhu'e
HULEIA N.W.R.
Pu'uwai — Kalāheo
NI'IHAU
Kaulakahi Channel

Kure Atoll
Midway Islands
MIDWAY ATOLL N.W.R.
Pearl and Hermes Atoll
NORTHWESTERN HAW
Lisianski I.
Laysan I.
Maro Reef

0 — 400 miles
0 — 400 kilometers
Oblique Mercator Projection

DANGER FROM BELOW

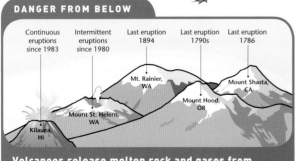

Continuous eruptions since 1983
Intermittent eruptions since 1980
Last eruption 1894
Last eruption 1790s
Last eruption 1786

Mt. Rainier, WA
Mount St. Helens, WA
Mount Hood, OR
Mount Shasta, CA
Kilauea, HI

Volcanoes release molten rock and gases from beneath Earth's crust, often with explosive force that can put people and property at great risk.

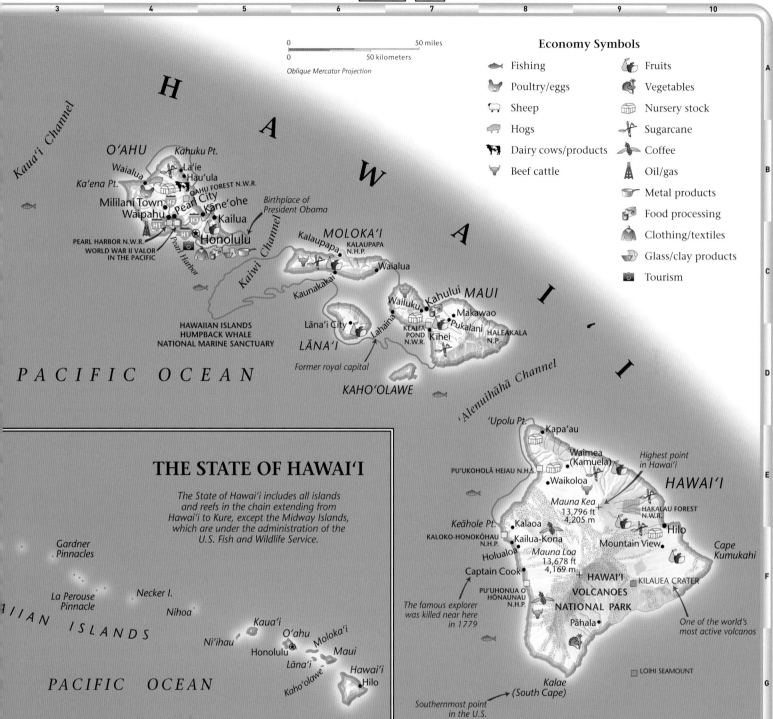

Economy Symbols

- Fishing
- Poultry/eggs
- Sheep
- Hogs
- Dairy cows/products
- Beef cattle
- Fruits
- Vegetables
- Nursery stock
- Sugarcane
- Coffee
- Oil/gas
- Metal products
- Food processing
- Clothing/textiles
- Glass/clay products
- Tourism

3 4 5 6 7 8 9 10

0 50 miles
0 50 kilometers
Oblique Mercator Projection

H A W A I I

O'AHU
Kahuku Pt.
Waialua
La'ie
Hau'ula
Ka'ena Pt.
OAHU FOREST N.W.R.
Mililani Town
Pearl City
Kāne'ohe
Waipahu
H2
Kailua
H3
H1
PEARL HARBOR N.W.R.
WORLD WAR II VALOR
IN THE PACIFIC
Honolulu
Pearl Harbor
Birthplace of
President Obama
Kaiwi Channel
Kaua'i Channel

MOLOKA'I
Kalaupapa
KALAUPAPA
N.H.P.
Waialua
Kaunakakai

HAWAIIAN ISLANDS
HUMPBACK WHALE
NATIONAL MARINE SANCTUARY

PACIFIC OCEAN

Lāna'i City
LĀNA'I
Lahaina
Former royal capital
Wailuku
Kahului
MAUI
Makawao
Pukalani
KEALIA
POND
N.W.R.
Kihei
HALEAKALA
N.P.

KAHO'OLAWE

'Alenuihāhā Channel

'Upolu Pt.
Kapa'au
Waimea
(Kamuela)
Highest point
in Hawai'i
PU'UKOHOLĀ HEIAU N.H.S.
Waikoloa
HAKALAU FOREST
N.W.R.
HAWAI'I
Keāhole Pt.
Kalaoa
Mauna Kea
13,796 ft
4,205 m
KALOKO-HONOKŌHAU
N.H.P.
Kailua-Kona
Hilo
Holualoa
Mountain View
Mauna Loa
13,678 ft
4,169 m
Captain Cook
Cape
Kumukahi
PU'UHONUA O
HŌNAUNAU
N.H.P.
The famous explorer
was killed near here
in 1779
**HAWAI'I
VOLCANOES
NATIONAL PARK**
KILAUEA CRATER
Pāhala
One of the world's
most active volcanos
LOIHI SEAMOUNT
Kalae
(South Cape)
Southernmost point
in the U.S.

THE STATE OF HAWAI'I

The State of Hawai'i includes all islands
and reefs in the chain extending from
Hawai'i to Kure, except the Midway Islands,
which are under the administration of the
U.S. Fish and Wildlife Service.

Gardner
Pinnacles
La Perouse
Pinnacle
Necker I.
Nihoa
HAWAIIAN ISLANDS
Kaua'i
Ni'ihau
O'ahu
Moloka'i
Honolulu
Maui
Lāna'i
Kaho'olawe
Hawai'i
Hilo

PACIFIC OCEAN

FIERY CREATION. Hawai'i is the fastest-
growing state in the U.S.—not in people,
but in land. Active volcanoes are constantly
creating new land as lava continues to flow.
The Pu'u 'O'o vent on Kilauea has added
more than 568 acres (230 ha) of new land
since it began erupting in 1983.

THE BASICS

Statehood
July 3, 1890; 43rd state

Total area (land and water)
83,569 sq mi (216,443 sq km)

Land area
82,643 sq mi (214,045 sq km)

Population
1,654,930

Capital
Boise
Population 218,281

Largest city
Boise
Population 218,281

Racial/ethnic groups
93.4% white; 0.8% African American; 1.5% Asian; 1.7% Native American; 12.2% Hispanic (any race)

Foreign born
5.9%

Urban population
70.6% (2010)

Population density
20.0 per sq mi (7.7 per sq km)

GEO WHIZ

Before the last ice age, woolly rhinos, giant ground sloths, and other huge mammals roamed what is now Idaho. Fossils of these prehistoric creatures are on display at the Museum of Idaho, in Idaho Falls.

Wood duck chicks born in Idaho and other Rocky Mountain states undergo an amazing rite of passage the day after they are born. To eat, they have to jump as much as 60 feet (18 m) from their tree-hole nest to the water below, where their mom awaits.

In preparation for their mission to the moon, Apollo astronauts visited Craters of the Moon National Monument to study its volcanic geology and experience its harsh environment.

Idaho

Some of the earliest Native American sites in what is now Idaho date back 10,000 to 12,000 years. In the 18th and early 19th centuries, contact between native people and Europeans brought not only trade and cultural change but also diseases that wiped out many native groups.

⬤ **WOOLLY RUSH HOUR.** Sheep fill a roadway in Idaho's Salmon River Valley. The herds move twice a year. In the spring they migrate north to mountain pastures. In the fall they return to the Snake River plains in the south.

Present-day Idaho was part of the 1803 Louisiana Purchase, and in 1805 it was explored during the famous Lewis and Clark expedition. In 1843 wagons crossed into Idaho on the Oregon Trail. The arrival of white settlers brought conflict with the Indians, which continued until 1890 when Idaho became a state. Today, farming plays an important role in Idaho's economy. Almost half of the land is planted with crops, especially wheat, sugar beets, barley, and potatoes. The state supports the use of alternative sources of energy, such as geothermal, wind, and biomass, including ethanol. The addition of manufacturing and high-tech industries has diversified the economy. The state's rugged natural beauty attracts tourists year-round.

SYRINGA (MOCK ORANGE)
MOUNTAIN BLUEBIRD

ANCIENT STAPLE FOOD

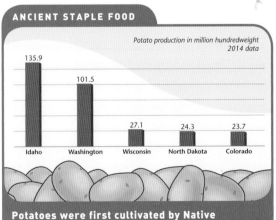

Potato production in million hundredweight
2014 data

135.9	101.5	27.1	24.3	23.7
Idaho	Washington	Wisconsin	North Dakota	Colorado

Potatoes were first cultivated by Native Americans in the mountains of South America. Today, Idaho leads in U.S. potato production.

⬤ **TIMBER!** More than 60 percent of Idaho's land area is tree-covered, much of it in national forests. Lumber and paper products, most of which are sold to other states, are important to the state economy.

ROLLING SPUDS. Growing more than 30 varieties of potatoes, Idaho leads the country in production of this staple food crop. About 60 percent of all potatoes grown in the state end up as french fries. Much of the rest goes to fresh-food markets and for making chips.

Economy Symbols

- Fishing
- Poultry/eggs
- Sheep
- Dairy cows/products
- Beef cattle
- Fruits
- Vegetables
- Vegetable oil
- Nursery stock
- Wheat
- Corn
- Vineyards
- Timber/forest products
- Furniture
- Mining
- Hydro-electricity
- Metal products
- Chemistry
- Food processing
- Computers/electronics
- Tourism

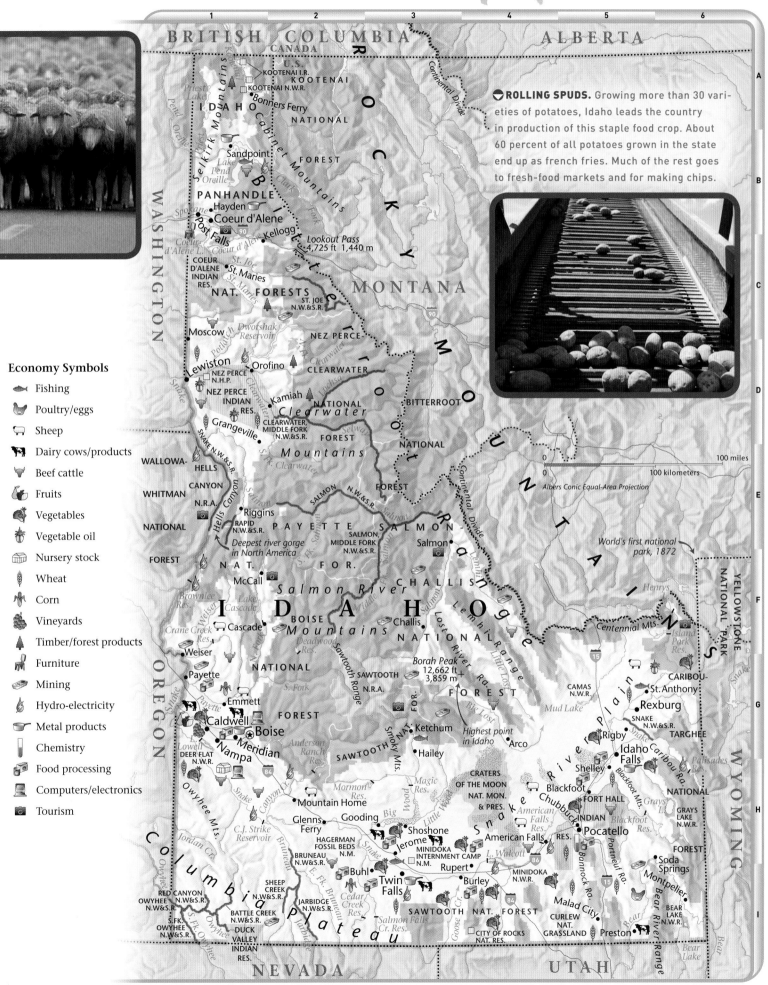

BRITISH COLUMBIA
ALBERTA
CANADA
U.S.

KOOTENAI I.R.
KOOTENAI N.W.R.
Bonners Ferry
IDAHO
KOOTENAI
NATIONAL
FOREST

Priest Lakes
Selkirk Mountains
Cabinet Mountains

Sandpoint
Lake Pend Oreille
PANHANDLE
Hayden
Coeur d'Alene
Post Falls
Kellogg
Lookout Pass
4,725 ft 1,440 m

Coeur d'Alene L.
COEUR D'ALENE INDIAN RES.
St. Joe
St. Maries
NAT. FORESTS
ST. JOE N.W.&S.R.

Moscow
Dworshak Reservoir
NEZ PERCE
CLEARWATER
BITTERROOT
NATIONAL

Lewiston
NEZ PERCE N.H.P.
Orofino
NEZ PERCE INDIAN RES.
Kamiah
Clearwater
NATIONAL

Grangeville
CLEARWATER, MIDDLE FORK N.W.&S.R.
FOREST
FOREST

WALLOWA-
HELLS
CANYON
WHITMAN
N.R.A.
NATIONAL
FOREST

Riggins
RAPID N.W.&S.R.
PAYETTE
SALMON N.W.&S.R.
SALMON-
Salmon
Deepest river gorge in North America
SALMON, MIDDLE FORK N.W.&S.R.
NAT.
FOR.

McCall
CHALLIS
Salmon River Mountains
BOISE
Challis
NATIONAL
Borah Peak 12,662 ft 3,859 m
World's first national park, 1872

Brownlee Res.
Lake Cascade
IDAHO
Cascade
Deadwood Res.
Centennial Mts.
Island Park Res.
YELLOWSTONE NATIONAL PARK

Crane Creek Res.
Weiser
NATIONAL
SAWTOOTH N.R.A.
CAMAS N.W.R.
St. Anthony
CARIBOU-
Rexburg

Payette
S. Fork
FOREST
Mud Lake
Highest point in Idaho
SNAKE N.W.&S.R.
Rigby
TARGHEE

Emmett
Caldwell
Boise
Meridian
Nampa
Anderson Ranch Res.
SAWTOOTH
Ketchum
Arco
Idaho Falls
Shelley
Blackfoot
FORT HALL INDIAN
CARIBOU

DEER FLAT N.W.R.
Hailey
CRATERS OF THE MOON NAT. MON. & PRES.
Pocatello
GRAYS LAKE N.W.R.
NATIONAL

L. Lowell
Mormon Res.
Magic Res.
American Falls
Chubbuck
American Falls Res.

Mountain Home
Gooding
Shoshone
Jerome
MINIDOKA INTERNMENT CAMP N.M.
American Falls
Soda Springs
FOREST

Glenns Ferry
HAGERMAN FOSSIL BEDS N.M.
Rupert
L. Walcott
Montpelier

C.J. Strike Reservoir
BRUNEAU N.W.&S.R.
Buhl
Twin Falls
Burley
MINIDOKA N.W.R.
Malad City
BEAR LAKE N.W.R.

Owyhee Mts.
SHEEP CREEK N.W.&S.R.
JARBIDGE N.W.&S.R.
Cedar Creek Res.
SAWTOOTH NAT. FOREST
CURLEW NAT. GRASSLAND
Preston
Bear Lake

RED CANYON OWYHEE N.W.&S.R.
BATTLE CREEK N.W.&S.R.
Salmon Falls Cr. Res.
CITY OF ROCKS NAT. RES.

S. FK. OWYHEE N.W.&S.R.
DUCK VALLEY INDIAN RES.

NEVADA
UTAH

WASHINGTON
OREGON
Columbia Plateau
MONTANA
Bitterroot Range
ROCKY MOUNTAINS
Snake River Plain
WYOMING

Continental Divide
Selway
Lochsa
Snake River
Spokane R.
Clark Fork

MONTANA

THE BASICS

Statehood
November 8, 1889; 41st state

Total area (land and water)
147,040 sq mi (380,831 sq km)

Land area
145,546 sq mi (376,962 sq km)

Population
1,032,949

Capital
Helena
Population 29,943 (2014)

Largest city
Billings
Population 110,263

Racial/ethnic groups
89.2% white; 0.6% African American; 0.8% Asian; 6.6% Native American; 3.6% Hispanic (any race)

Foreign born
2.0%

Urban population
55.9% (2010)

Population density
7.1 per sq mi (2.7 per sq km)

GEO WHIZ

The fossil of a turkey-size dinosaur is being called the missing link between Asian and North American horned dinosaurs. Paleontologist Paul Horner discovered the fossil while sitting on it during a lunch break at a dig near Choteau.

Montana is the only state with river systems that empty into the Gulf of Mexico, Hudson Bay, and the Pacific Ocean.

Grasshopper Glacier is littered with frozen locusts (which look like grasshoppers) that became trapped in the ice. Scientists believe this species became extinct about 200 years ago.

Montana

Long before the arrival of Europeans, numerous native groups lived and hunted in the plains and mountains of present-day Montana. Although contact between European explorers and Native Americans was often peaceful, Montana was the site of the historic 1876 Battle of the Little Bighorn, in which Lakota (Sioux) and Cheyenne warriors defeated George Armstrong Custer's troops. In the mid-19th century the discovery of gold and silver attracted many prospectors, and later cattle ranching became big business, adding to tensions with the Indians. Montana became the 41st state in 1889. Today, Indians still make up more than 6 percent of the state's population—only four other states have a larger percentage. Agriculture is important to the economy, producing wheat, hay, and barley as well as beef cattle. Mining and timber industries have seen a decline, but service industries and tourism are growing. Montana's natural environment, including Glacier and Yellowstone National Parks, remains one of its greatest resources.

WESTERN MEADOWLARK
BITTERROOT

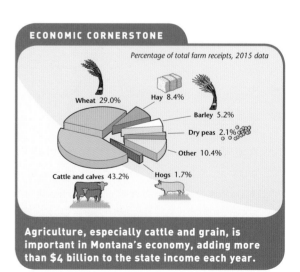

⬥ **STEP BACK IN TIME.** Just like in the past, Montana ranchers move their cattle herds from low winter pastures to higher elevations for summer grazing. Some ranches allow adventurous tourists to participate in the drives.

ECONOMIC CORNERSTONE

Percentage of total farm receipts, 2015 data

Wheat 29.0%
Hay 8.4%
Barley 5.2%
Dry peas 2.1%
Other 10.4%
Cattle and calves 43.2%
Hogs 1.7%

Agriculture, especially cattle and grain, is important in Montana's economy, adding more than $4 billion to the state income each year.

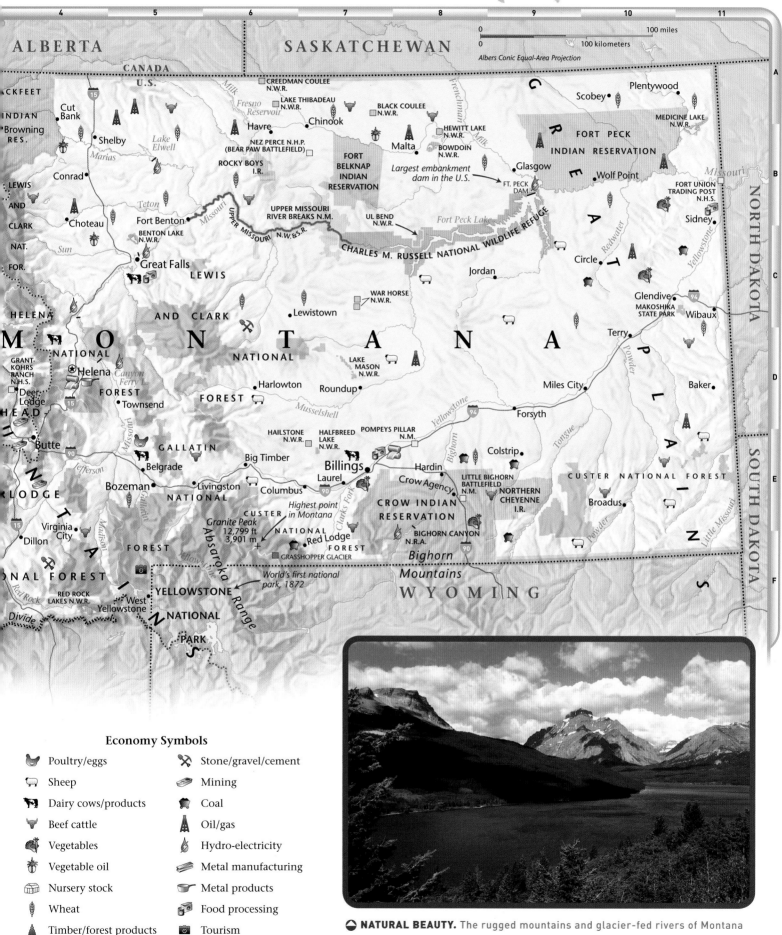

ALBERTA SASKATCHEWAN

100 miles
100 kilometers
Albers Conic Equal-Area Projection

CANADA
U.S.

CREEDMAN COULEE N.W.R.
LAKE THIBADEAU N.W.R.
Fresno Reservoir
BLACK COULEE N.W.R.
HEWITT LAKE N.W.R.
MEDICINE LAKE N.W.R.

BLACKFEET INDIAN RES.
Browning
Cut Bank
Shelby
Lake Elwell
Havre
Chinook
Malta
BOWDOIN N.W.R.
Scobey
Plentywood

LEWIS AND CLARK NAT. FOR.
Conrad
Marias
Choteau
Teton
NEZ PERCE N.H.P. (BEAR PAW BATTLEFIELD)
ROCKY BOYS I.R.
FORT BELKNAP INDIAN RESERVATION
Largest embankment dam in the U.S.
Glasgow
FT. PECK DAM
Wolf Point
FORT PECK INDIAN RESERVATION
Missouri
FORT UNION TRADING POST N.H.S.
Sidney

GREAT

Fort Benton
BENTON LAKE N.W.R.
Sun
Great Falls
UPPER MISSOURI RIVER BREAKS N.M.
UPPER MISSOURI N.W.&S.R.
UL BEND N.W.R.
Fort Peck Lake
CHARLES M. RUSSELL NATIONAL WILDLIFE REFUGE
Redwater
Circle
Yellowstone

HELENA
M O N T A N A
LEWIS AND CLARK NATIONAL FOREST
WAR HORSE N.W.R.
Lewistown
Jordan
Glendive
MAKOSHIKA STATE PARK
Wibaux

GRANT-KOHRS RANCH N.H.S.
Deer Lodge
Helena
Canyon Ferry L.
FOREST
Townsend
Harlowton
LAKE MASON N.W.R.
Roundup
Musselshell
Miles City
Powder
Terry
Baker

NORTH DAKOTA

BUTTE
Butte
Jefferson
GALLATIN
Belgrade
Bozeman
Madison
HAILSTONE N.W.R.
HALFBREED LAKE N.W.R.
Big Timber
POMPEYS PILLAR N.M.
Yellowstone
Forsyth
Colstrip
Tongue
CUSTER NATIONAL FOREST
Broadus

BEAVERHEAD
Virginia City
Dillon
GALLATIN NATIONAL FOREST
Livingston
Columbus
Clarks Fork
Billings
Laurel
Hardin
Crow Agency
CROW INDIAN RESERVATION
Bighorn
LITTLE BIGHORN BATTLEFIELD N.M.
NORTHERN CHEYENNE I.R.

Highest point in Montana
Granite Peak 12,799 ft 3,901 m
CUSTER NATIONAL FOREST
Red Lodge
GRASSHOPPER GLACIER
BIGHORN CANYON N.R.A.
Bighorn Mountains

RED ROCK LAKES N.W.R.
NATIONAL FOREST
Red Rock
Divide
West Yellowstone
Absaroka Range
World's first national park, 1872
YELLOWSTONE NATIONAL PARK

WYOMING
SOUTH DAKOTA
Little Missouri
Powder

Economy Symbols

Poultry/eggs	Stone/gravel/cement
Sheep	Mining
Dairy cows/products	Coal
Beef cattle	Oil/gas
Vegetables	Hydro-electricity
Vegetable oil	Metal manufacturing
Nursery stock	Metal products
Wheat	Food processing
Timber/forest products	Tourism
Printing/publishing	

NATURAL BEAUTY. The rugged mountains and glacier-fed rivers of Montana offer many opportunities to outdoor lovers, including hiking and backpacking as well as fishing in summer, skiing in winter, and year-round wildlife viewing.

THE BASICS

Statehood
October 31, 1864; 36th state

Total area (land and water)
110,572 sq mi (286,380 sq km)

Land area
109,781 sq mi (284,332 sq km)

Population
2,890,845

Capital
Carson City
Population 54,521

Largest city
Las Vegas
Population 623,747

Racial/ethnic groups
75.7% white; 9.3% African American; 8.5% Asian; 1.6% Native American; 28.1% Hispanic (any race)

Foreign born
19.1%

Urban population
94.2% (2010)

Population density
26.3 per sq mi (10.2 per sq km)

GEO WHIZ

The Applegate Trail, named for two brothers who first traveled it in 1846, offered a shorter alternative to the Oregon Trail. The Applegate Trail headed south from Idaho, across Nevada's Black Rock Desert into northern California, and then north into Oregon.

So many people claim to have seen extraterrestrials along a 98-mile (158-km) stretch of Nevada Highway 375 that the state transportation board named it Extraterrestrial Highway in 1996.

Nevada

Nevada's earliest settlers were native people about whom little is known. Around 2,000 years ago, they began establishing permanent dwellings of clay and stone perched atop rocky ledges in what today is the state of Nevada. This was what Spanish explorers saw when they arrived in 1776. In years following, many expeditions passing through the area faced challenges of a difficult environment and native groups protecting their land. In the mid-1800s gold and silver were discovered. In 1861 the Nevada Territory was created, and three years later statehood was granted. Today, the Nevada landscape is dotted with ghost towns—places once prosperous but now abandoned except for curious tourists. Mining is now overshadowed by other economic activities. Casinos, modern hotels, and lavish entertainment attract thousands of visitors each year. Hoover Dam, on the Colorado River, supplies water and power to much of Nevada as well as two adjoining states. But limited water promises to be a challenge to Nevada's future growth.

MOUNTAIN BLUEBIRD
SAGEBRUSH

TURNING BACK TIME. The Luxor, re-creating a scene from ancient Egypt, is one of the many hotel-casinos that attract thousands of tourists to the four-mile (6-km) section of Las Vegas known as the Strip.

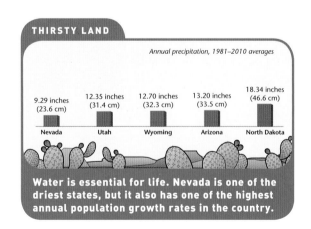

THIRSTY LAND

Annual precipitation, 1981–2010 averages

9.29 inches (23.6 cm)	12.35 inches (31.4 cm)	12.70 inches (32.3 cm)	13.20 inches (33.5 cm)	18.34 inches (46.6 cm)
Nevada	Utah	Wyoming	Arizona	North Dakota

Water is essential for life. Nevada is one of the driest states, but it also has one of the highest annual population growth rates in the country.

DESERT BEAUTY. A beavertail cactus thrives in the dry environment of Valley of Fire State Park. The park, Nevada's oldest, gets its name from red sandstone formations visible in the distance.

Economy Symbols

- 🐑 Sheep
- 🐄 Dairy cows/products
- 🐂 Beef cattle
- 🥬 Vegetables
- 🪴 Nursery stock
- 🍇 Vineyards
- 🖨 Printing/publishing
- ⚒ Stone/gravel/cement
- ⛏ Mining
- 🛢 Oil/gas
- 💧 Hydro-electricity
- 🚗 Motor vehicles/parts
- ⚙ Rubber/plastics
- 📷 Food processing
- 🔵 Electrical equipment
- 💻 Computers/electronics
- 🔬 Scientific instruments
- ✈ Aircraft/parts
- 📷 Tourism

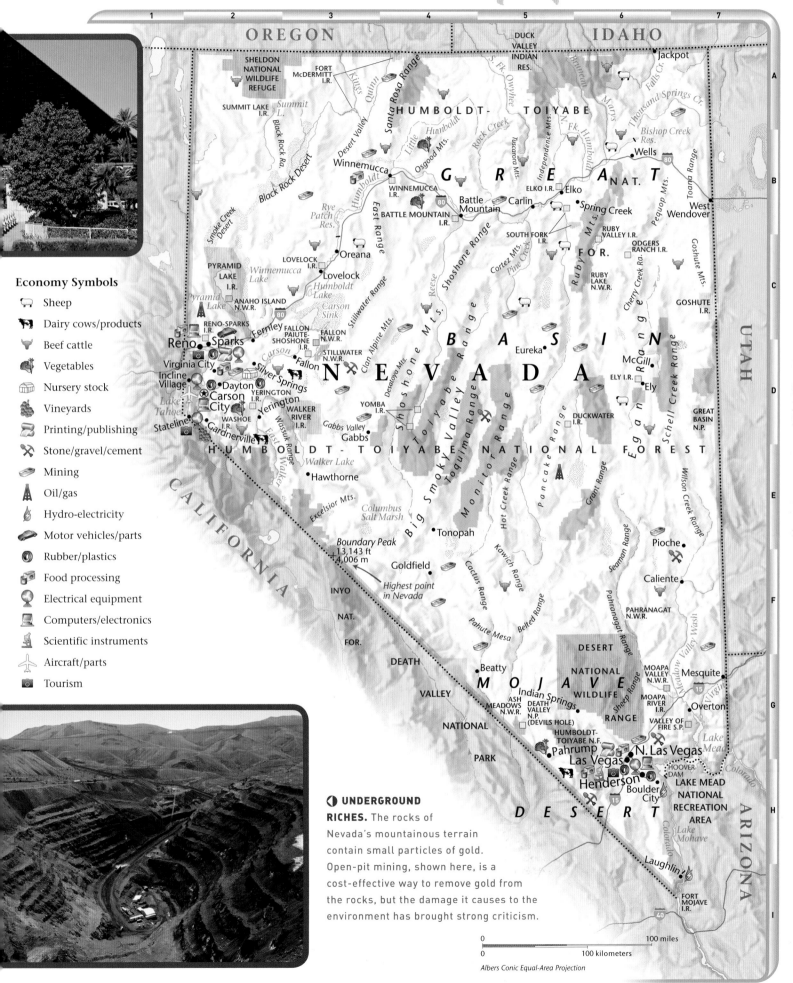

UNDERGROUND RICHES.
The rocks of Nevada's mountainous terrain contain small particles of gold. Open-pit mining, shown here, is a cost-effective way to remove gold from the rocks, but the damage it causes to the environment has brought strong criticism.

0   100 miles
0   100 kilometers

Albers Conic Equal-Area Projection

STATE OF OREGON

1859

THE BASICS

Statehood
February 14, 1859; 33rd state

Total area (land and water)
98,379 sq mi (254,799 sq km)

Land area
95,988 sq mi (248,608 sq km)

Population
4,028,977

Capital
Salem
Population 164,549

Largest city
Portland
Population 632,309

Racial/ethnic groups
87.6% white; 2.1% African
American; 4.4% Asian;
1.8% Native American;
12.7% Hispanic (any race)

Foreign born
9.8%

Urban population
81.0% (2010)

Population density
42.0 per sq mi (16.2 per sq km)

GEO WHIZ

To recover wetlands and save
two endangered fish species,
100 tons (90 t) of explosives
were used to blast through
levees so that water from the
Williamson River could again
flow into Upper Klamath Lake.

Crater Lake, at 1,932 feet (589 m),
is the deepest in the United
States. It fills a depression created when an eruption caused
the top of a mountain to collapse.
Wizard Island, at the center of
the 6-mile (10-km)-wide lake is
the top of the volcano.

Mount Hood, a dormant volcano
near Portland, is Oregon's highest peak, rising 11,239 feet (3,426
m). Its last major eruption was
in the 1790s, a few years before
the Lewis and Clark expedition
reached the region.

Oregon

Long before the Oregon Trail brought settlers from the eastern United States, Indians fished and hunted in Oregon's coastal waters and forested valleys. Spanish explorers sailed along Oregon's coast in 1543, and in the 18th century fur traders from Europe set up forts in the region. In the mid-1800s settlers began farming the rich soil of the Willamette Valley. Oregon achieved statehood in 1859, and by 1883 railroads linked Oregon to the East, and Portland had become an important shipping center. Today, forestry, fishing, and agriculture make up an important part of the state economy, but Oregon is making an effort to diversify into manu-facturing and high-tech industries. Dams on the Columbia River generate inexpensive electricity to support energy-hungry indus-tries, such as aluminum production. Computers, electronics, and research-based industries are expanding. The state's natural beauty—snowcapped volcanoes, old-growth forests, and a rocky coastline—makes tourism an important growth industry.

OREGON GRAPE
WESTERN MEADOWLARK

TOWER OF HISTORY.
The 125-foot (38-m)
Astoria Column, built in
1926 near the mouth of
the Columbia River, is
decorated with historic
scenes of exploration
and settlement along the
Pacific Northwest coast.

CHANGING LANDSCAPE.
Oregon's Pacific coast is a lesson
on erosion and deposition. Rocky
outcrops called sea stacks are
leftovers of a former coastline
that has been eroded by waves.
The sandy beach is a result of
eroded material being deposited
along the shore.

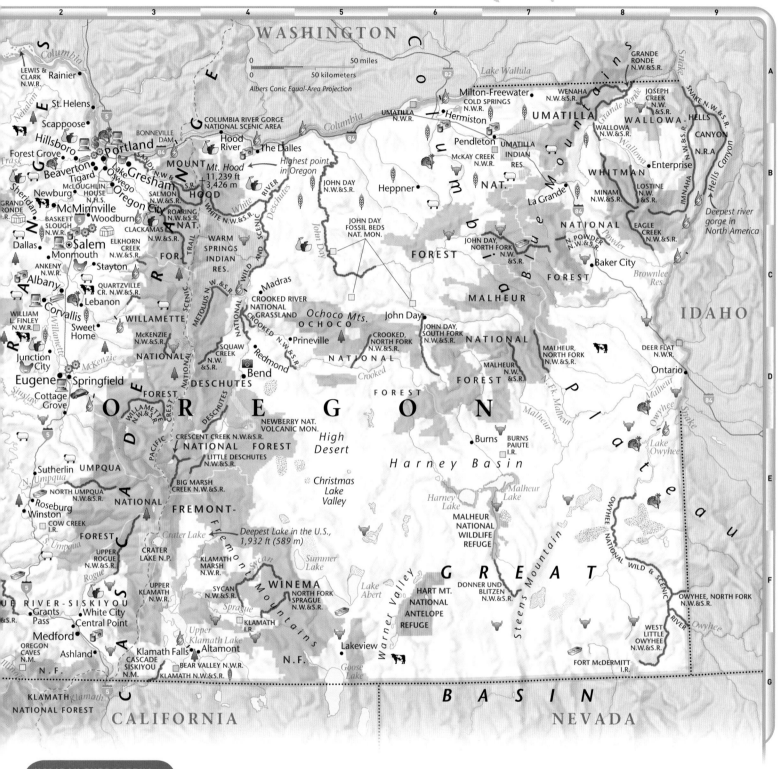

HOLIDAY EVERGREENS

Christmas trees harvested, 2012 data

- 6.5 million — Oregon
- 4.3 million — North Carolina
- 1.7 million — Michigan
- 1.0 million — Pennsylvania
- 0.6 million — Wisconsin

Oregon's marine west coast climate provides an ideal environment for growing firs and spruce for the lucrative Christmas tree market.

Economy Symbols

- Fishing
- Shellfish
- Poultry/eggs
- Sheep
- Dairy cows/products
- Fruits
- Vegetables
- Nursery stock
- Wheat
- Timber/forest products
- Mining
- Hydro-electricity
- Machinery
- Metal manufacturing
- Motor vehicles/parts
- Food processing
- Computers/electronics
- Tourism
- Finance/insurance

THE BASICS

Statehood
January 4, 1896; 45th state

Total area (land and water)
84,897 sq mi (219,882 sq km)

Land area
82,170 sq mi (212,818 sq km)

Population
2,995,919

Capital
Salt Lake City
Population 192,672

Largest city
Salt Lake City
Population 192,672

Racial/ethnic groups
91.2% white; 1.3% African American; 2.5% Asian; 1.5% Native American; 13.7% Hispanic (any race)

Foreign born
8.2%

Urban population
90.6% (2010)

Population density
36.5 per sq mi (14.1 per sq km)

GEO WHIZ

A giant duck-billed dinosaur is among the many kinds of dinosaur fossils that have been found in the Grand Staircase–Escalante National Monument. Scientists think the plant eater was at least 30 feet (9 m) long and had a mouthful of 300 teeth.

Drought and water withdrawals have caused the level of Lake Powell to drop to only 42 percent of its capacity, revealing the walls of Glen Canyon, which was submerged in 1983 when a dam created the lake.

Great Salt Lake is the largest natural lake west of the Mississippi River. The lake, which has a high level of evaporation, contains about 4.5 billion tons (4 billion t) of salt.

Utah

For thousands of years present-day Utah was populated by Native Americans living in small hunter-gatherer groups, including the Ute for whom the state is named. Spanish explorers passed through Utah in 1776, and in the early 19th century trappers came from the East searching for beavers. In 1847 the arrival of Mormons seeking freedom to practice their religion marked the beginning of widespread settlement of the territory. They established farms and introduced irrigation. Discovery of precious metals in the 1860s brought miners to the territory. Today, almost 65 percent of Utah's land is set aside by the federal government for use by the military and defense industries and as national parks, which attract large numbers of tourists annually. As a result, government is a leading employer in the state. Another important force in Utah is the Church of Latter-day Saints (Mormons), which has influenced culture and politics in the state for more than a century. Salt Lake City is the world headquarters of the church.

SEGO LILY
CALIFORNIA GULL

⬯ **NATURE'S HANDIWORK.** Arches National Park includes more than 2,000 arches carved by forces of water and ice, extreme temperatures, and the shifting of underground salt beds over a period of 100 million years. Delicate Arch stands on the edge of a canyon, with the snowcapped La Sal Mountains in the distance.

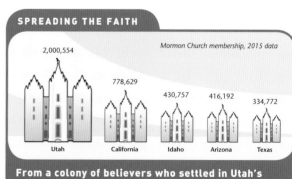

SPREADING THE FAITH

Mormon Church membership, 2015 data

2,000,554 — Utah
778,629 — California
430,757 — Idaho
416,192 — Arizona
334,772 — Texas

From a colony of believers who settled in Utah's Salt Lake basin in the 1840s, followers of the Mormon faith have expanded into nearby states.

◖ **MONUMENT TO FAITH.** Completed in 1893, the Salt Lake Temple is where Mormons gather to worship and participate in religious ceremonies. Church members regard temples as the most sacred places on Earth.

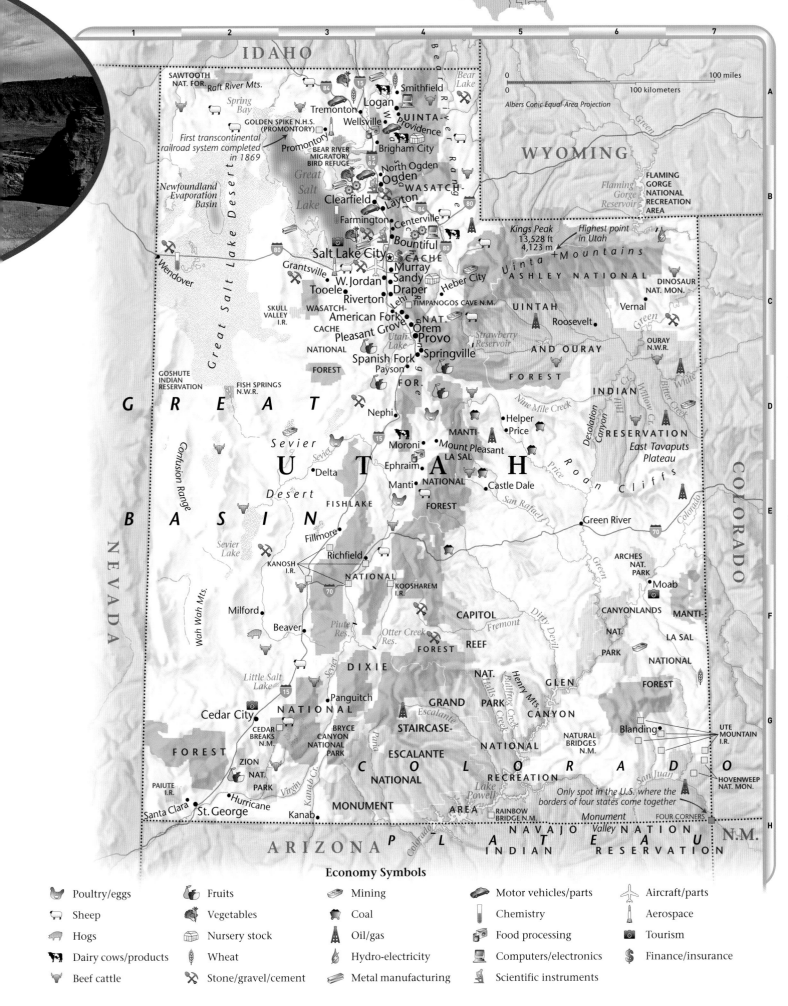

IDAHO

WYOMING

SAWTOOTH NAT. FOR.   Raft River Mts.

Spring Bay

GOLDEN SPIKE N.H.S. (PROMONTORY)

First transcontinental railroad system completed in 1869

Promontory

Newfoundland Evaporation Basin

Great Salt Lake

Tremonton
Wellsville
Logan
Smithfield
Providence
Brigham City

Bear Lake

UINTA

Bear River Range

North Ogden
Ogden
WASATCH
Clearfield
Layton
Farmington
Centerville
Bountiful

Flaming Gorge Reservoir

FLAMING GORGE NATIONAL RECREATION AREA

Kings Peak 13,528 ft 4,123 m   Highest point in Utah

Uinta Mountains

ASHLEY NATIONAL

DINOSAUR NAT. MON.

Wendover

Great Salt Lake Desert

Salt Lake City
Murray
Grantsville
W. Jordan   Sandy
Tooele   Draper
Riverton   Lehi
CACHE

Heber City
TIMPANOGOS CAVE N.M.

UINTAH

Roosevelt

Vernal

Green

AND OURAY

OURAY N.W.R.

SKULL VALLEY I.R.

WASATCH
CACHE

American Fork
Pleasant Grove
NAT.
Orem
Provo
Springville

Utah Lake

Strawberry Reservoir

FOREST

INDIAN

East Tavaputs Plateau

GOSHUTE INDIAN RESERVATION

NATIONAL

Spanish Fork
Payson

FOR.

Nine Mile Creek

RESERVATION

FISH SPRINGS N.W.R.

FOREST

Nephi

Desolation Canyon

Roan

White

Bitter Creek

G R E A T

Confusion Range

Sevier

Sevier

U T A H

Moroni
Ephraim
Manti

Helper
Price

MANTI-
Mount Pleasant
LA SAL

Castle Dale

Cliffs

San Rafael

Green River

Colorado

COLORADO

B A S I N

Delta

Desert

FISHLAKE

NATIONAL
FOREST

Price

NEVADA

Sevier Lake

Fillmore

Richfield

KANOSH I.R.

NATIONAL

KOOSHAREM I.R.

CAPITOL

Dirty Devil

ARCHES NAT. PARK

Moab

CANYONLANDS

MANTI-

Wah Wah Mts.

Milford

Beaver

Piute Res.

Otter Creek Res.

FOREST

REEF

NAT.

Fremont

Green

NAT. PARK

LA SAL

NATIONAL

Little Salt Lake

DIXIE

NAT.

GLEN

Henry Mts.

FOREST

Cedar City
CEDAR BREAKS N.M.

Panguitch

NATIONAL

BRYCE CANYON NATIONAL PARK

STAIRCASE-

GRAND

CANYON

Escalante

Halls Creek

Bullfrog Creek

Blanding

UTE MOUNTAIN I.R.

FOREST

ZION NAT. PARK

PAIUTE I.R.

Santa Clara   St. George

Hurricane

Virgin

ESCALANTE

NATIONAL

COLORADO

MONUMENT

Kanab

Paria

Kanab Cr.

RECREATION

NATURAL BRIDGES N.M.

NATIONAL

FOREST

Lake Powell

AREA

RAINBOW BRIDGE N.M.

Only spot in the U.S. where the borders of four states come together

Monument

San Juan

HOVENWEEP NAT. MON.

FOUR CORNERS

ARIZONA PLATEAU

NAVAJO NATION

Valley INDIAN RESERVATION

N.M.

Colorado

0   100 miles
0   100 kilometers
Albers Conic Equal-Area Projection

Economy Symbols

Poultry/eggs	Fruits	Mining	Motor vehicles/parts	Aircraft/parts
Sheep	Vegetables	Coal	Chemistry	Aerospace
Hogs	Nursery stock	Oil/gas	Food processing	Tourism
Dairy cows/products	Wheat	Hydro-electricity	Computers/electronics	Finance/insurance
Beef cattle	Stone/gravel/cement	Metal manufacturing	Scientific instruments	

THE EVERGREEN STATE:
WASHINGTON

THE BASICS

Statehood
November 11, 1889; 42nd state

Total area (land and water)
71,298 sq mi (184,661 sq km)

Land area
66,456 sq mi (172,119 sq km)

Population
7,170,351

Capital
Olympia
Population 49,218 (2014)

Largest city
Seattle
Population 684,451

Racial/ethnic groups
80.3% white; 4.1% African American; 8.4% Asian; 1.9% Native American; 12.4% Hispanic (any race)

Foreign born
13.2%

Urban population
84.1% (2010)

Population density
107.9 per sq mi (41.7 per sq km)

GEO WHIZ

The Olympic Peninsula is among the world's rainiest places, and its Hoh Rain Forest is one of Earth's few temperate rain forests.

Mount St. Helens, the most active volcano in the lower 48 states, is close to both Seattle and Portland, Oregon. The eruption in May 1980 reduced its elevation by 1,314 feet (401 m) and triggered the largest landslide in recorded history.

Orcas, also known as killer whales, are the world's largest dolphins. The 90 or so that call the waters of Puget Sound home have been placed on the government's Endangered Species List.

Washington

Long before Europeans explored the coast of the Pacific Northwest, Native Americans inhabited the area, living mainly off abundant seafood found in coastal waters and rivers. In the late 18th century Spanish sailors and then British explorers, including Captain James Cook, visited the region. Under treaties with Spain (1819) and Britain (1846), the United States gained control of the land, and in 1853 the Washington Territory was formally separated from the Oregon Territory. Settlers soon based their livelihood on fishing, farming, and lumbering. Washington became the 42nd state in 1889. The 20th century was a time of growth and development for the state. Seattle became a major Pacific seaport. The Grand Coulee Dam, completed in 1941, provided the region with inexpensive electricity. Today, industry, led by Boeing and Microsoft, is a mainstay of the economy. Washington leads the country in production of apples and sweet cherries, and the state is home to the headquarters of the popular Starbucks chain of coffee shops.

AMERICAN GOLDFINCH
COAST RHODODENDRON

HARVEST TIME. Once a semiarid grassland, the Palouse Hills north of the Snake River in eastern Washington is now a major wheat-producing area.

PACIFIC GATEWAY. The city of Seattle, easily recognizable by its distinctive Space Needle tower, is a major West Coast port and home to the North Pacific fishing fleet.

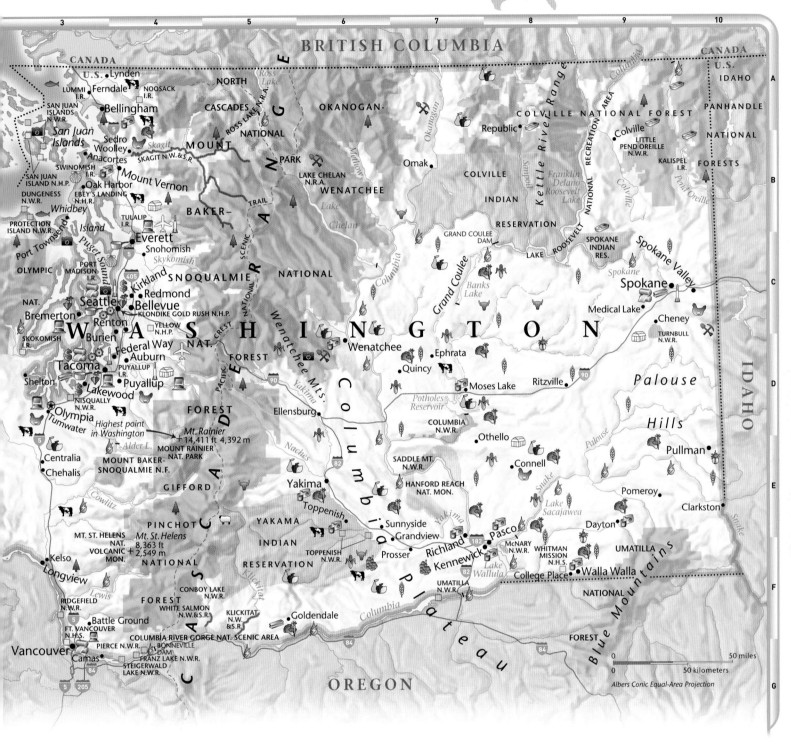

Economy Symbols

- Fishing
- Shellfish
- Poultry/eggs
- Sheep
- Dairy cows/products
- Beef cattle
- Fruits
- Vegetables
- Vegetable oil
- Nursery stock
- Wheat
- Corn
- Vineyards
- Timber/forest products
- Printing/publishing
- Stone/gravel/cement
- Mining
- Hydro-electricity
- Machinery
- Metal manufacturing
- Metal products
- Shipbuilding
- Food processing
- Computers/electronics
- Aircraft/parts
- Aerospace
- Tourism
- Finance/insurance

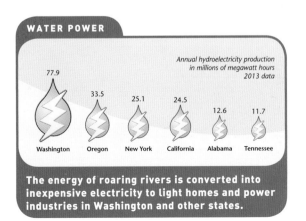

WATER POWER

Annual hydroelectricity production in millions of megawatt hours 2013 data

Washington	Oregon	New York	California	Alabama	Tennessee
77.9	33.5	25.1	24.5	12.6	11.7

The energy of roaring rivers is converted into inexpensive electricity to light homes and power industries in Washington and other states.

THE BASICS

Statehood
July 10, 1890; 44th state

Total area (land and water)
97,813 sq mi (253,335 sq km)

Land area
97,093 sq mi (251,470 sq km)

Population
586,107

Capital
Cheyenne
Population 63,335

Largest city
Cheyenne
Population 63,335

Racial/ethnic groups
92.7% white; 1.4% African American; 1.0% Asian; 2.7% Native American; 9.9% Hispanic (any race)

Foreign born
3.3%

Urban population
64.8% (2010)

Population density
6.0 per sq mi (2.3 per sq km)

GEO WHIZ

The successful reintroduction of wolves into Yellowstone National Park has become a worldwide model for saving endangered carnivores. At the end of 2014 there were at least 1,657 wolves in 282 packs living in Wyoming's northern Rockies.

The National Elk Refuge, in Jackson Hole, provides a winter home for more than 6,000 elk. The herd's migration from the refuge to their summer home in Yellowstone National Park is the longest elk herd migration in the lower 48 states.

Devils Tower, the country's first national monument, was featured in the science-fiction classic *Close Encounters of the Third Kind*.

Wyoming

When Europeans arrived in the 18th century in what would become Wyoming, various native groups were already there, living as nomads following herds of deer and bison across the plains. In the early 19th century fur traders moved into Wyoming, and settlers followed later along the Oregon Trail. Laramie and many of the state's other towns developed around old army forts built to protect wagon trains traveling through Wyoming. Today, fewer than 600,000 people live in all of Wyoming. The state's economy is based on agriculture—mainly grain and livestock production—and mining, especially energy resources. The state has some of the world's largest surface coal mines. In addition, the state is a source of petroleum, natural gas, industrial metals, and precious gems. The natural environment is also a major resource. People come to Wyoming for fishing and hunting, for rodeos, and for the state's majestic mountains and parks. Yellowstone, established in 1872, was the world's first national park.

WESTERN MEADOWLARK
INDIAN PAINTBRUSH

⊜ **WANT TO RACE?** Unique to the High Plains of the West, the pronghorn can sprint up to 60 miles an hour (97 km/h).

⬤ **DRAMATIC LANDSCAPE.** Rising more than 13,000 feet (3,900 m), the jagged peaks of the Tetons, one of the youngest western mountain ranges, tower over a barn on the valley floor.

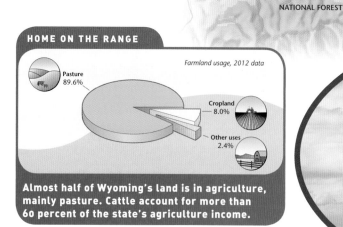

HOME ON THE RANGE

Farmland usage, 2012 data

Pasture 89.6%

Cropland 8.0%

Other uses 2.4%

Almost half of Wyoming's land is in agriculture, mainly pasture. Cattle account for more than 60 percent of the state's agriculture income.

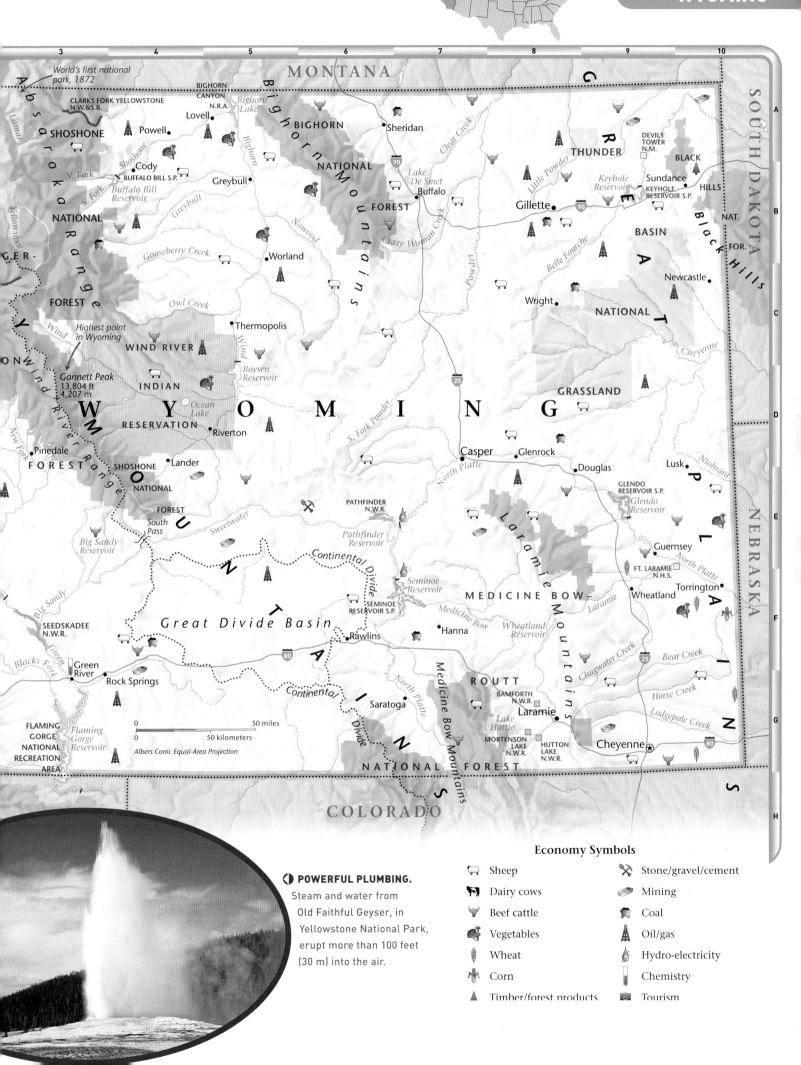

World's first national
park, 1872

MONTANA

SOUTH DAKOTA

NEBRASKA

COLORADO

Absaroka Range

SHOSHONE

NATIONAL

RANGE

FOREST

GER-

Yellowstone

Lamar

CLARKS FORK YELLOWSTONE
N.W.&S.R.

Lovell

Powell

Cody

BUFFALO BILL S.P.

Shoshone

N. Fork

S. Fork

Buffalo Bill
Reservoir

Greybull

BIGHORN
CANYON
N.R.A.

Bighorn
Lake

Bighorn

BIGHORN

NATIONAL

FOREST

Bighorn Mountains

Sheridan

Clear Creek

Lake
De Smet

Buffalo

Little Powder

THUNDER

Crazy Woman Creek

Gillette

DEVILS
TOWER
N.M.

Keyhole
Reservoir

Sundance

KEYHOLE
RESERVOIR S.P.

BLACK

HILLS

NAT.

Black Hills

FOR.

GREAT

Greybull

Gooseberry Creek

Worland

Nowood

Powder

Belle Fourche

BASIN

Newcastle

Wright

NATIONAL

Cheyenne

Owl Creek

Thermopolis

Highest point
in Wyoming

Wind

WIND RIVER

Gannett Peak
13,804 ft
4,207 m

INDIAN

Wind River Range

Wind

Boysen
Reservoir

S. Fork Powder

Ocean
Lake

GRASSLAND

W Y O M I N G

New Fork

Pinedale

FOREST

RESERVATION

SHOSHONE

Lander

Riverton

NATIONAL

Casper

Glenrock

Douglas

Lusk

Niobrara

GLENDO
RESERVOIR S.P.

Glendo
Reservoir

North Platte

Big Sandy
Reservoir

FOREST

South
Pass

Sweetwater

M
O
U
N

PATHFINDER
N.W.R.

Pathfinder
Reservoir

North Platte

Guernsey

FT. LARAMIE
N.H.S.

North Platte

Torrington

Wheatland

P
L
A
I
N
S

Big Sandy

SEEDSKADEE
N.W.R.

Continental Divide

T

SEMINOE
RESERVOIR S.P.

Seminoe
Reservoir

Laramie Mountains

Laramie

MEDICINE BOW-

Wheatland
Reservoir

Green

Blacks Fork

Green
River

Rock Springs

Great Divide Basin

A

Rawlins

Hanna

Medicine Bow

Bear Creek

Chugwater Creek

Horse Creek

I
N
S

Continental

North Platte

Medicine Bow Mountains

ROUTT

BAMFORTH
N.W.R.

Lodgepole Creek

FLAMING
GORGE
NATIONAL
RECREATION
AREA

Flaming
Gorge
Reservoir

Divide

Saratoga

NATIONAL   FOREST

Lake
Hattie

MORTENSON
LAKE
N.W.R.

Laramie

HUTTON
LAKE
N.W.R.

Cheyenne

0   50 miles
0   50 kilometers
Albers Conic Equal-Area Projection

POWERFUL PLUMBING.
Steam and water from
Old Faithful Geyser, in
Yellowstone National Park,
erupt more than 100 feet
(30 m) into the air.

Economy Symbols

Sheep		Stone/gravel/cement	
Dairy cows		Mining	
Beef cattle		Coal	
Vegetables		Oil/gas	
Wheat		Hydro-electricity	
Corn		Chemistry	
Timber/forest products		Tourism	

The Territories

ACROSS TWO SEAS

Listed below are the five largest* of the fourteen U.S. territories, along with their flags and key information. Two of these are in the Caribbean Sea, and three are in the Pacific Ocean. Can you find the other nine U.S. territories on the map?

U.S. CARIBBEAN TERRITORIES

PUERTO RICO

Total area: 5,325 sq mi (13,791 sq km)
Land area: 3,424 sq mi (8,868 sq km)
Population: 3,598,357
Capital: San Juan
Languages: Spanish, English

U.S. VIRGIN ISLANDS

Total area: 733 sq mi (1,898 sq km)
Land area: 134 sq mi (348 sq km)
Population: 103,574
Capital: Charlotte Amalie
Languages: English, Spanish or Spanish Creole, French or French Creole

U.S. PACIFIC TERRITORIES

AMERICAN SAMOA

Total area: 581 sq mi (1,505 sq km)
Land area: 76 sq mi (198 sq km)
Population: 54,343
Capital: Pago Pago
Language: Samoan, English

NORTHERN MARIANA ISLANDS

Total area: 1,976 sq mi (5,117 sq km)
Land area: 182 sq mi (472 sq km)
Population: 52,344
Capital: Saipan (Capitol Hill)
Languages: Philippine languages, Chamorro, English

GUAM

Total area: 571 sq mi (1,478 sq km)
Land area: 210 sq mi (543 sq km)
Population: 161,785
Capital: Hagåtña (Agana)
Languages: English, Filipino, Chamorro

OTHER U.S. TERRITORIES

Baker Island, Howland Island, Jarvis Island, Johnston Atoll, Kingman Reef, Midway Islands, Navassa Island, Palmyra Atoll, Wake Island

*Close-up views of the five largest territories are highlighted in enlarged inset maps labeled with a letter. You can see where each territory is by looking for its corresponding letter on the main map.

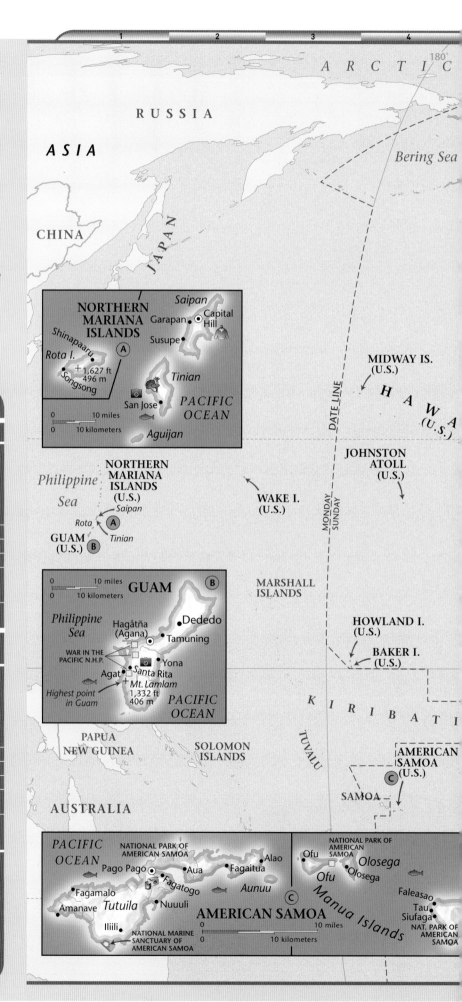

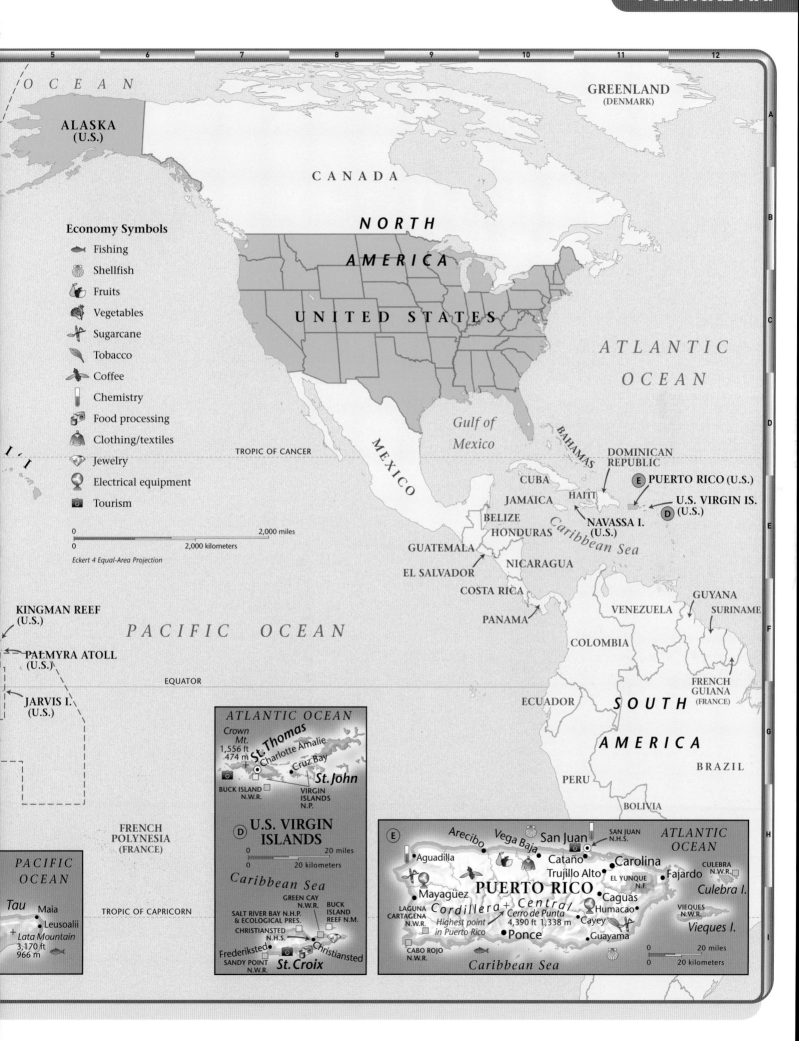

Economy Symbols

- Fishing
- Shellfish
- Fruits
- Vegetables
- Sugarcane
- Tobacco
- Coffee
- Chemistry
- Food processing
- Clothing/textiles
- Jewelry
- Electrical equipment
- Tourism

0 _____ 2,000 miles
0 _____ 2,000 kilometers

Eckert 4 Equal-Area Projection

OCEAN

ALASKA
(U.S.)

GREENLAND
(DENMARK)

CANADA

NORTH

AMERICA

UNITED STATES

ATLANTIC

OCEAN

TROPIC OF CANCER

Gulf of
Mexico

MEXICO

BAHAMAS

DOMINICAN
REPUBLIC

CUBA

PUERTO RICO (U.S.)

JAMAICA

HAITI

U.S. VIRGIN IS.
(U.S.)

BELIZE

NAVASSA I.
(U.S.)

HONDURAS

Caribbean Sea

GUATEMALA

NICARAGUA

EL SALVADOR

COSTA RICA

KINGMAN REEF
(U.S.)

VENEZUELA

GUYANA

SURINAME

PANAMA

COLOMBIA

PALMYRA ATOLL
(U.S.)

PACIFIC OCEAN

EQUATOR

FRENCH
GUIANA
(FRANCE)

JARVIS I.
(U.S.)

ECUADOR

SOUTH

BRAZIL

AMERICA

PERU

FRENCH
POLYNESIA
(FRANCE)

BOLIVIA

ATLANTIC OCEAN

Crown
Mt.
1,556 ft
474 m

St. Thomas

Charlotte Amalie

Cruz Bay

St. John

BUCK ISLAND
N.W.R.

VIRGIN
ISLANDS
N.P.

San Juan

SAN JUAN
N.H.S.

ATLANTIC
OCEAN

Arecibo

Vega Baja

Aguadilla

Cataño

Carolina

CULEBRA
N.W.R.

Trujillo Alto

EL YUNQUE
N.F.

Fajardo

PACIFIC
OCEAN

U.S. VIRGIN
ISLANDS

0 _____ 20 miles
0 _____ 20 kilometers

Mayagüez

PUERTO RICO

Caguas

Culebra I.

Tau

Maia

Caribbean Sea

LAGUNA
CARTAGENA
N.W.R.

Cordillera Central

Cerro de Punta
4,390 ft 1,338 m
Highest point
in Puerto Rico

Humacao

VIEQUES
N.W.R.

Leusoalii

GREEN CAY
N.W.R.

BUCK
ISLAND
REEF N.M.

Cayey

Vieques I.

Lata Mountain
3,170 ft
966 m

TROPIC OF CAPRICORN

SALT RIVER BAY N.H.P.
& ECOLOGICAL PRES.

CHRISTIANSTED
N.H.S.

Christiansted

Ponce

Guayama

Frederiksted

SANDY POINT
N.W.R.

St. Croix

CABO ROJO
N.W.R.

0 _____ 20 miles
0 _____ 20 kilometers

Caribbean Sea

◗ **PRESERVING TRADITION.** Young dancers from American Samoa, dressed in costumes of feathers and pandanus leaves, prepare to perform in the Pacific Arts Festival, which is held once every four years to promote Pacific cultures.

The Territories

ISLANDS IN THE FAMILY

Fourteen territories and commonwealths scattered across the Pacific and Caribbean came under U.S. influence after wars or various international agreements. Although they are neither states nor independent countries, the U.S. government provides economic and military aid. Puerto Rico's more than 3.5 million residents give it a population greater than that of 23 U.S. states. Many tourists seeking sunny beaches visit the U.S. Virgin Islands, purchased from Denmark for $25 million in 1917. American Samoa, Guam, and the Northern Mariana Islands in the Pacific have sizable populations, but several tiny atolls have no civilian residents and are administered by U.S. military or government departments. In most cases, citizens of these territories are also eligible for American citizenship.

⬦ **RELIC OF THE PAST.** Sugar mill ruins on St. John, in the U.S. Virgin Islands, recall a way of life that dominated the Caribbean in the 18th and 19th centuries. Plantations used slave labor to grow cane and make it into sugar and molasses.

WHERE THE PICTURES ARE

— Managaha Is.
p. 157

Aerial of San Juan
pp. 156-157

— Brown tree snake
p. 157

Sugar mill
p. 156

— Festival dancers
pp. 156-157

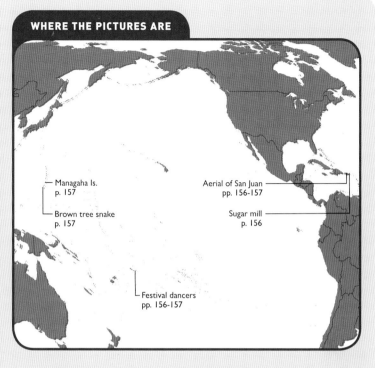

◖ **PACIFIC JEWEL.** Managaha Island sits in the blue-green waters of a lagoon formed by a long reef along Saipan's western coast. Marine biologists fear that portions of the reef are dying due to pollution. The lagoon holds wrecks from battles fought in Northern Mariana waters during World War II.

◖ **ATLANTIC PLAYGROUND.** Modern hotels, catering to more than four million tourists annually, rise above sandy beaches in San Juan, Puerto Rico. Founded in 1521, the city has one of the best natural harbors in the Caribbean.

◑ **UNWELCOME STOWAWAY.** The brown tree snake probably arrived in Guam on cargo ships in the 1950s. The snake has greatly reduced the island's bird and small mammal populations and causes power outages when it climbs electric poles.

U.S. FACTS & FIGURES

THE BASICS

Founding
1776

Total area (land and water)
3,796,742 sq mi (9,833,517 sq km)

Land area
3,531,905 sq mi (9,147,593 sq km)

Population
321,418,820

Capital
Washington, D.C.
Population 672,228

Largest city
New York
Population 8,550,405

Racial/ethnic groups
77.1% white; 13.3% African American;
5.6% Asian; 1.2% Native American;
17.6% Hispanic origin (any race)

Foreign born
13.5%

Urban population
80.7%

Population density
91.0 per sq mi (35.1 per sq km)

Language
No official national language;
language spoken at home: English
79.2%; Spanish 12.9%

Economy
Agriculture: 1.6%; Industry: 20.8 %;
Services: 77.6%

BALD EAGLE,
NATIONAL SYMBOL

Top States

Listed below are major producers of selected agricultural products, fish and seafood, and minerals.

Agricultural Products

Value of total U.S. agricultural production:
$421.5 billion (2014)

Top 10 Agricultural Producing States (based on cash receipts, 2014)

1. California
2. Iowa
3. Texas
4. Nebraska
5. Illinois
6. Minnesota
7. Kansas
8. Indiana
9. North Carolina
10. Wisconsin

Leading Agricultural Products and Top Producers (based on cash receipts, 2014)

Cattle and calves: Texas, Iowa, California, Nebraska, Kansas

Corn: Illinois, Iowa, Nebraska, Minnesota, Indiana

Milk/dairy products: California, Wisconsin, New York, Idaho, Pennsylvania

Soybeans: Illinois, Iowa, Indiana, Minnesota, Nebraska

Poultry and eggs: Georgia, North Carolina, Arkansas, Alabama, Mississippi

Hogs: Iowa, Minnesota, North Carolina, Illinois, Indiana

Fruit/tree nuts: California, Washington, Florida, Oregon, Michigan

Vegetables/melons: California, Florida, Washington, Idaho, Arizona

Potatoes: Idaho, Washington, Wisconsin, North Dakota, California

Fish and Seafood

Value of total U.S. seafood catch: $5.1 billion (2012)

Volume of wild catch: 9.5 billion lb (4.3 billion kg)

Volume of farmed catch: 662 million lb (300 million kg)

Top 5 States in Fish and Seafood (based on value of commercial landings, 2012)

1. Alaska
2. Massachusetts
3. Maine
4. Louisiana
5. Washington

Leading Fish and Seafood Products (based on U.S. consumption habits)

1. Pollock
2. Salmon
3. Shrimp
4. Crab

Minerals

Leading Fossil Fuels and Top Producers

Petroleum: Texas, North Dakota, California, Alaska, Oklahoma (2013)

Natural gas: Texas, Louisiana, Wyoming, Oklahoma, Colorado (2011)

Coal: Wyoming, West Virginia, Kentucky, Pennsylvania, Illinois (2014)

Nonfuel Minerals

Value of total U.S. nonfuel mineral production: $78.3 billion (2015)

Top 10 Nonfuel Mineral Producing States (based on value, 2015)

Nevada, Arizona, Texas, Minnesota, Wisconsin, California, Alaska, Utah, Florida, Michigan

Important Nonfuel Minerals and Top States in Terms of Production

Copper: Arizona, Utah, New Mexico, Nevada, Montana

Crushed stone: Texas, Pennsylvania, Missouri, Ohio, Florida

Gold: Nevada, Alaska, Utah, Colorado, California (2011)

Iron ore: Michigan, Minnesota

Molybdenum: Colorado, Idaho, Arizona

Salt: Louisiana, Texas, New York, Kansas, Utah

Sand and Gravel: Texas, California, Minnesota, Washington, Michigan

Silver: Alaska, Nevada

Zinc: Alaska, Washington, Pennsylvania, North Carolina

Extremes

Strongest Surface Wind in U.S.

231 miles an hour (372 km/h), Mount Washington, New Hampshire, April 12, 1934

World's Tallest Living Tree

Hyperion; a coast redwood in Redwood National Park, California, 379.1 ft (115.55 m) high

World's Oldest Living Tree

Methuselah: a bristlecone pine, California; 4,789 years old

World's Largest Gorge

Grand Canyon, Arizona: 290 mi (466 km) long, 600 ft to 18 mi (183 m to 29 km) wide, 1 mile (1.6 km) deep

Highest Temperature in U.S.

134°F (56.6°C), Death Valley, California, July 10, 1913

Lowest Temperature in U.S.

Minus 80°F (-62.2°C), at Prospect Creek, Alaska, January 23, 1971

Highest Point in U.S.

Denali (Mount McKinley), Alaska: 20,320 ft (6,194 m)

Lowest Point in U.S.

Death Valley, California: 282 feet (86 m) below sea level

Longest River System in U.S.

Mississippi-Missouri: 3,710 mi (5,971 km) long

Rainiest Spot in U.S.

Wai'ale'ale (mountain), Hawai'i: average annual rainfall 460 in (1,168 cm)

Metropolitan Areas With More Than 5 Million People

A metropolitan area is a city and its surrounding suburban areas.

1. New York, pop. 20,182,305
2. Los Angeles, pop. 13,340,068
3. Chicago, pop. 9,551,031
4. Dallas–Fort Worth, pop. 7,102,796
5. Houston, pop. 6,656,947
6. Washington, D.C., pop. 6,097,684
7. Philadelphia, pop. 6,069,875
8. Miami, pop. 6,012,331
9. Atlanta, pop. 5,710,795

GLOSSARY

aquaculture raising fish or shellfish in controlled ponds or waterways for commercial use

atoll a circular coral reef enclosing a tropical lagoon

arid climate type of dry climate in which annual precipitation is generally less than 10 inches (25 cm)

biomass total weight of all organisms found in a given area; organic matter used as fuel

bituminous coal a soft form of coal used in industries and power plants

bog a poorly drained area with wet, spongy ground

broadleaf forest trees with wide leaves that are shed during the winter season

canal an artificial waterway that is used by ships or to carry water for irrigation

center-pivot irrigation an irrigation system that rotates around a piped water source at its middle, often resulting in circular field patterns

city proper an incorporated urban place with boundaries and central government

continental climate temperature extremes with long cold winters and heavy snowfall

continental divide an elevated area that separates rivers flowing toward opposite sides of a continent

Creole a modified form of a language, such as French or Spanish, used for communication between two groups; spoken in some Caribbean islands

delta lowland formed by silt, sand, and gravel deposited by a river at its mouth

desert vegetation plants such as cactus and dry shrubs that have adapted to conditions of low, often irregular precipitation

fork in a river, the place where two streams join

Fortune 500 company top 500 U.S. companies ranked by revenue

fossil remains of or an impression left by the remains of plants or animals preserved in rock

geothermal energy a clean, renewable form of energy provided by heat from Earth's interior

grassland areas with medium to short grasses; found where precipitation is not sufficient to support tree growth

gross domestic product (GDP) the total value of goods and services produced in a country in a year

highland climate found in association with high mountains where elevation affects temperature and precipitation

hundredweight in the U.S., a commercial unit of measure equal to 100 pounds

ice age a very long period of cold climate when glaciers often cover large areas of land

intermittent river/lake a stream or lake that contains water only part of the time, usually after heavy rain or snowmelt

lava molten rock from Earth's interior that flows out on the surface during volcanic activity

levee an embankment, usually made of earth or concrete, built to prevent a river from overflowing

lignite low-grade coal used mainly to produce heat in thermal-electric generators

marine west coast climate type of mild climate found on the mid-latitude west coast of continents poleward of the Mediterranean climate

Mediterranean climate type of mild climate found on the mid-latitude west coast of continents

mesa a high, extensive, flat-topped hill; an eroded remnant of a plateau

metropolitan area a city and its surrounding suburbs or communities

mild climate moderate temperatures with distinct seasons and ample precipitation

nursery stock young plants, including fruits, vegetables, shrubs, and trees, raised in a greenhouse or nursery

pinnacle a tall pillar of rock standing alone or on a summit

plain a large area of relatively flat land that is often covered with grasses

plateau a relatively flat area, larger than a mesa, that rises above the surrounding landscape

population density the average number of people living on each square mile or square kilometer of a specific land area

precipitate process of depositing dissolved minerals as water evaporates, as in limestone caves

rangeland areas of grass prairie that are used for grazing livestock

reactor a device that uses controlled nuclear fission to divide an atomic nucleus to generate power

Richter scale ranking of the power of an earthquake; the higher the number, the stronger the quake

Rust Belt a region made up of northeastern and midwestern states that have experienced a decline in heavy industry and an out-migration of population

scale on a map, a means of explaining the relationship between distances on the map and actual distances on Earth's surface

stalactite column of limestone hanging from the ceiling of a cave that forms as underground water drips down and evaporates, leaving dissolved minerals behind

stalagmite column of limestone that forms on the floor of a cave when underground water drips down and evaporates, leaving dissolved minerals behind

staple main item in an economy; also, main food for domestic consumption

subtropical climate type of mild climate found in the southeastern areas of continents

Sunbelt a region made up of southern and western states that are experiencing major in-migration of population and rapid economic growth

temperate rain forest forests in the coastal Pacific Northwest region of the U.S. with heavy rainfall and mild temperatures

territory land that is under the jurisdiction of a country but that is not a state or a province

tropical zone the area bounded by the Tropic of Cancer and the Tropic of Capricorn, where it is usually warm year-round

tundra vegetation plants, often stunted in size, that have adapted to periods of extreme cold and a short growing season; found in polar regions and high elevations

urban area associated with a town or city in which most people are engaged in nonagricultural employment

volcanic pipe a vertical opening beneath a volcano through which molten rock has passed

wetland land that is either covered with or saturated by water; includes swamps, marshes, and bogs

POSTAL ABBREVIATIONS

AK- Alaska	DE- Delaware	KY- Kentucky	MS- Mississippi	OH- Ohio	UT- Utah
AL- Alabama	FL- Florida	LA- Louisiana	MT- Montana	OK- Oklahoma	VA- Virginia
AR- Arkansas	GA- Georgia	MA- Massachusetts	NC- North Carolina	OR- Oregon	VI- U.S. Virgin Islands
AS- American Samoa	GU- Guam	MD- Maryland	ND- North Dakota	PA- Pennsylvania	VT- Vermont
AZ- Arizona	HI- Hawai'i	ME- Maine	NE- Nebraska	PR- Puerto Rico	WA- Washington
CA- California	IA- Iowa	MI- Michigan	NH- New Hampshire	RI- Rhode Island	WI- Wisconsin
CO- Colorado	ID- Idaho	MN- Minnesota	NJ- New Jersey	SC- South Carolina	WV- West Virginia
CT- Connecticut	IL- Illinois	MO- Missouri	NM- New Mexico	SD- South Dakota	WY- Wyoming
DC- District of	IN- Indiana	MP- Northern	NV- Nevada	TN- Tennessee	
Columbia	KS- Kansas	Mariana Islands	NY- New York	TX- Texas	

MAP ABBREVIATIONS

°E .... degrees East	ME. .... Maine	OREG. .... Oregon
°N .... degrees North	mi .... miles	p., pp. .... page, pages
°S .... degrees South	MICH. .... Michigan	PA. .... Pennsylvania
°W .... degrees West	MINN. .... Minnesota	Pen. .... Peninsula
°C .... degrees Celsius	MISS. .... Mississippi	Pk. .... Peak
°F .... degrees Fahrenheit	MO. .... Missouri	Pres. .... Preserve
ALA. .... Alabama	MONT. .... Montana	Pt. .... Point
ARIZ. .... Arizona	Mt., Mts. .... Mount, Mountain, Mountains	R. .... River
ARK. .... Arkansas	N. .... North	Ra. .... Range
Br. .... Branch	Nat. .... National	Res. .... Reservoir
CALIF. .... California	NAT. MEM. .... National Memorial	RES. .... Reservation
COLO. .... Colorado	NAT. MON., N.M. .... National Monument	R.I. .... Rhode Island
CONN. .... Connecticut	NAT. RES. .... National Reserve	S. .... South
Cr. .... Creek	N.B. .... National Battlefield	S.C. .... South Carolina
D.C. .... District of Columbia	N.B.P. .... National Battlefield Park	S. DAK. .... South Dakota
DEL. .... Delaware	N.B.S. .... National Battlefield Site	S.H.P. .... State Historical Park
E. .... East	N.C. .... North Carolina	S.H.S. .... State Historical Site
Fk. .... Fork	N. DAK. .... North Dakota	S.P. .... State Park
FLA. .... Florida	NEBR. .... Nebraska	Sprs. .... Springs
ft .... feet	NEV. .... Nevada	sq km .... square kilometers
Ft. .... Fort	N.F. .... National Forest	sq mi .... square miles
GA. .... Georgia	N.G. .... National Grassland	St., Ste. .... Saint, Sainte
GDP .... Gross Domestic Product	N.H. .... New Hampshire	Str., Strs. .... Strait, Straits
I., Is. .... Island, Islands	N.H.A. .... National Historical Area	TENN. .... Tennessee
ILL. .... Illinois	N.H.P. .... National Historical Park	TVA .... Tennessee Valley Authority
IND. .... Indiana	N.H.S. .... National Historical Site	U.S. .... United States
INDIAN RES., I.R. .... Indian Reservation	N.J. .... New Jersey	VA. .... Virginia
KANS. .... Kansas	N. MEX. .... New Mexico	VT. .... Vermont
km .... kilometers	N.M.P. .... National Military Park	W. .... West
KY. .... Kentucky	N.P. .... National Park	WASH. .... Washington
L. .... Lake	N.R.A. .... National Recreation Area	WIS. .... Wisconsin
LA. .... Louisiana	N.W.R. .... National Wildlife Refuge	W. VA. .... West Virginia
m .... meters	N.W.&S.R. .... National Wild & Scenic River	WYO. .... Wyoming
MASS. .... Massachusetts	N.Y. .... New York	
MD. .... Maryland	OKLA. .... Oklahoma	

OUTSIDE WEBSITES

The following websites will provide additional valuable information about topics included in this atlas. Additional sites can be found by putting topics of interest into your favorite search engine.*

General information:
States: *www.state.al.us* (This is for Alabama; for each state insert the two-letter state abbreviation where "al" is now.)
Washington, D.C.: *www.dc.gov*
Territories: *www.cia.gov/library/publications/resources/the-world-factbook*
American Samoa: *www.americansamoa.gov*
Guam: *ns.gov.gu*
Northern Marianas: *www.saipan.com/government.html*
Puerto Rico: *welcome.topuertorico.org*
U.S. Virgin Islands: *www.vi.gov*

Natural Environment:
Biomes: *www.blueplanetbiomes.org*
Climate: *www.eoearth.org*
Climate change: *www3.epa.gov/climatechange*

Climate:
www.noaa.gov/climate
www.world-climates.com
www.cpc.ncep.noaa.gov

Natural Hazards:
General: *www.usgs.gov/hazards*
Droughts: *droughtmonitor.unl.edu/*
Earthquakes: *earthquake.usgs.gov*
Hurricanes: *www.nhc.noaa.gov*
Tornadoes: *www.tornadoproject.com*
Tsunamis: *www.tsunami.noaa.gov*
Volcanoes: *www.geo.mtu.edu/volcanoes/Volcanoes/Index.html*
Wildfires: *www.nifc.gov* and *www.fs.fed.us/fire*

Population:
Population clock: *www.census.gov*
States: *quickfacts.census.gov/qfd/index.html*
Cities: *www.city-data.com*
Population movement: *census.gov/library/publications/2014/demo/p20-574.html*
Foreign-born population: *census.gov/library/publications/2012/acs/acs-19.html*

Energy:
www.eia.gov/energyexplained/index.cfm
www.nrdc.org/energy/renewables/
profile.usgs.gov/myscience/upload_folder/ci2015Jun1012005755600Induced_EQs_Review.pdf

Check with an adult before going on the Internet.

PLACE-NAME INDEX

Map references are in boldface (**59**) type. Letters and numbers following in lightface (G6) locate the place-names using the map grid. (Refer to page 7 for more details.)

Benton, AR — Canyons of the Ancients Nat. Mon.

Cap Rock Escarpment — Conemaugh

Confusion Range — Eleven Point N.W.&S.R.

Georgetown, SC — Holton

Koyukuk, North Fork N.W.&S.R. — Manti

Manua Islands — Mystic Seaport

N — Paint N.W.&S.R.

Painted Desert — Rainy Lake

Raisin — Seaman Range

Sunnyvale — Walnut Creek

Walnut Ridge — Zuni (river)

Published by National Geographic Partners, LLC.
All rights reserved. Reproduction of the whole
or any part of the contents without written
permission from the publisher is prohibited.

Since 1888, the National Geographic Society
has funded more than 12,000 research, exploration,
and preservation projects around the world. The Society
receives funds from National Geographic Partners, LLC,
funded in part by your purchase. A portion of the
proceeds from this book supports this vital work.
To learn more, visit natgeo.com/info.

NATIONAL GEOGRAPHIC and Yellow Border Design
are trademarks of the National Geographic Society,
used under license.

For more information, visit nationalgeographic.com, call
1-800-647-5463, or write to the following address:

National Geographic Partners
1145 17th Street N.W.
Washington, D.C. 20036-4688 U.S.A.

Visit us online at nationalgeographic.com/books

For librarians and teachers: ngchildrensbooks.org

More for kids from National Geographic:
kids.nationalgeographic.com

For information about special discounts for bulk
purchases, please contact National Geographic Books
Special Sales: specialsales@natgeo.com

For rights or permissions inquiries, please contact
National Geographic Books Subsidiary Rights:
bookrights@natgeo.com

Art directed by Kathryn Robbins
Designed by Nicole Lazarus

National Geographic supports K–12 educators
with ELA Common Core Resources.
Visit natgeoed.org/commoncore for more information.

Trade paperback ISBN: 978-1-4263-2831-2
Reinforced library binding ISBN: 978-1-4263-2832-9

Printed in Hong Kong
17/THK/1

The publisher would like to thank everyone
who worked to make this book come together:
Angela Modany, associate editor; Martha Sharma, writer/
researcher; Suzanne Fonda, project manager; Lori
Epstein, photo director; Mike McNey, map production;
Sean Philpotts, production director; Anne LeongSon,
design production assistant; Sally Abbey, managing
editor; Joan Gossett, editorial production manager; Molly
Reid, production editor; and Stuart Armstrong, illustrator.

Photo Credits

Abbreviations for terms appearing below: IS = iStockphoto; NGS = National Geographic Creative;
SS = Shutterstock
Art for state flowers and state birds by Robert E. Hynes.
Locator globe, p. 14, created by Theophilis Britt Griswold.
Front cover, (wolf), Holly Kuchera/SS; (oranges), ANCH/SS; (Washington Monument), Gary Blakeley/SS;
(Arches National Park), Lunamarina/Dreamstime; **Back cover,** (bison), MilousSK/SS; (Statue of Liberty),
EyeWire; (Grand Canyon), Erik Harrison/SS; (girl), Jupiterimages/Getty Images

Front of the Book

2 (far left), Freerk Brouwer/SS; 2 (left), PhotoDisc; 2 (right), Brandon Laufenberg/IS; 2 (far right), Richard
Nowitz/NGS; 3 (far left), Joel Sartore/NGS; 3 (left), Jeremy Edwards/IS; 3 (right), Eileen Hart/IS; 3 (far right),
PhotoDisc; 4 (left), PhotoDisc; 4 (right), Brian J. Skerry/NGS; 4-5, Lenice Harms/SS; 5 (left), italianestro/SS; 5
(right), James Davis Photography/Alamy; 5 (lo), Digital Stock; 9 (a), Lane V. Erickson/SS; 9 (b), Elena Elisseeva/
SS; 9 (c), SNEHIT/SS; 9 (d), Nic Watson/SS; 9 (e), FloridaStock/SS; 9 (F), Sai Yeung Chan/SS; 9 (g), TTphoto/
SS; 10, Lowell Georgia/NGS; 12 (a), George F. Mobley/NGS; 12 (b), Skip Brown/NGS; 12 (c), Jan Brons/SS; 12
(d), Michelle Pacitto/SS; 12 (e), Tammy Bryngelson/IS; 13 (a), Carsten Peter/NGS; 13 (b), Mark Thiessen/NGS;
13 (c), Michael Nichols/NGS; 13 (d), Steven Collins/SS; 13 (e), Robert Madden/NGS; 16, Ira Block/NGS; 18 (UP),
Penny De Los Santos; 18 (lo left), Steven Clevenger/Corbis; 18-19, Sarah Leen/NGS; 21, Douglas Peebles/Danita
Delimont/Getty Images; 22 (left), PhotoDisc; 22-23, PhotoDisc; 23 (UP), Orhan Cam/SS

The Northeast

25 (lo), EyeWire; 28 (UP), Michael Melford/NGS; 28 (lo left), Rudi Von Briel/Photo Edit; 28 (lo right), Les Byerley/
SS; 29 (UP), Donald Swartz/IS; 29 (lo), Tim Laman/NGS; 30 (UP), David L. Arnold/NGS; 30 (lo), David L. Arnold/
NGS; 31, Catherine Karnow/NGS; 32 (lo left), Kevin Fleming/NGS; 32 (lo right), Stephen R. Brown; 32-33,
Stephen St. John/NGS; 34 (lo), David Cannings-Bushell/IS; 34-35, PhotoDisc; 35 (lo), Roy Toft/NGS; 36 (UP),
Jeremy Edwards/IS; 36 (lo), Justine Gecewicz/IS; 37, James L. Stanfield/NGS; 38 (UP), Sarah Leen/NGS; 38 (lo),
Tim Laman/NGS; 39, Darlyne A. Murawski/NGS; 40 (UP), Medford Taylor/NGS; 40 (lo), Steven Phraner/IS; 41
(UP), Richard Nowitz/NGS; 42 (UP), Richard Nowitz/NGS; 42 (lo left), Iconica/Getty Images; 42 (lo right), Matt
Rainey/Star Ledger/Corbis; 42-43, Mike Derer/Associated Press; 44 (up), Glenn Taylor/IS; 44 (lo), James P. Blair/
NGS; 45, Kenneth Garrett/NGS; 46 (UP), Kenneth Garrett/NGS; 46 (lo), Jeremy Edwards/IS; 47, William Albert
Allard/NGS; 48 (up left), Todd Gipstein/NGS; 48 (lo), Onne van der Wal/Corbis; 48-49, Ira Block/NGS; 50 (UP),
Michael S. Yamashita/NGS; 50-51, David McLain/Aurora/Getty Images; 51 (right), LynnHuman/SS

The Southeast

56 (UP), Klaus Nigge/NGS; 56 (lo left), Tyrone Turner; 56 (lo right), Richard T. Nowitz/Corbis; 56-57, Skip Brown/
NGS; 57 (center), Robert Clark/NGS; 57 (lo), Raymond Gehman/NGS; 58 (UP), sacherjj/E+/Getty Images; 58 (lo),
NASA; 60 (UP), Harrison Shull/Aurora/Getty Images; 60 (lo), Joel Sartore/NGS; 61, Cary Wolinsky/NGS; 62 (UP),
David Burnett/NGS; 62 (lo), Brian J. Skerry/NGS; 62-63, NASA; 64 (up left), William S. Weems/NGS; 64 (up right),
PhotoDisc; 64 (lo), Micheal Melford/NGS; 66, Melissa Farlow/NGS; 67 (lo), Randy Olson/NGS; 68 (UP), Tyrone
Turner/NGS; 68-69, Jason Major/IS; 70 (UP), Jim West/Alamy Stock Photo; 70 (LO), Ira Block/NGS; 71, Elena
Vdovina/IS; 72 (lo left), Jack Fletcher/NGS; 72 (lo right), Pete Souza/NGS; 73, Raymond Gehman/NGS; 74 (UP),
Terry Healy/IS; 74-75, Planetpix/Alamy Stock Photo; 75 (right), Raymond Gehman/NGS; 76, Melissa Farlow/NGS;
77 (up left), Dennis R. Dimick/NGS; 77 (up right), Jodi Cobb/NGS; 78 (UP), Robert Clark/NGS; 78 (up), Medford
Taylor/NGS; 78 (lo), Richard Nowitz/NGS; 80 (UP), James L. Stanfield/NGS; 80 (lo), Joel Sartore/NGS; 81, Robert
Pernell/SS

The Midwest

86 (UP), James L. Stanfield/NGS; 86 (lo), Jim Richardson/NGS; 86-87, JAMES P. BLAIR/NGS; 87 (up left), Nadia
M. B. Hughes/NGS; 87 (up right), Sean Martin/IS; 87 (lo right), Aga/SS; 88 (UP), Chas/SS; 88 (lo left), Raymond
Boyd/Getty Images; 88-89, Lenice Harms/SS; 90 (UP), IS; 90 (lo), Melissa Farlow/NGS; 92 (UP), Joel Sartore/
NGS; 92 (lo), Madeleine Openshaw/SS; 93, Tom Bean/NGS; 94, Cotton Coulson/NGS; 95, Phil Schermeister/NGS;
96 (UP), Kevin Fleming/Corbis; 96 (lo), Vince Ruffa/SS; 97, Geoffrey Kuchera/SS; 98 (UP), Joel Sartore/NGS; 98
(lo), Medford Taylor/NGS; 99, Lawrence Sawyer/IS; 100 (lo), PhotoDisc; 100 (up left), Phil Schermeister/NGS; 101
(up left), Sarah Leen/NGS; 102 (UP), Joel Sartore/NGS; 102 (lo), Joel Sartore/NGS; 103, Sarah Leen/NGS; 104
(UP), Farrell Grehan/NGS; 104 (lo), Beverley Vycital/IS; 105, Annie Griffiths Belt/NGS; 106 (UP), PhotoDisc; 106
(LO LE), Ronald T. Bennett; 106 (lo right), Robert J. Daveant/SS; 108, Carol M. Highsmith/Library of Congress;
109, Dan Westergren/NGS; 110 (up left), Paul Damien/NGS; 110 (up right), Medford Taylor/NGS

The Southwest

116 (lo left), Penny De Los Santos; 116 (UP), Joseph H. Bailey/NGS; 116-117, Anton Foltin/IS; 117 (lo), Joel Sartore/
NGS; 117 (UP), Photodisc; 118 (UP), Joel Sartore/NGS; 118 (lo), George Burba/SS; 120 (center), James P. Blair/
NGS; 120 (up right), italianestro/SS; 120 (lo), Lynn Johnson/NGS; 122, Joel Sartore/NGS; 123, Annie Griffiths
Belt/NGS; 124 (UP), Sarah Leen/NGS; 124 (lo), Diane Cook & Len Jenshel/NGS

The West

130 (UP), PhotoDisc; 130 (lo), PhotoDisc; 130-131, Digital Stock; 131 (UP), Phillip Holland/SS; 131 (center right),
Digital Stock; 131 (lo), Joel Sartore/NGS; 132 (UP), Joel Sartore/NGS; 132 (lo), Blue Poppy/Flickr RF/Getty
Images; 134 (UP), Vacclav/SS; 134 (lo), Randy Olson/NGS; 136 (UP), PhotoDisc; 136 (lo), PhotoDisc; 138, Andrew
Zarivny/SS; 139, Charles Wood/REX SS; 140 (lo), Joel Sartore/NGS; 140-141, Michael Melford/NGS; 141, J.
Cameron Gull/SS; 142 (lo), William Albert Allard/NGS; 143, SS; 144 (lo), Danita Delimont/Alamy Stock Photo;
144-145, Andy Z./SS; 145 (lo), Raymond Gehman/NGS; 146 (UP), Jennifer Lynn Arnold/SS; 146 (lo), Peter Kunasz/
SS; 148 (lo), Eunika Sopotnicka/IS/Getty Images; 148-149, PhotoDisc; 150 (left), PhotoDisc; 150 (right), Digital
Stock; 152 (UP), Michael Rubin/SS; 152 (lo), Digital Stock; 153, PhotoDisc

The Territories and Back of the Book

156 (left), Kendra Nielsam/SS; 156 (upright), James Davis Photography/Alamy; 156-157, Ira Block/NGS; 157 (UP),
VisionsofParadise.com/Alamy; 157 (lo right), Gerry Ellis/Minden/Getty Images

Map Acknowledgments

2-3, 24-25, 52-53, 82-83, 112-113, 126-127, Blue Marble: Next Generation NASA Earth Observatory; 10-11,
climate data adapted from Peel, M. C., Finlayson, B. L., and McMahon, T. A.: Updated world map of the Köppen-
Geiger climate classification, Hydrol. Earth Syst. Sci., 11, 1633-1644, 2007, National Snow & Ice Data Center:
nsidc.org, NOAA's National Centers for Environmental Information: www.ncei.noaa.gov; 12-13, data from Billion
Dollar Weather Disasters 1980-2007 (map), NOAA's National Centers for Environmental Information; 16-17,
Landscan 2014 Population Dataset created by UT-Battelle, LLC, the management and operating contractor
of the Oak Ridge National Laboratory acting on behalf of the U.S. Department of Energy under Contract No.
DE-AC05-000R22725. Distributed by East View Geospatial: geospatial.com and East View Information Services:
eastview.com/online/landscan; 18-19, United States Atlas of Renewable Resources, National Renewable
Energy Laboratory, US Census Bureau: www.census.gov; 20-21, EIA (U.S. Energy Administration), Rubinstein,
J. L., and A. B. Mahani (2015). Myths and Facts on Wastewater Injection, Hydraulic Fracturing, Enhanced Oil
Recovery, and Induced Seismicity. Seismol. Res. Lett. 86, no. 4, doi: 10.1785/0220150067.